Ages of Discord

A STRUCTURAL-DEMOGRAPHIC ANALYSIS
OF AMERICAN HISTORY

Peter Turchin

Beresta Books

Beresta Books
Published by BERESTA BOOKS LLC
Chaplin, Connecticut, U.S.A.

AGES OF DISCORD:
A STRUCTURAL-DEMOGRAPHIC ANALYSIS OF AMERICAN HISTORY

Copyright © 2016 by Peter Turchin

Library of Congress Cataloging-in-Publication Data
Turchin, Peter, 1957–
Ages of Discord: A Structural-Demographic Analysis of American History / Peter Turchin
p. cm.
Includes bibliographical references and index
1. History – United States.   2. Social Dynamics – Mathematical Models.
3. Power Elites – Cooperation.   4. Political Violence – Social aspects.
5. Inequality – Effects on Social Structures.   I. Title

Preface

Is America headed in the wrong direction? An increasing proportion of Americans are saying "yes". For what it's worth, the subjective mood of gloom (and even doom) is buttressed by a variety of data trends—too many for comfort.[1]

Inequality of both income and wealth has been increasing in the US since the 1970s. As a result, there are many more wealthy Americans—the number of multimillionaires quadrupled between 1983 and 2007. At the same time, the real (inflation-adjusted) wage of American men today is lower than 40 years ago. Today, median-wage earners have to work twice as many months to earn the price of a median home, compared with 30 years ago. Between 1999 and 2015, the suicide rate rose by 24 percent. Things are so bad that the life expectancy of middle-aged, white Americans is declining—a shocking statistic in a modern postindustrial country not at war.

Signs of government dysfunction and gridlock abound. The effects of rampant political polarization among the political class are particularly visible in the Senate, which has been inundated by a wave of filibusters. Whereas during the 1960s nearly all judges nominated for US District Courts were confirmed by the Senate, today half of the nominations are rejected. In 2016 the intransigent Senate refused to consider the President's nominations for the Supreme Court, so currently (as of summer of 2016) we have only eight supreme justices.

The American infrastructure is fraying, the politics are becoming more poisonous, and the trust in government has plummeted. On top of this, there is an epidemic of domestic terrorism, although it is not often acknowledged as such by the media or political elites. Every year, greater numbers of Americans, armed with guns, go on shooting rampages killing strangers and passers-by. The incidence of such indiscriminate mass murder has increased twentyfold over the past 40 years, and nobody can explain why. No wonder that, according to the latest NBC/*Wall Street Journal* poll, 70 percent of Americans think that "things are off on the wrong track".

Troubling trends of this kind are constantly discussed by politicians, public intellectuals, and social scientists. But most commentators see only a small slice of the overall problem. Indeed, what do increasingly frequent

---

1   All data trends mentioned in the Preface will be discussed and referenced in the main body of the book.

shooting rampages have to do with the polarization in Congress? Or falling life expectancies for large segments of the American population? Is there a connection between too many multimillionaires and more filibusters in the Senate?

In this book I will argue that the trends listed above, and many others, are indeed interrelated. Analysis by my colleagues and me of historical states shows that complex, large-scale human societies tend to go through cycles of alternating integrative and disintegrative phases. Long periods of relative equity, prosperity, and internal peace are succeeded by periods of inequity, immiseration, and political instability, frequently ending in state collapses, revolutions, and civil wars. Each of the "secular" phases, integrative and disintegrative, unfolds over several human generations. The typical period of the overall secular cycle is around two centuries, although there is a lot of variability, depending on the type of society in question, starting conditions, and chance events.

What is particularly relevant to the questions with which I started this Preface, is that while post-crisis dynamics can take many routes, the pre-crisis periods tend to have the same characteristic features, shared across many societies and even different historical eras. The American polity today has a lot in common with the Antebellum America of the 1850s; with *Ancien Régime* France on the eve of the French Revolution; with Stuart England during the 1630s; and innumerable other historical societies that went through integrative/disintegrative cycles. Can it really be true that the troubles of our days are not so new, and many historical societies experienced them previously? I will marshal empirically supported theory and a lot of data to show that this is, indeed, the case.

However, unlike historical societies, we are in a unique position to take steps that could allow us to escape the worst. Societal breakdown and ensuing waves of violence can be avoided by collective, cooperative action. My goal is to present in this book the best current understanding of why political violence in states waxes and wanes in long cycles. This understanding is encapsulated in what has become known as *Structural-Demographic Theory* (SDT), whose empirical adequacy has been tested on a number of historical societies. As we shall see in this book, the SDT helps us answer why the various trends mentioned earlier changed direction from favorable to unfavorable in America around the 1970s. Such understanding is the key to developing reforms that would reverse these negative trends, and move us to a more equitable, prosperous, and peaceful society.

Acknowledgments

I would like to thank Radek Szulga, Ross Hartshorn, and Jim Bennett, who read and commented on a complete draft of the manuscript. Over the years, I have profited from many discussions with my colleagues. Here is an incomplete list (please forgive me if I have left you out): Mark Ames, Paul Gilje, Herb Gintis; Jim Bennett, Kevin Feeney, and the rest of the Seshat crew; Andrey Korotayev, Sergey Nefedov, and other members of the Russian Cliodynamics community; and my colleagues in the Evolution Institute: David Sloan Wilson, Jerry Miller, Joe Brewer, and Robert Kadar. I'd like also to thank Alexander Dibrov, MD, for drawing my attention to data on the overproduction of medical degrees (Figure 13.3).

Many years ago, when I was not yet sure that I should pursue this project, Jack Goldstone, the father of the Structural-Demographic Theory, gave me the encouragement I needed to start me on this long road. As I wrote, I revisited his magisterial *Revolution and Rebellion in the Early Modern World* many, many times, and never failed to be impressed by the prescience of his book in respect of subsequent developments in structural theories of revolution and internal war.

During the preparation of this volume for publication, I have been ably helped by a talented team: Agathe Dupeyron, who chased down many hard-to-find facts and bits of data; Simon Reynolds, whose editing skills made the manuscript immeasurably more readable; Greg Laszczyk, who typeset it; and Marta Dec, who designed the cover.

As always, my greatest debt of gratitude is to my wife Olga, whose support and encouragement sustained me during the long (but, thanks to her, never lonely) years of working on the book.

Table of Contents

List of Tables

List of Figures

PART ONE

A Theoretical Introduction

Multi-Secular Cycles in Historical and Modern Societies

Introduction: Human Societies Are Fragile

At 4:30am on April 12, 1861, Confederate batteries opened fire on Fort Sumter, located on an island in the middle of Charleston harbor, South Carolina. After 34 hours of bombardment, the commander of the U.S. troops defending the fort, Major Robert Anderson, gave the order to strike the flag: the first battle of the American Civil War was over. Curiously, there were no casualties, a strange beginning for the bloodiest war in American history.

That this war happened at all is itself strange. Both sides spoke the same language and professed the same religion. There was no shortage of food or land, with a huge and lightly populated Western frontier ready to absorb millions of settlers. Even stranger, it happened in a democracy. For the first 80 years of the American polity, its democratic institutions had sufficed to resolve the inevitable clashes of interests found in any large society. Political crises were defused within the constitutional framework—in other words, without violence. In 1861, however, these institutions failed catastrophically. By this point, the American political elites had lost their ability to cooperate in finding a compromise that would preserve the commonwealth. And instead of defusing the crisis, popular elections in which Abraham Lincoln won the presidency triggered the conflagration.

What is particularly astounding is how myopic the American political leaders and their supporters were on the eve of the Civil War, especially those from the Southern states. They gleefully wrecked the Union, without realizing what a heavy personal cost that would mean for most of them.

When news of Fort Sumter's surrender reached Richmond, Virginia, wild celebrations filled the streets and a crowd took down the United States flag from the capitol, replacing it with the Confederate one (Epperson 2005). Within days, Virginia left the Union and joined the Confederacy of the seven deep-south states that had seceded before Fort Sumter. Similar events took place in North Carolina and Tennessee. One wonders what they thought of their initial eagerness to join in the conflict four years and 620,000 corpses later. In the 1860s, Americans learned that large-scale complex societies are actually fragile, and that a descent into a civil war can be rapid.

Today, 150 years later, this lesson has been thoroughly forgotten. As I discuss in Chapter 11, the degree to which cooperation among the American political elites has unraveled during the past decade is eerily similar to what happened in the 1850s, the decade preceding the Civil War. The divisive issues are different (although the fault-line between the North and the South endures), but the vehemence and the disregard for the consequences of failing to compromise are the same. Of course, nobody expects another Civil War. But the political leaders of antebellum America also could not have imagined in their wildest dreams the eventual consequences of the choices they made during the 1850s. As another historical example, it is doubtful that when the Assembly of French Notables rejected royal proposals for the state budget in 1788, they intended to start the French Revolution, in which many of them would lose their heads to the guillotine. Just because we cannot imagine our actions leading to disaster, it doesn't mean that such a disaster cannot happen.

Perhaps human beings have become more civilized in the past two centuries, as the psychologist Steven Pinker argues in *The Better Angels of Our Nature*. A political crisis in the United States in the twenty-first century may not result in the same magnitude of slaughter that France saw during the Revolution and Terror, and the United States in the Civil War. But given the stakes, are we willing to bet on it? And wouldn't it be better to figure out what ails our society so that we can fix it?

The real difference between us and our predecessors is that today we are rapidly gaining much better understanding of the inner workings of societies. We have better theories and data to help us figure out what makes societies function better, and what causes dysfunction. This understanding is a result of multidisciplinary research by a diverse group of scientists, who include anthropologists, sociologists, economists, mathematicians, evolutionary biologists, psychologists, historians, and archaeologists. We need all those disciplines, and a few others, to discover both the general principles that govern historical dynamics—how states rise and fall—and special circumstances that make each society unique. We call this new discipline *Cliodynamics*, from *Clio*, the muse of history in Greek mythology, and *dynamics*, the science of why things change (Turchin 2003b).

Although our understanding of historical dynamics is by no means complete, we now know enough to be worried, very worried, about the direction in which the United States is moving. Back in 2010, writing for the leading science journal, *Nature*, I used Cliodynamics to predict that "the next decade is likely to be a period of growing instability in the United States and western Europe". As I write this *Introduction*, we are half way through the decade and, as we will see in the following chapters, the troubling trends that I identified in 2010 are showing no signs of reversing themselves. The presidential election season of 2016 has hammered that message home in a particularly clear way.

This book explains why we should be worried about the current course taken by American society and how we can use history to plan a better future. And this brings me to the topic of the next section.

Does History Have Lessons?

Science can yield deep understanding of the world, and such understanding translates into our ability to build and fix things. Thus, we know how to construct and fly spaceships and cure many diseases (and even eradicate some). Unfortunately, understanding of the dynamics and functioning of societies is nowhere near the point where it can be used in practical applications. In fact, our interventions to solve particular societal problems at times just make things worse. As I pointed out earlier, the American political leaders who allowed the Civil War to happen had no idea of the magnitude of the disaster they were about to experience.

As we shall see later in the book, something happened to American society during the 1970s. Several previously positive social, economic, and political trends suddenly reversed their direction. Each of these turn-around points has been noticed and commented on by social scientists and media commentators. However, what is not broadly appreciated is that these trend reversals were related. A human society is a *dynamical system*, and its economic, social, and political subsystems do not operate in isolation.

A well-meaning intervention to fix one particular problem is likely to have unexpected and, often, undesirable consequences (although, one hopes, not a disaster on the scale of the French Revolution and Terror). The only way to avoid such undesirable consequences is to gain a deep understanding of the fundamental mechanisms affecting functioning of complex macrosocial systems.

Such an understanding is the goal of Cliodynamics (Turchin 2003b, 2008a). Cliodynamics is one of the historical sciences, similar to astrophysics, geology, paleontology, evolutionary biology, and linguistics. Generally speaking, manipulative experiments (when we change some condition and detect its effect by a comparison with unmanipulated controls) are impossible in historical sciences. Instead, progress is made by formulating general theories whose predictions can be tested with historical data, constructing large databases, capitalizing on natural experiments (Diamond and Robinson 2010), and designing *mensurative* experiments—planned comparisons between the predictions of two or more rival theories and data (Turchin 2006a). An explicitly historical approach is the key (which is why these disciplines are termed historical).

Such a focus on history, however, will strike many social scientists and, especially, policy-makers as seriously misguided. We live in such a rapidly changing world that surely history cannot have any real lessons for us. There is a marked tendency among policy-makers to deal with economic or political crises of today as though they were completely new and unprecedented. Such blindness to history often leads us to repeat old mistakes. Investors, for example, have been caught in one speculative frenzy after another throughout the centuries. Eventually, such financial bubbles always burst, but in the heady days before the crash the majority blithely believes that "this time is different" (Reinhart and Rogoff 2009).

In fairness to policy-makers, traditional history has generally failed to provide useful guidance for public policy. It is easy enough to buttress one's argument for a proposed course of action by "cherry picking" examples from the historical record. The problem is, there are usually just as many examples supporting the opposite course. The same historical evidence can be used to make entirely different, and sometimes diametrically opposed arguments. As an example, recently a number of books have drawn parallels between today's America and the Roman Empire. One is by Thomas Madden (2008), *Empires of Trust: How Rome Built—and America Is Building—a New World*. Another is *Ancient Rome and Modern America* by Margaret Malamud (2008). Yet another is by Cullen Murphy (2008) asking *Are We Rome?* Its subtitle, *The Fall of an Empire and the Fate of America*, suggest that America faces the same destiny as ancient Rome. But Vaclav Smil (2010) argues precisely the opposite, as his title indicates: *Why America is Not a New Rome*.

History has lessons for us, but these lessons must be extracted in an indirect way. What we need is *theory* in the broadest sense, which includes general principles that explain the functioning and dynamics of societies and models that are built on these principles, usually formulated as mathematical equations or computer algorithms. Theory also needs empirical content that deals with discovering general empirical patterns, determining the empirical adequacy of key assumptions made by the models, and testing model predictions with the data from actual historical societies. A mature, or "developed" theory, thus integrates models with data; developing such a theory for history is the main goal of Cliodynamics. Practical applications become possible only as a result of progress towards understanding the general principles governing social dynamics.

This research program raises two fundamental questions. First, are there general principles of social dynamics? Second, even supposing we discover such principles by studying historical societies, will they still apply to the very different societies of today? In the following sections I address these questions; my focus is on why we sometimes see waves of sociopolitical instability that may, when extreme, cause state breakdown and collapse.

Complex Dynamics of Sociopolitical Instability

Empirical Patterns

Recent research indicates that the dynamics of sociopolitical instability in pre-industrial states are not purely random; history is not just "one damned thing after another", as Arnold Toynbee famously said in response to another historian (Toynbee 1957: 267). There is a regular, albeit dynamically complex, pattern involving at least two cycles superimposed on each other (plus exogenous stochasticity on top of that). This dynamical pattern is apparent in Figures 1.1a and 1.1b. First, there are long-term waves of political instability with durations of a century or more that are interspersed with relatively stable periods. Second, note how the instability waves tend to look "saw-toothed"—there is a shorter oscillation with an average period of c.50 years (because the data in Figure 1.1 are sampled at 25-year intervals, a period twice that produces the pattern of alternating ups and downs). In this chapter I focus on the long waves, while deferring the discussion of shorter oscillations to Chapter 2 (*Wheels within Wheels: Modeling Complex Dynamics of Sociopolitical Instability*).

These data and analyses suggest that a typical historical state goes through a sequence of relatively stable political regimes separated by unstable periods characterized by recurrent waves of internal war. The characteristic length of both stable (or *integrative*) and unstable (or *disintegrative*) phases is a century or longer, and the overall period of the cycle is around two to three centuries (Figure 1.1).

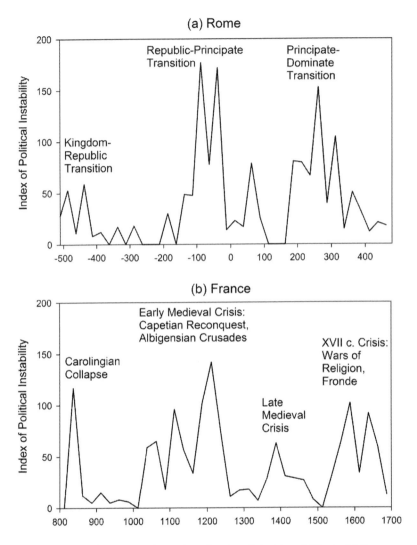

FIGURE 1.1. Long-term dynamics of sociopolitical instability in (a) Rome, 510BCE–480CE and (b) France, 800–1700 (data from Sorokin 1937). Data are plotted per 25-year interval. "Index of Political Stability" combines measures of duration, intensity, and scale of political instability events, coded by a team of professional historians (see Sorokin 1937 for details). The Roman trajectory is based on only instability events that occurred in Italy.

Historians' time divisions tend to reflect this pattern of multi-secular (or *secular*, for brevity) cycles. For example, Roman history is usually separated into Regal (or Kingdom), Republican, Principate, and Dominate periods. Transitions between these periods, in all cases, involved prolonged waves of sociopolitical instability (Figure 1.1a).

Similarly, the Germanic kingdoms that replaced the Roman Empire after it collapsed in the West went through a sequence of secular cycles that roughly corresponded to the dynasties that ruled them (Table 1.1). The instability waves have also been noted by historians, and sometimes given specific labels. The best known are the Crisis of Late Middle Ages between 1300 and 1450 (Tuchman 1978, Bois 1984, 2000) and the Crisis of the Seventeenth Century (Trevor-Roper 1966). The 17th century's crisis affected polities across the whole of Eurasia (Goldstone 1991), although the precise dates varied from region to region. In France, for example, the crisis unfolded during the century following 1560 (see Table 1.1 and Figure 1.1b).

TABLE 1.1 A summary of the chronological sequence of secular cycles in Western Europe. This chronology focuses on the dominant state within Western Europe: first on the Roman Empire, then medieval German empires, and finally France (modified from Turchin and Nefedov 2009: Table 10.1). The only exception is the Late Antiquity, when two parallel cycles for the Eastern Roman Empire and the Franks are shown. The naming convention is to use the dynasty that ruled during the integrative phase for the whole secular cycle (thus, the dates of dynasties and cycles do not correspond precisely).

Dominant Polity	Secular cycle	Integrative phase	Disintegrative phase
Rome	Regal	650–500 BCE	500–350 BCE
Rome	Republican	350–130 BCE	130–30 BCE
Rome	Principate	30 BCE–165 CE	165–285
Eastern Roman Empire	Dominate*	285–540	540–700
Frankish Empire	Merovingian*	480–640	640–700
Frankish Empire	Carolingian	700–820	820–920
German Empire	Ottonian-Salian	920–1050	1050–1150
France	Capetian	1150–1315	1315–1450
France	Valois	1450–1560	1560–1660
France	Bourbon	1660–1780	1780–1870

* Merovingian cycle in the West and the Dominate cycle in the Eastern Roman Empire

Secular cycles are also observed in other world regions: in China with its dynastic cycles (Figure 1.2), in the Middle East (Nefedov 1999), and in Southeast Asia (Lieberman 2003). In fact, it is a general dynamic pattern that is observed in all agrarian states for which the historical record is accurate enough (Turchin 2003b, Korotayev et al. 2006, Turchin and Nefedov 2009).

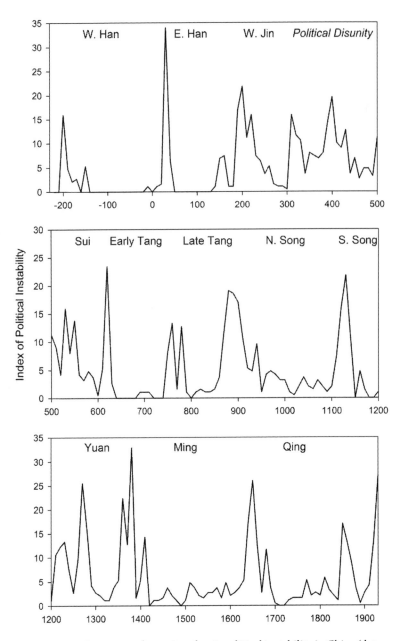

FIGURE 1.2. Long-term dynamics of sociopolitical instability in China (data from Lee 1931). Data are plotted per 25-year interval. "Index of Political Stability" refers to the number of instability events (civil wars, peasant uprising, major outbreaks of banditry, etc.) per 5-year interval. Note that unlike in Figure 1.1, where labels are assigned to instability waves, here labels indicate internally stable periods, associated with a unifying dynasty.

As noted above, the dynamical pattern of sociopolitical instability in agrarian societies is complex: it involves at least two types of cycles superimposed on each other (and exogenous stochasticity on top of that). Note that instability waves in Figures 1.1a and 1.1b appear "saw-toothed": on the scale of 25 years, there is a pattern of alternating ups and downs. However, unlike the secular waves, 50-year cycles are not a universal feature of agrarian societies. For example, they do not show up in the Chinese data (Figure 1.2).

Explaining the Historical Patterns

Strong empirical patterns suggest that instability dynamics in agrarian societies may be governed by general mechanisms. One possible explanation of why agrarian societies experience periodic state breakdowns is the Structural-Demographic Theory (Goldstone 1991, Turchin 2003b). According to this theory, population growth in excess of the productivity gains of the land has several effects on social institutions. First, it leads to persistent price inflation, falling real wages, rural misery, urban migration, and increased frequency of food riots and wage protests. Second, rapid expansion of population results in *elite overproduction*—an increased number of aspirants for the limited supply of elite positions. Increased intraelite competition leads to the formation of rival patronage networks vying for state rewards. As a result, elites become riven by increasing rivalry and factionalism. Third, population growth leads to expansion of the army and the bureaucracy and to rising real costs. States have no choice but to seek to expand taxation, despite resistance from the elites and the general populace. Yet, attempts to increase revenues cannot offset the spiraling state expenses. Thus, even if the state succeeds in raising taxes, it is still headed for fiscal crisis. As all these trends intensify, the end result is state bankruptcy and consequent loss of military control; elite movements of regional and national rebellion; and a combination of elite-mobilized and popular uprisings that expose the breakdown of central authority.

Sociopolitical instability resulting from state collapse feeds back on population growth via depressed birth rates and elevated mortality and emigration. Additionally, increased migration and vagrancy spread the disease by connecting areas that would have stayed isolated during better times. As a result, epidemics and even pandemics strike disproportionately often during the disintegrative phases of secular cycles (Turchin 2008b). Instability also has a negative impact on the productive capacity of a society. Lacking strong government to protect them, peasants cultivate only fields that are near fortified settlements or other strongpoints (e.g., hilltop settlements). Conversely, the strong state protects the productive population from external and internal (banditry, civil war) threats, and thus allows the whole cultivable area to be put into production.

Recent research has shown that the predictions of the Structural-Demographic Theory find much empirical support in detailed case-studies of medieval and early-modern England and France, ancient Rome, and Muscovy-Russia (Turchin and Nefedov 2009). Furthermore, wherever we can find quantitative data on the key structural-demographic variables, we find that relationships between them conform to those postulated by the theory. Thus, the structure of dynamical feedbacks between population growth and sociopolitical instability is precisely as postulated by the model: population pressing against Malthusian limits causes instability to rise, while high instability depresses population growth leading to population decline or stagnation (Turchin 2005). Other empirically strong feedbacks between variables include the negative relationship between the supply of labor and real wages, and the positive association between popular immiseration and elite expansion (reflected in growing numbers of elites and an increase in their incomes). The data also indicate that one of the most reliable predictors of state collapse and high political instability is elite overproduction (Turchin and Nefedov 2009:314).

I have already commented above that secular cycles are not cycles in the strict mathematical sense. The period of oscillation is not fixed; instead, there is a statistical tendency for instability waves, or vigorous population growth periods, to recur on a characteristic time-scale. It would be strange if it were otherwise—the structural-demographic model describes only one set, albeit an important one, of factors affecting population and instability dynamics. Amelioration of the climate or a technological advance may increase the carrying capacity, prolonging the population growth phase and postponing the onset of instability. Successful conquest followed by colonization of the newly acquired lands may have the same effect.

While the overall *dynamics* are complex, the dynamical feedbacks between variables, that is, *mechanisms* that generate the dynamics, are often characterized by a high degree of determinism. One example (out of a multitude documented in Turchin and Nefedov 2009) is an uncannily close relationship between population pressure on resources and popular immiseration (inverse real wage) shown in Figure 1.3.

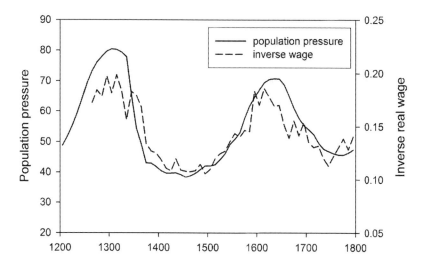

FIGURE 1.3. The relationship between population pressure on resources and popular immiseration in England, 1200–1800 (Turchin and Nefedov 2009: Figure 3.10). Population pressure is expressed as population numbers in relation to the carrying capacity; popular immiseration is the inverse of real wages (for details of calculations, see Turchin and Nefedov 2009:108–110).

From Agrarian to Industrial Societies

Reformulating the Theory for Modern Societies

I started this chapter by asking whether history has any lessons for us today. Some may respond that while it is all well and good that the dynamics of agrarian societies are governed by mechanisms we can identify and quantify, the dynamics of modern societies are probably governed by a different set of mechanisms, thanks to the dramatic effect of the Industrial Revolution on the structure and dynamics of those societies. According to this argument, any lessons of history are obsolete.

Clearly, at least some of the relationships postulated by the Structural-Demographic Theory have been made obsolete. In particular, we hardly expect population increase to result in starvation in Western industrialized states. But perhaps other aspects of the theory may be more robust with respect to changes brought about by the Industrial Revolution. Can the theory be reformulated in a way that would make it useful for describing the dynamics of industrialized societies?

This question has both a theoretical and an empirical part. The rest of this chapter will be devoted to the theoretical reformulation and Chapter 2 will approach this question from a more formal modeling perspective, while chapters in Parts II–IV will empirically test the theoretical predictions, using the United States as the case study.

The starting point for a reformulation of the Structural-Demographic Theory is provided by the three theory-motivated and empirically-supported generalizations discussed at the end of *Secular Cycles* (Turchin and Nefedov 2009:313–14): (1) the Neo-Malthusian principle, (2) the principle of elite over-production, and (3) the structural-demographic causes of political instability. The Neo-Malthusian principle that sustained population growth inevitably leads to falling living standards and popular immiseration, has, clearly, been challenged the most by the agrarian-industrial transition. However, it can be restated in more general terms of supply and demand (Borjas 2009): when the supply of labor exceeds its demand, its price should decrease (depressing living standards for the majority of population). In agrarian economies, demand for labor is limited by the availability of cultivable land, so unchecked population growth inevitably leads to falling living standards. In modern economies, by contrast, the demand for labor is much more dynamic and can change as a result of technological advances, investments in physical and human capital, and growing demand for goods and services resulting from increasing per capita consumption. Additionally, modern societies are much more interconnected globally, and the balance of supply and demand for labor in any particular country can be affected by international flows of people and jobs. Thus, the set of factors affecting living standards in modern societies is much more complex than in agrarian. Nevertheless, to a first approximation, there should be two principal components in its long-term dynamics. First, there should be a monotonic trend to higher popular wellbeing resulting from scientific and technical progress. Second, around that trend there may be oscillations reflecting the shifting balance between the demand for and the supply of labor. The first proposition is hardly controversial, and the second leads to a hypothesis that can be tested empirically (and will be, using the US data).

The principle of elite overproduction is also a consequence of the law of supply and demand. The elites (in both agrarian and capitalist societies) are consumers of commoner labor. Low labor costs lead not only to declining living standards for a large segment of the population (employees, especially unskilled ones), but also to a favorable economic conjuncture for the elites (more specifically, for the economic segment of the elites—employers). There are several important consequences of this development. First, the elites become accustomed to ever greater levels of consumption. Furthermore, competition for social status fuels "conspicuous consumption" (Veblen 1973 [1899]). Thus, the minimum level of consumption necessary for maintaining the elite status exhibits runaway growth. Second, the numbers of elites, in relation to the rest of the population, increase. A favorable economic conjuncture for the employers enables large numbers of intelligent, hard-working, or simply lucky workers to accumulate wealth and then attempt to translate it into social status. As a result, upward mobility into the ranks of the elites will greatly surpass downward mobility. Additionally, there may be increased biological reproduction within elite families, although this mechanism was of greater importance in pre-industrial societies and, especially, societies with widespread polygyny among the elites (such as the Islamic ones). The third consequence is that the twin processes of declining living standards for the commoners and increasing consumption levels for the elites will drive up socioeconomic inequality.

As a result of the growth in elite appetites and numbers, the proportion of the total economic pie consumed by them will increase. However, there are limits on how far this process can go. Eventually, increasing numbers of elites and elite aspirants will have to translate into declining consumption levels for some, leading to the condition that has been termed *elite overproduction* (this is reminiscent of population growth leading to overpopulation). Intraelite competition for limited elite positions in the economy and government will become more fierce. Competition will be particularly intense for government positions whose supply is relatively inelastic (or completely inelastic—there can be only one President, nine Supreme Court Justices, and one hundred Senators). Since the number of power positions is limited, a growing segment of elites/elite aspirants must be denied access to them. These "surplus" elites must challenge the established elites for access to elite positions, or acquiesce in downward mobility. A democratic system of government may allow for nonviolent rotation of political elites, but ultimately this depends on the willingness of some segments of established elites and/or elite aspirants to give up their elite positions and status. Thus, elite overproduction increases the probability of violent intraelite conflict. One common response by the established elites under these conditions is to close ranks and exclude other elite aspirants from power, which causes the latter to organize as *counter-elites*. A classic example of this dynamic is the closing of the Roman patriciate (*la serrata del patriziato*) to new members in the early Republic (de Sanctis 1953), which was followed by a lengthy struggle between the established elites (patricians) and counter-elites (wealthy and socially prominent plebeians). Another example is *la Serrata del Maggior Consiglio* (the Great Council of Venice) in 1297, followed by other measures which by the 1320s had achieved the closing of the Venetian patriciate (Chojnacki 1994).

Elite overproduction leading to intraelite competition and conflict is, thus, one of the chief causes of political instability. Two other causes are popular discontent resulting from falling living standards, and fiscal crisis. These three causes interact in producing conditions ripe for political violence. Thus, one common tactic employed by the counter-elites is to mobilize the masses against the established elites, something made possible by deep-running popular discontent. On the other hand, elite overproduction contributes to the financial difficulties of the state, because impoverished members of the elites, seeking to secure resources to maintain their status, put enormous pressure on the state to provide employment for them, tipping state finances further into the red.

Our investigation of structural-demographic crises in the eight agrarian states suggested that the three structural-demographic causes of sociopolitical instability are not equal in their importance:

> The demographic-structural theory proposes three principal causes of the onset of a disintegrative trend (that is, a lengthy period of heightened instability): overpopulation, elite overproduction, and the fiscal crisis of the state. As we discussed in Section 10.4, however, some causal factors are relatively more important than others. In particular, a factor that appears to be always associated with high instability (at least, in the eight case studies that we examined) is the elite overproduction. Overpopulation, by contrast, results in popular immiseration and discontent, but as long as the elites remain unified, peasant insurrections, slave rebellions, or worker uprisings have little chance of success, and are speedily suppressed. Furthermore, when population declines during the disintegrative periods, there is often a substantial lag time between population density reaching a low level and the time when internal peace and order are restored. The third component, the fiscal crisis of the state, is usually present, but sometimes is missing as triggering factor leading to civil war (see Section 10.4). Thus, overpopulation and fiscal crisis are important contributing factors, but the dominant role in internal warfare appears to be played by elite overproduction leading to intraelite competition, fragmentation, and conflict, and the rise of counter-elites who mobilize

popular masses in their struggle against the existing order. (Turchin and Nefedov 2009:314)

Table 1.2 summarizes the predictions of the structural-demographic theory that should survive the agrarian/industrial transition.

TABLE 1.2 The three fundamental predictions of the structural-demographic theory that will be tested on the empirical material of the United States (c.1780–2010).

Prediction	Brief explanation
Labor oversupply principle	When the supply of labor exceeds its demand, the price of labor decreases, depressing the living standards for the majority of population, thus leading to **popular immiseration**, but creating favorable economic conditions for the elites.
Elite overproduction principle	Favorable economic conjuncture for the elites results in increasing numbers of elites and elite aspirants, as well as runaway growth of elite consumption levels. **Elite overproduction** results when elite numbers and appetites exceed the ability of the society to sustain them, leading to spiraling intraelite competition and conflict.
Instability principle	Chief causes of sociopolitical instability (in order of importance) are (1) **elite overproduction** leading to intraelite competition and conflict, (2) **popular immiseration**, resulting from falling living standards, and (3) the **fiscal crisis of the state**.

Structural-Demographic Theory is not Neo-Malthusianism

One common misconception equates structural-demographic theory (SDT) with Malthusianism. Indeed, the insights of Thomas Robert Malthus do form an important part of SDT. However, the theory integrates key Malthusian ideas with those of Marx and Weber (Turchin and Nefedov 2009: Chapter 1). SDT is a novel synthetic theory and its predictions can differ significantly from those of traditional Malthusianism, or of Marxism. For example, Malthusian theory predicts that a dramatic population decline, such as that which resulted from the Black Death epidemic in 1347–52 in Western Europe, should cause a rise in living standards, cessation of political instability, and resumption of robust population growth. These consequences should follow the relaxation of population pressure on resources without a significant time lag. In the SDT, by contrast, cessation of political instability occurs not when overpopulation is reversed, but when, in addition, the conditions of elite overproduction no longer obtain. In Western European societies with militarized elites this process takes time—several generations were required for the surplus elites to disappear as a result of being killed off in civil wars and low biological and social reproduction (that is, massive downward social mobility). Thus, the SDT predicts a lengthy period of political instability following population decline (this is known as the depression phase of the secular cycle). The century-long period of political instability following the Black Death in Western Europe, thus, is consistent with the predictions of the SDT, but not Neo-Malthusianism.

More generally, because in this book I am applying the theory to an industrializing and, eventually, post-industrial state, we should expect that the Malthusian component of the SDT would lose much of its salience. To emphasize this, I named the first SDT prediction in Table 1.2 *Labor Oversupply Principle*.

The "demographic" in the SDT, thus, does not mean "Malthusian". It refers to the characteristics of the non-elite population (from the Ancient Greek, *demos*, the people), primarily their wellbeing (and its inverse, popular immiseration). The "structural" part is even more important in understanding the onset of instability waves, because the theory pays a lot of attention to social structures (elite-general population interactions) and political structures (the state-elite-population interactions).

Organization of the book

The overall purpose of this book is to test the predictions of the Structural-Demographic Theory against the empirical material of the United States from its formation (c.1780) to the present. The three theoretical propositions discussed in the previous section (the effect of labor oversupply on living standards, the elite overproduction principle, and the structural-demographic causes of sociopolitical instability, see Table 1.2) provide the focus for empirical tests, but these are not the only theoretical predictions that will be addressed. There are other insights from the application of the structural-demographic theory to pre-industrial societies that are worth pursuing, although in a more informal way than the three main predictions. For example, I have already mentioned the general pattern of the dynamics of sociopolitical instability in historical society, resulting from the superposition of 50-year cycles on secular waves. Does this pattern hold for the United States? Examination of historical societies also yielded a number of insights not only about how they descend into crisis, but also what social mechanisms enable them to end civil wars and enter the next integrative phase. Rather than formalizing these observations as specific hypotheses ahead of time (as I did with the three propositions) I will bring them up informally when discussing relevant periods of the American history (a detailed list of these predictions can be found in Turchin and Nefedov 2009: Table 1.1).

The approach taken in this book mirrors the organizing scheme used in our previous study of agrarian states (Turchin and Nefedov 2009). After discussing modeling approaches in Chapter 2, Part II presents a systematic survey of the data on the dynamics of the fundamental variables of the structural-demographic model. A chapter is devoted to each of the following topics: demography and wellbeing, social structure (specifically, the numbers and consumption levels of the elites), the state strength and collective solidarity, and sociopolitical instability. These variables are fundamental in the sense that it is the feedback interactions between them that generate secular cycles (Turchin and Nefedov 2009:29–30). Next, once the general outlines of the structural-demographic dynamics have been established, I shift the focus to examining how these variables have interacted with each other during different eras of American history. Accordingly, Part III proceeds systematically through the first secular cycle (1780–1930), while Part IV does the same for the current cycle (1930 to the present).

2

Modeling Structural-Demographic Processes

This chapter presents a general theoretical framework for modeling structural-demographic processes. In the following pages I explain how several models that appear in subsequent chapters are related to each other, as well as to models developed earlier for the dynamics of agrarian states (Turchin 2003b). If you are not interested in mathematical details, by all means skip this chapter and go directly to Part II.

Dynamical Feedbacks: an Overview

Structural-demographic theory represents complex (state-level) human societies as systems with three main compartments (the general population, the elites, and the state) interacting with each other and with socio-political instability via a web of nonlinear feedbacks (Figure 2.1). The focus on only these structural components is not quite as great an oversimplification as it may appear, because each component has a number of attributes that change dynamically in response to changes in other structural-demographic variables.

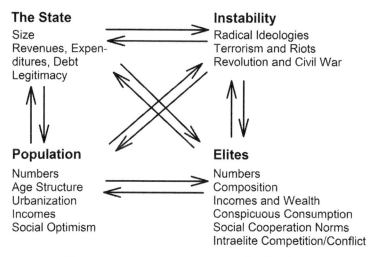

FIGURE 2.1 The complex web of interactions postulated by the structural-demographic theory.

The dynamics of population *numbers*, for example, are affected by other attributes of the general population, such as incomes and consumption levels (the Malthusian effect) and also positively by *social optimism* (when it is high, people tend to marry earlier and have more children) and negatively by *sociopolitical instability* (especially in its extreme forms, such as civil war, which results in elevated death rates and depressed birth rates). *Age structure* is affected by fluctuations in the population growth rate. Thus, a sudden release from the "Malthusian Trap", occurring as part of modernization processes, may generate a period of very rapid population growth that, after a time-lag of 20–25 years, results in what is known as "youth bulges"—unusually large cohorts of youths aged in their twenties (Korotayev et al. 2011). Youth bulges tend to be politically highly destabilizing, because a sudden increase in new workers joining the labor force tends to depress their employment prospects and wages (Easterlin 1980, Macunovich 2002). Furthermore, young adults in the 20–29 age cohort are particularly susceptible to radicalization. Both of these processes contribute to the mobilization potential of the population (Goldstone 1991).

Urbanization dynamics are in many ways similar to age structure. Rapid population growth in rural areas creates a "population surplus"—potential workers who can find no employment in the villages and are forced to migrate to cities, where they are concentrated in a structural setting that facilitates collective action (Goldstone 1991). Thus, rapid population growth in excess of employment opportunities can lead to declining standards of living, a youth bulge, and rapid urbanization—all processes that increase the mobilization potential of the population and thus are inherently destabilizing.

Turning now to the various attributes of the elite compartment in the structural-demographic model (Figure 2.1), the first and most important one is simply their *numbers* (for a discussion of how to define and measure elite numbers see *Approaches to Studying the US Elites* in Chapter 4). Elite numbers are affected by two general processes: the same demographic mechanisms (birth and death) that govern the dynamics of general population numbers; and social mobility. As I discussed in the previous chapter, one of the most important factors affecting social mobility is the oversupply of labor, which creates a favorable economic conjuncture for upward social mobility (intelligent, hard-working, and lucky commoners accumulating wealth and then attempting to translate it into elite status).

Elite *composition* refers to the relative numbers of established elites (those who have inherited their wealth and social status), new elites (who have moved into the upper class by their own efforts), aspirant elites (individuals aspiring to elite status by virtue of their newly acquired wealth or educational credentials; this category also includes any second and subsequent children of established elite families who are in danger of losing elite status), and counter-elites (radicalized aspirant elites, whose hopes of elite position/status have been frustrated).

Elite *incomes* are affected by the economic conjuncture (depressed real wages for commoners translate into increased revenues for the elites), by elite numbers (greater numbers result in a smaller average slice of the total economic pie), and by state expenditure (since the state is the source of many elite positions). *Wealth* is another important attribute because it is closely related to power (most directly, it is the economic form of power, but it can also be translated into political and ideological forms). Wealth is often a better indicator of the economic status of the elites, because it tends to fluctuate less on annual basis. Additionally, "wealth gives a better picture of differences in access to resources" (Stiglitz 2012: 2).

Elite overproduction, the presence of more elites than the society can provide positions for, is inherently destabilizing. It reduces average elite incomes and increases *intraelite competition/conflict* because of large numbers of elite aspirants and counter-elites. Additionally, intraelite competition drives up *conspicuous consumption*, which has an effect of inflating the level of income that is deemed to be necessary to maintain elite status. Competition also plays a role in the unraveling of *social cooperation norms* (this factor will be dealt with at greater length later in this chapter).

This discussion of population and elite compartments highlights three important classes of their attributes: some measure of size or numbers, the economic aspects, and cultural or ideological aspects. The state compartment similarly is characterized by its *size* (measured perhaps by the total number of state employees or, alternatively, by the proportion of GDP going to the state), its economic health (*revenues, expenditures, debt*), and by an ideological aspect (state *legitimacy* as measured, for example, by the degree of trust in state and national institutions). The instability compartment is somewhat different because it is a process, rather than a societal subsystem, but it also has a "size" aspect (frequency of comparatively minor forms of political violence such as *terrorism and riots*; an outbreak of much more serious forms such as *revolution and civil war*) and a cultural/ideological aspect (growth or decline of *radical ideologies*).

This overview, even if brief and focusing only on the most important interactions, nevertheless indicates the rich complexity of the structural-demographic theory. The downside of this complexity is the difficulty of translating the theory from words into mathematical language, a necessary step for testing its logical coherence (in other words, checking whether the postulated dynamical behavior indeed arises from the premises). In principle, it is possible to build a very complicated model that would attempt to capture all the interactions postulated by the verbal theory. However, experience in many scientific fields, including natural and social sciences, shows such a research program to be self-defeating. Large complex models not only require many arbitrary decisions and the estimation of a multitude of difficult-to-measure parameters, they also tend to be structurally unstable, so that a small change in one parameter value results in a large change in the dynamics of the model. For this reason, the only feasible way to deal with such complex systems is to build a spectrum of models, each addressing a somewhat different aspect of the problem, and each simple enough to avoid the pitfalls of large, unwieldy models (large parameter numbers and structural instability). As Einstein famously said, a model should be as simple as possible, but no simpler than that.

There are two complementary approaches to building models of manageable complexity. In the first we focus on the short- and medium-term dynamics by modeling the development of a particular variable, or a particular compartment of the model. The question is, how changes in other variables contribute to the dynamics of the focal variable. Of particular interest are trend reversals: can the theory explain why sociopolitical instability, for example, declined for some decades, and then abruptly began growing? Because our focus is on a particular variable, to keep the model simple we do not include all, or even any of the feedback loops describing how it affects other variables. For this reason such models are "dynamically incomplete" and are not suitable for investigating long-term dynamics of the system. For example, explosive growth of political violence will eventually have consequences for other compartments, which will react by trying to bring it down, but we do not include such feedback effects in the model explicitly.

The second approach is to construct dynamically complete models, with the purpose of investigating long-term dynamics of the system. However, in order to be of manageable complexity, such dynamically complete models must keep the number of dynamical feedbacks that are investigated to an absolute minimum and drastically simplify how each link is modeled.

In the rest of the chapter I follow both of these approaches. I begin with a model whose goal it is to understand the genesis of secular instability waves. Next, I develop a cultural evolution model for trend reversals in social mood. I am interested, in particular, in the factors that underlie the increase, or decrease in the frequency of social cooperation norms. Both of these models are dynamically incomplete and focus on the middle-term time horizon. After that, I turn my attention to dynamically complete models. Of main interest is modeling and understanding why the long-term dynamics of sociopolitical instability are characterized by a complex mixture of two periodicities (50-year cycles superimposed on longer secular waves).

Quantifying Social Pressures for Instability

Political Stress Index

One of the main goals of structural-demographic theory (indeed, its *raison d'être*) is to understand and predict the dynamics of sociopolitical instability. Ultimately, we are interested in explaining why, and when, states collapse, revolutions and rebellions happen, and civil wars break out. The onset of a revolution or a civil war, however, only partially depends on deep structural forces explicitly modeled in the theory. The timing of such events is also affected by historical contingency, accidents, and acts of human free will (for a general discussion, see Turchin 2006b: Chapter 12). As Jack Goldstone (1991) proposed, we can put these two kinds of explanations within a single theoretical framework by distinguishing between *structural causes* of revolutions and *specific triggers* that set in motion the chain of events leading to a revolution.

It's like an earthquake. As tectonic forces build up within a fault line, an earthquake becomes increasingly probable. However, for that earthquake to occur, it has to be triggered—perhaps by a small slip between the plates deep underground. Most such tiny ruptures have no lasting effects, but occasionally one will trigger a cascade of other breakages, which eventually may (or may not) amplify into a huge earthquake. Because in this scenario large events have trivial causes, it is extremely difficult, if not impossible, to predict exactly when and where an earthquake will strike (such inherent unpredictability also characterizes many other types of physical system—hurricanes, for example, and indeed, weather in general). This comparison suggests that in human social systems, which are even more complex than the physical ones, it would be futile to aim for precise prediction of such dramatic events as revolutions (or stock market collapses, to give another familiar example of a macroscopic breakdown triggered by the initially negligible effects of individual investment decisions). As social pressures build up, we may recognize that the chance of a social rupture is increasing, but predicting exactly when and where it will occur, or even its magnitude, may not be possible. The focus of structural-demographic theory is on the structural causes, with specific triggers modeled as stochastic factors.

In his analysis of the social causes of the English Revolution, Goldstone (1991: 141–145) proposed that we can quantify pressures for crisis with a "Political Stress Indicator", *PSI* or Ψ. Here I follow the general logic of this approach, but with several modifications, particularly of the functional forms he proposed.

Political Stress Index reflects the representation of social systems as three subsystems (population-elites-state). It combines the sources of pressure for instability arising from each subsystem: Mass Mobilization Potential (MMP), Elite Mobilization Potential (EMP), and State Fiscal Distress (SFD). I assume that these three components are combined in the index multiplicatively:[2]

$$\Psi = \text{MMP}\times\text{EMP}\times\text{SFD}$$

Social pressures arising from popular distress are indexed with Mass Mobilization Potential (MMP), which has three subcomponents: relative wages, urbanization rate, and the effect of age structure:

$$\text{MMP} = w^{-1}\frac{N_{\text{urb}}}{N}A_{20-29}$$

where w^{-1} is the inverse relative wage (related to the "misery index", see Turchin and Nefedov 2009) and N_{urb}/N is the proportion of total population (N) within the cities (N_{urb}). The last term, A_{20-29}, is the proportion of the cohort aged between 20 and 29 years in the total population. This quantity reflects the role of "youth bulges" in the genesis of instability waves.

I use a similar approach to quantify the second component of Ψ, which deals with the elite overproduction and competition, EMP:

$$\text{EMP} = \varepsilon^{-1}\frac{E}{sN} = \frac{1}{s}\varepsilon^{-1}e$$

When dealing with the elites, we omit the effect of youth cohorts, primarily because it is undesirable to include this parameter twice in Ψ (since it is already incorporated into MMP). The first term on the right hand side, ε^{-1}, is the inverse relative elite income (average elite income scaled by GDP per capita), which is analogous to w^{-1} of the working population. Recollect that

---

2   This formulation effectively assigns the same weight to all three components. Ideally, it would be better to use exponents in a way similar to the Cobb-Douglas function used by economists. However, there is no theoretical or empirical basis for assigning values to exponents, and therefore we use a simple product in the formula. In any case, because all three components tend to move together (although with some time lags), the qualitative result is not strongly affected by allowing different exponents.

high ε^{-1} (and low ε) and can result either from too small a pie that the elites divide among themselves, or too many elites dividing the pie, leading to a high level of intraelite competition. Low ε^{-1}, on the other hand, means a low level of competition for economic resources among the elites. In other words, ε^{-1} is a measure of intraelite competition in the economic domain.

The second term measures the effect of intraelite competition in the political domain, specifically for government offices. It assumes that the demand for elite positions is proportional to the elite numbers, E. The supply of such positions will grow in proportion to the total population (N). The proportionality constant s is the number of government employees per total population (which is allowed to change dynamically). I further define relative elite numbers (relative to the total population) as $e = E/N$. Assuming that s doesn't change too much, the dynamics of EMP will be primarily driven by the product, $\varepsilon^{-1}e$, which reflects two aspects of elite overproduction and intraelite competition, in the economic and political domains.

The third component of Ψ, State Fiscal Distress, has two parts. One is a measure of national debt scaled either in relation to the GDP or, perhaps, in relation to the tax revenues of the state. The second part measures the degree of trust that the population and elites have in the state institutions and its ability to service the debt (this variable is related to a more general variable, the state legitimacy). Of particular importance is the confidence of investors, who buy government bonds, that their investment will be repaid. Confidence is inversely related to the interest rate on government securities (e.g., low confidence means that the state is forced to pay a higher interest rate). Thus, one way to operationalize SFD is as the proportion of the state revenues that is devoted to servicing national debt. Note, however, that the interest rate can be a very dynamic quantity, and can suddenly increase if the investors begin to doubt the ability of the state to service the debt. Historically, a rapid loss of confidence has been followed by rising costs of borrowing, sometimes causing SFD to increase above 1. When the total state revenues are insufficient to service the debt, government fiscal collapse ensues (unless the country is rescued by international lenders). Because the confidence of state bond investors is highly volatile and very difficult to predict, I will use a measure of public distrust in the state institutions (see Chapter 5). The formula for SFD is thus

$$\text{SFD} = \frac{Y}{G}(1-T)$$

where Y is the total state debt, G is the GDP, and T is the proportion of the population expressing trust in the state institutions (thus $1 - T$ is the proportion expressing *distrust* in the state institutions).

The various building blocks of Ψ usually don't develop independently of each other. In particular, structural-demographic variables reflecting attributes of general wellbeing and elite dynamics are interconnected by a series of feedback loops. In the next section I construct a mathematical model that attempts to capture these feedback loops and the resulting dynamics. This model has two goals. First, I presented above a verbal argument explaining the structural-demographic antecedents of instability waves. The logical coherence of this argument needs to be tested with a formal model. Second, readers who have not had extensive experience with nonlinear dynamical systems may not appreciate how easy it is for them to transform monotonic, one-directional inputs into dynamically more complex outputs, characterized by bifurcations and oscillations. In particular, the model illustrates how monotonic increases in such driving variables as the growth of labor supply may engineer a trend reversal in other variables, for example, sociopolitical instability. What the model will show is that an exogenous intervention is not necessary to cause a trend reversal—it can arise as a result of endogenous processes involving nonlinear feedbacks.

Dynamics of Real Wages

I begin building the model with a focus on the economic aspect of popular wellbeing—primarily, real wages (inflation-adjusted wages). The general modeling approach that I will use is fairly standard in Macroeconomics (e.g. Blanchard 1997:305ff). The main factor under consideration is typically the relationship between wages and unemployment or, alternatively, the balance of labor supply and demand (Blanchard 1997:310). To this purely economic model I add a component that reflects the action of extra-economic (non-market) forces. Such an approach yields a more general model, which can be used not only to model wages and levels of consumption in free-market societies, but in more general settings. (However, in this book my focus is on industrializing and industrialized societies, so I will not devote much theoretical effort to developing the more general aspects).

The starting point for building a model for the dynamics of real wages is gross domestic product per capita (GDPpc). This quantity is often, and somewhat misleadingly, referred to as "per capita income". As a result of industrialization, the real GDP per capita often increases by an order of magnitude and it stands to reason that such a huge increase in the average per capita income should have an effect on how much individual workers earn. However, as we shall see in the empirical parts of the book, trends in real wages can diverge substantially from the GDPpc trend (this happens in a cyclic manner, reflecting different phases of secular waves).

There are two broad groups of reasons why increasing GDP does not necessarily translate into real wage growth. The first reflects the operation of market forces. The economic mechanism is the law of supply and demand, which states that when the supply of labor (S) exceeds demand for it (D), the price of labor (that is, real wage) should decrease. Thus, real wage W is a function not only of GDP per capita, G/N (where G is GDP and N is the total population), but also of the balance of demand and supply, D/S.

A few additional words of explanation on D and S (and I will have more to say about how we can estimate these quantities in Chapters 9 and 12, where this general model will be applied to the antebellum and contemporary periods). Labor supply S is simply the total number of people who would like to work. The U.S. Department of Labor publishes yearly statistics on the American Labor Force. However, it's important to note that during the periods of prolonged economic recession, many potential workers become discouraged and stop seeking jobs. As a result, the actual labor supply will be higher than the number of people actively seeking work.

Labor demand D is also difficult quantity to estimate. To a first approximation, we may assume that it is the total GDP divided by average worker productivity. Because in any given quarter GDP may fluctuate due to such factors as business cycles, it is better to use "potential" or "trend" level of output (Samuelson and Nordhaus 1998:376), which smoothes over such short-term fluctuations. Potential level of output, however, may be difficult to estimate when demand for labor greatly exceeds labor supply. Under such conditions of labor shortage, the actually realized level of output could be substantially lower than the potential GDP.

The additional group of factors affecting real wage dynamics are non-market or "extra-economic" forces. They reflect the operation of three non-economic sources of social power: coercive, political, and ideological. Coercive and political factors (power relations) often operate synergistically with ideological factors (prevailing social norms and institutions), so for simplicity I fold them into a single variable, C (standing for "culture" or alternatively "coercion", depending on the modeling context; later on I will say a few words about how this model may be adapted to pre-industrial societies).

The general model of real wages, W, takes the following form:

(2.1)
$$W_{t+\tau} = a \left(\frac{G_t}{N_t} \right)^{\alpha} \left(\frac{D_t}{S_t} \right)^{\beta} C_t^{\gamma}$$

The subscripts index time (years). The three main components, GDPpc, demand/supply ratio, and culture are combined in an admittedly phenomenological fashion. The reason for using this form is apparent when we take logarithms ($A = \log a$):

(2.2)
$$\log W_{t+\tau} = A + \alpha \log \left(\frac{G_t}{N_t} \right) + \beta \log \left(\frac{D_t}{S_t} \right) + \gamma \log C_t + \text{error terms}$$

which recasts the model in the form suitable for regression analyses. Note the addition of the error terms, which may include autocorrelation and moving average components. This functional form implies that the influences of the three factors on log-transformed wages are combined linearly and additively—in other words, this is the simplest possible model to use. Log-transforming W makes sense on both theoretical and statistical grounds. The theoretical motivation is explained in Chapter 2 of Turchin (2003a). Briefly, the null model for many growth processes, including economic growth, is the exponential law. As a result, if we want to linearize the outcome of growth and investigate factors that influence it, we need to take logarithms. Log-transformation of the dependent variable also tends to stabilize variance, which is a plus in regression analyses. In short, if we don't have a functional form that arises from an explicitly mechanistic theory, the form (2.1) is the way to go. This accounts for its popularity in biological and economic applications (in economics, for example, the Cobb-Douglas function is a special case of this form).

Exponents α, β, and γ (the regression coefficients in the linearized form) measure relative contributions of the three factors to the growth of real wage. The parameter $A = \log a$ has no interpretation; it is simply a reflection of how independent variables are scaled. The final parameter, τ, which appears in the subscript of W, measures the degree of "stickiness" of wages. Changing conditions, as reflected especially in D/S and C factors, will shift the equilibrium to which W will start moving. However, W is an inertial variable and it takes several years for it to equilibrate. I model this lagged response phenomenologically with τ. The lag τ should be at least 3 years (typical length of contracts negotiated between management and unions) and probably no longer than 10 years, but the best value for this parameter will need to be determined empirically.

Model (2.1) is a general formulation. Its specific form will vary depending on the economic relations characterizing the studied society. For example, in countries with command economies, such as the USSR at its height, the forces of labor supply and demand (the D/S ratio) will have no effect on wages. The general model simplifies to

$$W_t = C_t \left(\frac{G_t}{N_t} \right)$$

where C_t reflects the decisions of central planners on what proportion of the GDP to devote to personal consumption, and what to investment and to the state (see Allen 2003 for a history of the Soviet industrialization as an example).

In economies based on slavery, the equation is even more simplified, $W_t = C_t$. In other words, the consumption levels of slaves are set by their owners, who take into consideration such factors as how much they need to spend on maintaining their property in working condition. The G/N ratio has no effect because there is no expectation that slaves will share the fruits of a growing economy. However, the balance of supply versus demand for slaves may have an indirect effect. If supply is deficient, slave owners may decide to spend more on their working force to reduce mortality and increase reproduction.

An alternative simplification of the model omits the term involving extra-economic forces and focuses entirely on labor supply/demand dynamics:

$$W_{t+\tau} = a \left(\frac{G_t}{N_t} \right)^\alpha \left(\frac{D_t}{S_t} \right)^\beta$$

Such a formulation is appropriate for "pure" capitalist systems. I will use this equation in Chapter 9, because the economic system of nineteenth-century America provides a good approximation to such a pure market-driven system. In the twentieth century, however, cultural factors played an increasingly important role (sometimes driving wages above the level set by economic forces, and at other times below it). Chapter 12 will devote a section to estimating the dynamics of C_t. Further elaborations of the modeling framework (Eqn 2.1) are, therefore, deferred to these two modeling chapters.

Elite Dynamics

Elite numbers, E, can change as a result of two processes: endogenous population growth (the balance between births and deaths) and social mobility (from and to the general population, N). Accordingly, the equation for E is:

(2.3) $$\dot{E} = rE + \mu N$$

where r is per capita rate of population growth and μ is the coefficient capturing the balance of upward and downward social mobility between the general population compartment and the elite compartment of the model.

The rate of net social mobility, μ, should be *inversely* related to the relative wage (wage scaled by GDP per capita), because if wages do not keep up with economic growth, the elites dispose of an increasingly large amount of surplus. A favorable economic conjuncture for employers, thus, creates greater upward mobility opportunities for entrepreneurial commoners. I assume that

$$\mu = \mu_0 \left(\frac{w_0}{w} - 1 \right)$$

where w is the relative wage and μ_0 and w_0 are scaling parameters. Parameter μ_0 modulates the magnitude of response in social mobility to the availability of surplus. Parameter w_0 is the level at which there is no net upward mobility (when $w = w_0$, $\mu = 0$). The more w falls below that level, the more positive the term on the right hand side will be, and the more vigorous upward social mobility. Conversely, when w increases above w_0, upward social mobility is choked off, and the net mobility is downwards (out of the elite compartment into the general population).

Combining these two equations, we have the following model for the dynamics of elite numbers:

(2.4) $$\dot{E} = rE + \mu_0 \left(\frac{w_0 - w}{w} \right) N$$

If the demographic rate of elite increase is the same as that characterizing the general population, then this equation can be simplified by focusing on *relative elite numbers, e = E/N*. After some algebra we have

$$\dot{e} = \mu_0 \frac{w_0 - w}{w}$$

In other words, the rate of change of relative elite numbers is simply the net rate of social mobility (assuming that the elites do not differ in their demography from commoners).

The final component in the model is a calculation of how the average elite income changes with time. I will assume that the elites divide among themselves the amount of surplus produced by the economy. This surplus is $G - WL$, where G is the total GDP (in inflation-adjusted dollars), W is the real wage, and L is the size of labor force. This formulation assumes that the total economic output is divided among the elites and commoners with little or no role for the state. It is a reasonable approximation for nineteenth-century

America, when the economic footprint of the state was quite insignificant (a few percentage points of the GDP). However, for the twentieth century a more elaborate approach is required, which tracks the state and private sectors separately.

Dividing this quantity by the elite numbers (E) we obtain average surplus per elite. Finally, we scale average surplus per elite by the GDP per capita, or *relative elite income*:

$$\varepsilon = \frac{1}{g} \frac{G - WL}{E}$$

which simplifies to

(2.5)
$$\varepsilon = \frac{1 - w\lambda}{e}$$

where w is the relative wage of workers (scaled by GDP per capita), e is relative elite numbers (elites as a proportion of the total population), and $\lambda = L/N$ proportion of the total population that is employed. Because the total population includes children and the elderly, $\lambda \approx 0.5$. This parameter can fluctuate as a result of greater or lesser labor force participation and due to changes in the unemployment rate, but generally speaking such fluctuations stay within fairly narrow bounds, so the dynamics of ε are mostly determined by w and e.

Equations 2.1–2.5 describe the general model of worker-elite interactions, which will serve as the basis for more specific models in Chapters 9 and 12 dealing with social pressures for instability during the nineteenth and twentieth centuries, respectively.

Explaining Trend Reversals

The Importance of Social Mood

Cultural (social, ideological) factors can influence more than just real wages (as discussed in the previous section). Generally speaking, they are a part of the complex web of interacting forces, postulated by the structural-demographic theory, and therefore can have wide-ranging effects on all aspects of the social system. However, cultural factors are difficult to operationalize and quantify, which probably explains why quantitative historians have a tendency to focus on more easily measurable factors, such as population numbers, prices and wages, or biological measures of wellbeing. Such an emphasis served "the new economic history" (Fogel 1966), or cliometrics, very well (as witness the Nobel Memorial Prize in Economics shared by Robert Fogel and Douglass North in 1993 for their research in economic history).

Structural-demographic theory also deals with "hard" variables: population numbers, inflation and real wages, economic inequality, and incidence of political violence. Yet, analysis of historical societies (Turchin 2003b, 2009) suggests that "soft", difficult-to-quantify factors, such as social mood (Casti 2010) and changing cultural attitudes also play a key role. The role of cultural factors is particularly important during the Disintegrative Trend Reversals (when a Disintegrative Trend is succeeded by an Integrative Trend).

As an example, consider the swing of the social mood in Ancient Rome towards the end of the disintegrative phase of the first century BCE:

> In addition to the elevated elite mortality and depressed reproduction rates there must have been another, difficult to detect process—acquiescence to downward mobility. There must have been many potential elite aspirants who saw that the likely consequence of their pursuit of higher status would be an untimely death on battlefield or in a purge. They, therefore, could decide to be content with whatever modest status they already had, and chose to stay away from politics. An example of such a choice is Marcus Aemilius Lepidus, consul in 46 BCE and a member of the Second Triumvirate along with Mark Anthony and Octavian. In 36 Lepidus and Octavian had a falling out. "Octavian boldly entered the camp of Lepidus and persuaded the legions to desert. Then he stripped Lepidus of any real power and committed him to comfortable retirement at the lovely seaside town of Circeii in Latium. Lepidus lived there peacefully for another twenty-four years" (Ward 2003). It is hard to imagine a Pompey or a Caesar accepting such a comfortable retirement from the struggle, but people vary in how much they are driven by ambition. Another example is T Pomponius Atticus, Cicero's confidant, publisher, and banker. This equestrian had more wealth than many senators, but chose to stay away from politics. During the turbulent years of 88–65 he moved to Greece, where he was safe from Rome's political storms. After returning to Rome, he patronized the arts and literature and made so many important contacts that he was protected on all sides during the subsequent civil wars (Ward 2003). At lower levels of the Roman social hierarchy there must have been many such Lepidi or Attici who, perhaps after a brush with death in the civil war, decided to return to their estates; and their numbers probably increased as

the futility of internal war was demonstrated over and over again. The poet Tibullus exclaimed (probably in 32 BCE): "I don't want to die young and for nothing!" (Le Glay 1997). Vergil's *Georgics* are filled with longing for peace: "so many wars throughout the world ... the fields going to waste in the farmer's absence" (quoted from Wells 1992).

After the last period of civil war, the twenty years of "*discordia, non mos, non ius*" that began in 49, Italy was exhausted and ready to welcome a regime that offered peace (Brunt 1971). A century of sociopolitical instability had dealt with the problem of elite overproduction and also induced in Romans a powerful longing for peace. The rule of Augustus, as a result, rested on a broad popular consensus. For example, when Augustus in 23 BCE gave up the annual consulship he held since 31, the people of Rome, fearing the diminution of his authority, rioted trying to force him to accept the office (Wells 1992). The secular disintegrative trend reversed itself, and a new cycle of the Principate commenced (Turchin and Nefedov 2009: 207–8).

Similar swings in the public mood, underlying the shift from disintegrative to integrative dynamics can be detected in other societies at the end of secular cycles, for example, in France at the end of both the Capetian and Valois cycles (Turchin and Nefedov 2009: 138 and 173–4). Here's how a new cooperative mood took root among the French elites in the seventeenth century, and helped to bring the disintegrative phase of the Valois cycle to an end:

> It is clear that the assumption of personal rule by Louis XIV in 1661 marked an important turning point in the history of France. The most dramatic development was the consolidation of the elites around the center, which ended intraelite conflict that plagued the preceding hundred years and channeled elite energies to wars of external conquest. The internal workings of how this consensus between the elites and the state was achieved has been admirably probed by William Beik (1985, 2005) using as an example the provincial aristocracy of Languedoc. Essentially, the last period of high sociopolitical instability, peaking with the Fronde of 1648–53, forced the elites to understand that they needed military, diplomatic, and economic protection of the center (Beik 1985). Between 1560 and 1660 various factions fighting in civil wars were either entirely composed of the

elites, or were elite-mobilized popular uprisings. After 1660 the elites withdrew leadership and uprisings dramatically declined (Beik 1985). Later popular uprisings, such as the rebellion of Cévennes peasants (1702–4) lacked support among the elites, and were easily put down.

The new consensus allowed the government of Louis XIV to raise taxes to an unprecedented level in French history (see Figure 5.2). The elites were, of course, the primary beneficiaries. First, comparative distribution of tax flow between crown and regional elites in 1647 and 1677 (Beik 1985) shows that at least in Languedoc the regional elites were able to increase the share of taxes that remained in the province. Second, the lion's share of taxes went into financing the wars of Louis XIV, which meant improved employment for the sword nobility. Furthermore, at least during the late seventeenth century, Louis's program of external conquest was highly successful (Turchin and Nefedov 2009: 173–4).

A Cultural Multilevel Selection Framework for Trend Reversals

As the example of sixteenth-century France makes clear, the key process that resulted in the reversal of the disintegrative trend was the consolidation of national elites and their willingness to cooperate with the monarchy. A very general theoretical framework for making sense of how such a cooperative state of affairs might become established is cultural evolution and, more specifically, cultural multilevel selection (CMLS) theory (Richerson and Boyd 2005, Wilson 2007, Bowles and Gintis 2011). This theory allows us to conceptualize how some cultural attitudes (or social norms) may increase in frequency, while other variants decrease. Thus, one set of social norms is willingness to cooperate with other interest groups for the sake of the common good, readiness to compromise, and generalized trust that the authorities and social institutions will "do the right thing". The alternative set is pervasive social distrust, unwillingness to compromise, and resolve to advance the partisan goals of one's interest group. An "interest group" here may mean an ethnic or religious community, an economic class (e.g., employees versus employers), regional and local communities focusing on their parochial agendas, and other kinds of special interest groups.

The overall level of social cooperation within a polity at any given time, therefore, should be greatly influenced by the relative frequency of "broadly cooperative" versus "narrowly partisan" attitudes. Note that a partisan attitude is also a cooperative social norm, but cooperation is directed towards one's narrow group, rather than towards society as whole. This distinction is similar to the one Robert Putnam (2000) makes between "bridging" and "bonding" types of social capital. The question is, what mechanisms are responsible for the change in relative frequencies of cooperative versus partisan norms?

Social theorists have suggested several. One mechanism, with a long pedigree, is the Simmel-Coser principle: conflict between groups tends to increase internal cohesion (Simmel 1955, Coser 1956). Conflict sharpens boundaries between groups and strengthens group consciousness (Coser 1956:34). Thus, competition between groups tends to promote within group cooperation. This is sometimes known as "parochial altruism" (Choi and Bowles 2007).

The second, and related mechanism, is that the cultural distance between two competing groups tends to increase both the intensity of the conflict, and the degree of internal cohesion within each group. A review of anthropological evidence by Solometo (2006:27–30) indicates that cultural distance between groups affects warfare intensity. As an example, the Jívaro of South America recognize two different types of armed conflict. Wars waged against other Jívaro are essentially lengthy blood feuds, in which deaths are limited. Conflicts between neighboring tribes that "speak differently", on the other hand, typically take the form of "wars of extermination". Recently, I collected data on the historical incidence of genocide, focusing on the fates of populations of cities falling to a siege, or assault. The data indicate that genocide was an order of magnitude more frequent in wars between culturally very dissimilar steppe nomads and settled agriculturalists, compared with civil wars between culturally similar groups (Turchin 2011).

Cultural dissimilarity *within a group*, by contrast, tends to decrease the capacity for within-group cooperation (Putnam 2007, for a critical review, see Portes and Vickstrom 2011). One reason for this effect is that people tend to trust those who are similar to them. But probably an even more important reason is that establishing and sustaining cooperative ability critically depends on prosocial norms (Richerson and Henrich 2012). Different ethnic groups often evolve their own ways of cooperating, and establishing cooperation in a heterogeneous group can become a difficult problem of coordinating between incompatible mechanisms of achieving consensus and sustaining collective action.

Finally, competition *within* groups also has a corrosive effect on the tendency of the group to generate and sustain collective action. As Steven Frank (2003) argues, "When opportunities for competition against neighbors are limited within groups, individuals can increase their own success only by enhancing the efficiency and productivity of their group. Thus, characters that repress competition within groups promote cooperation and enhance group success." A study by Kay et al (2004) showed that exposing exper-imental subjects to objects that evoke competition (e.g., a businessman to a briefcase) increased the cognitive accessibility of the construct of com-petition and decreased cooperation (increased the amount of money that participants retained for themselves in the Ultimatum Game). Additional, although indirect, evidence for this comes from numerous studies suggesting that economists and economics students are much more likely to free-ride than representatives of other academic professions (Marwell and Ames 1981, Frank et al. 1993). And there is evidence that high levels of inequality within groups (which can be thought of as a proxy for within-group competition) also decrease cooperation (see Chapter 4 in Turchin 2016).

These four mechanisms, (1) competition between groups, (2) competi-tion within groups, (3) cultural distance between competing groups, and (4) cultural homogeneity within groups are not the only processes that can affect the spread of cooperation norms. However, these four processes are interesting because historical evidence suggests that all of them play a role in trend reversals during secular cycles, and because they happen to be con-nected by one of the most important formulas in multilevel selection theory, so in a certain sense they are just four aspects of a single, more fundamental mechanism.

The mathematical formula I am referring to is the Price equation (Price 1970, 1972, Bowles 2006, see also Okasha 2007, Gardner 2008). A useful way to write it for our purposes is as follows (Bowles 2009):

(2.3) $$\Delta p = V_S \beta_S - \overline{V}_I \beta_I$$

Here p refers to the frequency of agents holding broadly cooperative attitudes, and $(1 - p)$, correspondingly, the frequency of narrowly partisan agents; Δp is the rate of change of p. The right-hand side shows how the four factors (competition between and within groups, and cultural variation within and between groups) determine whether the frequency of broadly cooperative norms will increase, or decrease. The approach here is explicitly multilevel, so we represent human societies as consisting of interest groups nested within it. Here we are concerned with just two hierarchical levels, but in principle the analysis can be extended to an arbitrary number of levels.

Subscripts reference the hierarchical level of a (potentially) cooperating group. Thus, S is the level of the overall society (or the whole polity; we can also apply the analysis to just the governing elites, which may be appropriate for certain historical societies in which cooperation from peasants was neither expected nor particularly desired). The subscript I refers to "interest groups" nested within the overall polity.

An "interest group" is a social group whose members are united by a common set of goals, which they attempt to achieve by cooperating together. Generally speaking, such groups include religious cults, ethnic groups, professional associations, mutual-aid societies, and economic organizations such as corporations. For structural-demographic dynamics the most relevant groups are class-based organizations (e.g., AFL-CIO and the Chamber of Commerce), lobbying groups, and political parties. Political organizations include not only established parties (e.g., Democrats and Republicans), but also such movements as the Tea Party or Occupy Wall Street, and even radical organizations that may aim to overthrow the state, or secede from it.

V_S and V_I are cultural variances. V_S quantifies the variation among societies; it is a measure of cultural distance between competing polities. V_I is the cultural variance between interest groups and measures cultural dissimilarity within a polity (the bar over V_I indicates a weighted average over all polities). The two quantities on the right hand side are coefficients measuring competition, with β_S quantifying the strength of between-society competition and β_I, similarly, measuring the strength of within-society competition between different interest groups. Note the negative sign before β_I. It's there because within-society competition works *against* the spread of the broadly cooperative norms.

Putting it all together, Eqn (2.3) specifies whether broadly cooperative norms (at the level of the whole society) are favored, or whether the opposite occurs (partisan norms are favored to spread). It all depends on the balance of forces favoring each kind of norm and on the structure of cultural variation.

Within the field of cultural evolution the Price equation has been used primarily to understand cultural multilevel selection. In such settings, a cultural norm spreads because one group outcompetes the other. For example, if a polity with more cooperative norms and institutions conquers another, it may impose these norms on the defeated society. As an example, the British Empire conquered India and transmitted to it such institutions as democratic forms of governance. Cultural group selection can also operate without conquest. When one polity clearly does better than another, people within the society that is falling behind in competition may collectively decide to adopt some of the institutions of the successful society. An example of this could be Russia's abandoning a state-run economy in favor of a more market-oriented one, after losing economic competition with the United States.

While the dynamics of intersocietal competition are largely outside the scope of the Structural-Demographic Theory, similar processes of cultural selection may operate within societies. At the interest group level, if one political party successfully deploys a smear campaign against a rival party, and wins the election, in the next electoral round the defeated party may also decide to adopt smear tactics (this is an example of a partisan norm spreading at the expense of more broadly cooperative norm).

Such copying of practices that enhance success in between-group competition is a legitimate form of cultural group selection (see also Richerson and Henrich 2012). Furthermore, this form of cultural group selection may be of relevance in explaining secular trend reversals. However, another set of processes that can affect the dynamics of cooperative norms, in addition to cultural group selection, is what is known as *biased transmission* (Richerson and Boyd 2005).

The biased transmission scenario focuses on the likelihood of people adopting one or the other cultural variant due to innate or cultural preferences (Richerson and Boyd 2005: 66). These preferences themselves evolved as a result of gene-culture coevolution and, therefore, the insights of the Price equation also apply to this scenario, although in an indirect way. In particular, the four factors, corresponding to the four entities on the right-hand side of Eqn (2.3), should "prime" individuals either for broadly cooperative norms, or for partisan norms. Changing conditions such as presence or absence of external threat, the level of internal competition, and cultural similarity/dissimilarity at various levels should tilt the "mental landscape" in ways favoring either cooperative or partisan norms.

Using this conceptual framework, we see that integrative trend reversals occur under the conditions of elevated competition within a polity, resulting from both overpopulation and elite overproduction. As we documented in *Secular Cycles* (Turchin and Nefedov 2009), intrapolity competition drives up economic inequality, both between classes (commoners and elites) and within classes, and decreases cooperation both between classes and within classes. Growing rates of crime and political violence are the visible manifestations of declining social cooperation (Roth 2009).

Increased cultural heterogeneity of the elites is often an additional factor affecting the decline of cooperation during this phase of the secular cycle.

Typically, elite overproduction is due in large part to vigorous upward mobility from the ranks of commoners. As a result, the ranks of elites are swelled with individuals coming from very different socioeconomic and educational backgrounds. Cultural misunderstanding and mistrust between old aristocracy and "parvenus" may contribute to intraelite fragmentation. Furthermore, the integrative phases of secular cycles are often correlated with periods of successful territorial expansion. If the elites from newly conquered territories, who are likely to have a different ethnic background from the core ethnic group, are admitted to the elite ranks, the cultural diversity among the elites is further increased. Eventually, the new elites are culturally assimilated, but this is a lengthy, time-consuming process.

During disintegrative trend reversals, these processes work in reverse. Abatement of elite overproduction decreases intraelite competition. Additionally, there is another curious dynamic that tends to increase intraelite homogeneity, the "closing of the patriciate", in which the established elites close their ranks to newcomers and dramatically reduce, or even reverse upward social mobility. This is a very frequent occurrence during the reversal from disintegrative to integrative trends.

One example of this dynamic is the formation of the Roman patriciate during the fifth century BCE. Although the tradition maintains that the patriciate originated during the regal period, modern historians believe that the patricians were the individuals who expelled the king and held office during the early years of the republic, and then attempted to arrogate to themselves and their descendants exclusive rights of access to positions of political and sacred power (Cornell 1995:251). This process was described by De Sanctis (1953) as *serrata del patriziato*, or "the closing of the patriciate" (in turn, reflecting the process that occurred in medieval Venice).

Another example is the reforms undertaken by several early modern monarchies to restrict entry into the nobility. For example, the French Crown officials periodically inspected the credentials of individuals claiming noble status. Whereas during the expansion of the sixteenth century, only about one percent of family heads were permanently "condemned" (denied noble status), during the disintegrative trend reversal of the late seventeenth century six percent were condemned (Turchin and Nefedov 2009: Table 5.2 and see the discussion on pp. 166–8). Similar efforts by the Russian monarchy, in which impoverished nobles were forced into the class of state peasants, helped to reduce the numbers of Russian gentry from the peak of 80,000 in the 1580s to 23,000 around 1700 (Turchin and Nefedov 2009: Table 8.2).

External war often played an important role in increasing or sustaining cooperation among the elites, as well as cooperation between the elites, the state, and sometimes even commoners. During integrative phases, governments in collaboration with the elites often used external war to bring about periods of national consolidation. Additionally, successful wars of conquest yielded abundant rewards to be shared between the state and the elites. During disintegrative phases, meddling by external powers could cause a backlash in which rival factions of the elites forgot their divisions and cooperated in expelling the common enemy. One example of this dynamic at work was the disintegrative trend reversal at the end of the medieval French cycle (Turchin and Nefedov 2009:137–41). However, because external wars are affected by a much broader set of factors than the internal dynamics of the polity in question, they should be treated as largely an exogenous mechanism. As an example, the September 11, 2001 terrorist attacks caused Americans to close the ranks and increased internal cohesiveness and cooperation, even if the effect did not last very long. One manifestation of this brief moment of internal solidarity was reflected in a spike of "trust in government" as measured by the Pew Research Center (see Figure 5.3).

In summary, Eqn (2.3) offers a conceptual framework for making sense of cultural dynamics during secular trend reversals. Chapters 7 and 8 will apply this framework to the Jackson Era trend reversal, and Chapter 9 to the Progressive Era trend reversal.

Wheels within Wheels: Modeling Complex Dynamics of Sociopolitical Instability

In *Complex Dynamics of Sociopolitical Instability* (Chapter 1) I noted that the dynamical pattern characterizing sociopolitical instability in historical societies (see, for example Figure 1.1) is more complex than just a sequence of secular integrative (relatively stable) and disintegrative (relatively unstable) phases. The jagged, "saw-toothed" nature of the trajectory suggests that there is another, shorter cycle superimposed on the longer multi-century oscillations. Because the time step of instability data, plotted in Figure 1.1, is 25 years, a series of alternating highs and lows corresponds to an average period of c.50 years. Indeed, a spectral analysis of the Roman data suggests that there are two frequencies dominating these fluctuations, with periods of c.300 and 50 years (Figure 2.2a). The French series also has two peaks, one with the period of 300 years and another at 67 years, somewhat longer than in the Roman data (Fig. 2.2b). The shorter cycles are particularly prominent during the dis-integrative phases of the longer (secular) cycle.

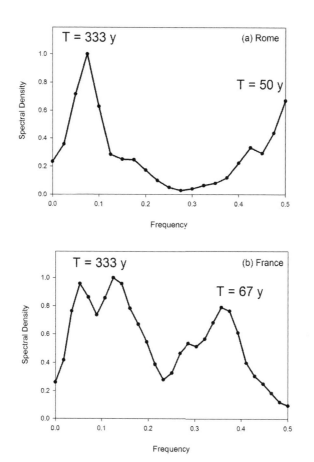

FIGURE 2.2 Spectral analysis of sociopolitical instability data in Figure 1.1.
(a) Rome. (b) France.

These observations suggest that there is an additional process (which is not part of the Structural-Demographic Theory) that needs to be taken into account when studying sociopolitical instability. In my earlier publications I referred to this shorter-term oscillation as the "fathers-and-sons" cycles (Turchin 2003b, 2006b). The operation of this mechanism is especially ap-parent during the prolonged disintegrative secular trends, which are charac-teristic of secular cycles in Europe.

The empirical observation is that disintegrative trends are not periods of continuous civil war; instead, they have internal structure with decades when sociopolitical instability is particularly high, interspersed with decades of relative pacification. To illustrate this dynamic, consider the disintegrative trend of late-medieval France, somewhat misleadingly called the Hundred Years War, although the "Hundred Years of Hostility" (Braudel 1988) might be a better description. During the late-medieval crisis in France "good" reigns alternated with "bad" (Turchin 2006b: 243–47). Thus, the reign of John II (1350–64) was a period of social dissolution and state collapse, while that of his son Charles V (1364–1380) was a time of national consolidation and territorial reconquest. The next reign, that of Charles VI (1380–1422) was yet another period of social disintegration and collapse. It was followed by a period of internal consolidation and national resurgence under Charles VII (1422–1461), which finally lifted France out of the late medieval depression.

This is a general dynamical pattern of alternation between very turbulent and relatively peaceful spells that is observed repeatedly during the secular disintegrative phases. A possible explanation is swings in the collective social mood (Turchin 2006b: Chapter 9). Episodes of internal warfare often develop in ways similar to epidemics or forest fires. In the beginning of the conflict, each act of violence triggers chains of revenge and counter-revenge, and conflict escalates in an accelerating, explosive fashion. Once the conflict has entered the phase of general civil war, however, it triggers a kind of a backlash. As violence drags on and on, often for years, the most violent leaders and their psychopathic followers are gradually killed off. The rest of the population begin to yearn for an end to fighting and return of stability.

In other words, this explanation proposes that collective violence "burns out", much like an epidemic or a forest fire. Even though the fundamental causes that brought on the conflict in the first place may still be operating, the prevailing social mood swings in favor of cessation of conflict at all costs, and an uneasy truce gradually takes hold. Those people, like the generation of Charles the Wise, who directly experienced civil war, become "immunized" against it, and while they are in charge, they keep things stable. The peaceful period may last for a human generation—between 20 and 30 years. Eventually, however, the conflict-scarred generation dies off or retires, and a new cohort arises, people who have not experienced the horrors of civil war, and are not immunized against it.

If the long-term social forces that brought about the first outbreak of internal hostilities are still operating, then the society will slide into a second civil war. As a result, periods of intense conflict tend to recur with a period of roughly two generations (40–60 years). These swings in the social mood may be termed "bi-generation cycles" because they involve alternating generations that are either prone to conflict, or not. Another example of such social mood swings, also with a period of roughly 50 years, has been noted, for example, by Arthur M. Schlesinger Jr. (1986).

This verbal theory sounds plausible. However, when dealing with cycles that result from nonlinear feedback loops, verbal theories should always be checked with formal mathematical models. More specifically, the verbal explanation treats the population as consisting of discrete, not-overlapping "generations". Yet the age-structure of human populations is characterized by smoothly overlapping generations, without any clear-cut break points between them. We cannot simply impose generations on human social systems; we need to investigate mathematically whether they will arise naturally as a result of age-structured population and social dynamics.

A Model of Social Contagion

To answer the question posed above, I developed a simple age-structured model of social contagion. The model is inspired by the theoretical framework used in epidemiology, known as the SIR models (May and Anderson 1991). The SIR refers to the representation of the modeled population as composed of three compartments: Susceptible, Infectious, and Recovered individuals. The mathematical theory of epidemics offers a natural framework for modeling the dynamics of such cultural traits as social attitudes and norms, because individuals learn them socially, from others—just as epidemics spread as a result of people infecting each other with germs. Many discussions in cultural evolution employ epidemiological metaphors. For example, the proponents of memetics often speak of memes jumping from brain to brain (Dawkins 1976). However, it is worth stressing that the model in this section does not assume presence of cultural "replicators", such as memes. In fact, the model makes no assumption about the form that cultural information takes. It simply tracks how individuals change their state as a result of interacting with others in the population.

There are three kinds of individual in the model. The first is the "naïve" type, corresponding to the susceptibles in the epidemiological framework. This is the class into which individuals are put when they become adults (the model tracks only individuals who are active adults; so children and the elderly past the retirement age are not modeled and have no effect on the dynamics). Naïve individuals can become "radicalized" by being exposed to individuals of the radical type (corresponding to infectious individuals in the SIR framework). The process of radicalization can occur as a result of encountering a radical and becoming converted to his or her ideology. This process of social contagion is of central importance in the model.

The social contagion model is quite general and can be used for many purposes, such as the spread of rumors, fads, panics, innovations, and many other kinds of cultural trait. However, my primary goal here is to understand the dynamics of sociopolitical instability. The proportion of radicals in the total population is thus the key variable that we need to track. When a high proportion of the population is radicalized, sociopolitical instability will be very high. Under such conditions, riots are easily triggered and readily spread, terrorist and revolutionary groups thrive and receive support from many sympathizers, and the society is highly vulnerable to an outbreak of civil war. Thus, the proportion of radicals in the population can serve as a proxy for sociopolitical instability.[3]

Alternatively, or additionally to contracting a radical ideology, a naïve individual can also become radicalized by being exposed to violence resulting from radical activities. Note that all radicals will usually not belong to a single "Radical Party". During periods of high political instability there are typically many issues dividing the population and the elites. Thus, there are many factions of radicals, warring with each other. Some become left-wing extremists, others join right-wing organizations. Additionally, there are likely to be feuds or outright hostilities even among factions at the same end of the political spectrum.

The model does not track different factions of radicals, only their numbers (proportion of the overall population). The more radicals there are, the more likely it is that a naïve individual will be exposed to political violence and become radicalized as a result. For example, someone whose relative or friend has been killed in a terrorist act perpetrated by right-wing extremists might join a left-wing revolutionary group. This second route to radicalization is also a kind of social contagion (but mediated by violence, instead of radical ideology). Both routes result in similar dynamics, so I will model them with one general functional form.

The third type of individual in the model is the "moderate" (corresponding to "recovered" in the SIR framework). This comprises former radicals who have become disenchanted with radicalism and internecine warfare,

---

3   However, there is likely to be a nonlinear relationship between these two variables, because as the proportion of radicals in the population grows, it becomes increasingly easy for them to link up and organize, potentially leading to a threshold effect on the levels of political violence. For reasons of parsimony, the current model does not incorporate this realistic mechanism.

and have come to the conclusion that the society needs to pull together and overcome its differences. The moderates differ from the naïves in that they value peace and order above all, and work actively to bring it about. In other words, naïve individuals don't have an active political program, radicals work actively to increase instability, and moderates work actively to dampen it out. Another way of thinking about the difference between radicals and moderates is in terms of the theory described earlier in this chapter (see *A Cultural Multilevel Selection Framework for Trend Reversals*): radicals are holders of partisan norms, whereas moderates hold broadly cooperative norms.

Dynamical equations describing how the rates at which individuals pass into and out of the three compartments are:

(2.4)
$$S_{a+1,t+1} = (1-\sigma_t)S_{a,t}$$
$$I_{a+1,t+1} = (1-\rho_t)I_{a,t} + \sigma_t S_{a,t}$$
$$R_{a+1,t+1} = R_{a,t} + \rho_t I_{a,t}$$

The state variables are the proportions of naïve individuals in the population (S), of radicals (I), and of moderates (R; following the SIR convention of susceptibles–infected–recovered). Subscripts refer to age (a) and time (t); thus, $a = 1, \dots T$ where T is the maximum age (and the number of age classes). For example, $R_{25,1951}$, is the proportion of moderates in the age class 25 in year 1951.[4]

Equations (2.4) are simply an accounting device, keeping track of flows between different compartments. Thus, all individuals leaving the naïve compartment (at the rate σ_t) must be added to the radicalized compartment (keeping track of their age class). Similarly, all individuals leaving the radicalized compartment (at the rate ρ_t) are added to the moderate compartment. All the action is in the two coefficients, which are modeled as follows:

(2.5)
$$\sigma_t = \left(\alpha - \gamma \sum_a R_{a,t}\right)\sum_a I_{a,t} \qquad 0 \le \sigma_t \le 1$$
$$\rho_t = \delta \sum_a I_{a,t-\tau} \qquad 0 \le \rho_t \le 1$$

The first equation says that the social contagion rate, σ_t, increases together with the total number of radicals ($\Sigma I_{a,t}$, summing over all age classes). In other words, the more radicals there are, the more likely it is that a naïve individual will become radicalized. However, there is an additional effect of the

---

4   Note that "age class 25" does not mean that individuals within it are 25 years old. The actual age depends on when "adulthood" starts. So if the model begins to track individuals when they turn 21, age class 25 will correspond to individuals who are 45 years old.

moderate presence: "infection" by radicalism declines as moderates increase in numbers and exert their moderating, instability-suppressing influence to reduce the probability that a naïve will become radicalized.

The second equation models the effect of the level of political violence on the probability of a radical becoming disgusted with radicalism and turning into a moderate. Because I proxy instability by the number of radicals, the equation for ρ_t includes the sum of radicals in all age classes. However, note that there is a time delay, τ. This parameter reflects the observation that high levels of political violence do not instantly translate into the social mood of revulsion against violence and desire for internal peace. Violence acts in a cumulative fashion; many years of high instability, or even outright civil war have to pass before the majority of the population begin to yearn for order earnestly. Including a time delay is admittedly a phenomenological approach to modeling this process; an alternative would be to add sociopolitical instability and explicitly model its effect on the rate of transition from radical to moderate compartment. However, to keep the current model parsimonious, I chose the simpler, even if less mechanistic, approach.

Equations (2.4) and (2.5) define the dynamics of the model. In addition, we need boundary and initial conditions. For initial conditions I put everybody in the naïve class and then add a radicalization "inoculum" by moving a small fraction of naïves into the radicalized compartment (because naïves can catch the radicalization "virus" only from radicals, without such an inoculum everybody would simply stay in the naïve compartment). Boundary conditions are constructed similarly. At every time step a constant fraction is added to the first age class in the naïve compartment, $S_{1,t} = 1/T$, where T is the number of age classes (this ensures that the proportions of all age classes in all compartments add up to 1). At the other end, individuals moving into age class $T + 1$ are simply eliminated (they die off or retire from active political life).

The model is quite parsimonious and has only five parameters: α, γ, δ, τ, and T. Parameter α indicates the likelihood that an encounter between a radical and a naïve will result in the naïve becoming radicalized, while γ measures the suppressive effect of moderates on radicalization rate. Parameter δ translates the intensity of radicalism into the rate at which radicals turn into moderates. Parameter τ measures the time scale at which exposure to violence acts to cause the backlash against it, and T is the period of adult activity.

Solving the age-structured social contagion model on the computer indicates that it readily produces bi-generational "fathers-and-sons" cycles, for a wide variety of parameter combinations. The anatomy of a typical 50-year cycle is depicted in Figure 2.3.

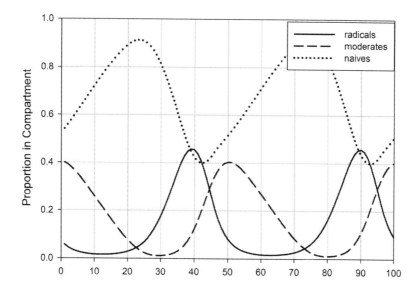

FIGURE 2.3 Dynamics of the age-structured social contagion model for parameters α = 0.3, γ = 1, δ = 0.5, τ = 10, and T = 35. Solid curve: the proportion of radicals (summing up all age classes) in the population. Broken and dotted curves: proportions of moderates and naïves, respectively.

The cycle starts when the number of radicals is low and that of moderates high. Few naïves are radicalized because they rarely encounter a radical, and the radicalization rate is low, thanks to the presence of many moderates. For the next 25 years the number of radicals continues to stay low, and the overall society enjoys a period of internal peace and stability. However, and more ominously, during this period the number of moderates declines as moderates retire from active political life. There are few new moderates because they arise only when radicals become disenchanted with radicalism, and the levels of political violence are too low to cause such disenchantment and, anyway, there are few radicals to convert to moderates. As a result, around the midpoint of the peaceful phase the number of radicals begins to increase, although initially very gradually.

Meanwhile, the number of naïve individuals grows, primarily due to moderates retiring and new individuals becoming adults. Around year 25, however, naïves start turning into radicals in increasing numbers. The growth of radicalism enters an autocatalytic phase (more radicals means greater numbers of naïves becoming exposed, while fewer moderates cannot exert a dampening influence on this process). The numbers of radicals explode, so that the second half of the cycle is characterized by elevated sociopolitical instability.

Sociopolitical instability reaches a peak around year 40 and then starts to decline. This decline is because increasing numbers of radicals become disenchanted, as a result of high levels of political violence, leading to the rise of moderates. By the end of the cycle (year 50), the moderates reach their peak. Their collective influence results in the suppression of radicals, radicalism, and instability, signaling the start of a peaceful phase (and the beginning of the next cycle).

The main lesson from this modeling exercise is that it is not necessary to assume that there are distinct (or even self-aware) "generations". Generations arise as a side-effect of age structure and the dynamics of social contagion. Thus, most individuals who become adults during the peaceful phase (the first 25 years of the cycle) will never become radicals or moderates. Thirty years into the cycle, over 80 percent are naïves (Figure 2.3). On the other hand, individuals who enter adulthood during the next 25-year period, the instability phase, have a high chance of becoming first radicalized and then "burntout", and make the transition into moderates. Half or more of those cohorts who are in the young adult stage during the acceleration phase of instability (25–40 years into the cycle) will travel the radicalization-moderation path.

In the real world, oscillations in the social mood should be even more extreme than in the model, because most people who catch the radicalism virus tend to do so during their young adulthood years, from other individuals of a similar age. The model (2.4–2.5) does not incorporate such age-dependency in the dynamical rates. The important point is that even with minimalist assumptions about the radicalization and moderation rates (with only three parameters, α, γ, and δ, modulating these two processes, the model still can generate bi-generational cycles for a wide variety of parameters.

The period of these cycles depends primarily on the two time parameters, τ and T. The model-predicted trajectory in Figure 2.3 was generated by assuming that the total length of active political life is $T = 35$ years. If people become adults at the age of 21, then their active period is 21–55 years old. Increasing this parameter by 10 years (active years are 21–65) lengthens the cycle period from 50 to 55 years. Decreasing this period makes cycles shorter and eventually leads to stability (with an oscillatory approach to the stable equilibrium). The time-lag in the effect of instability on the moderation rate has a similar effect. For example, for $\tau = 15$, the cycle rises to 60 years, while decreasing τ eventually stabilizes the dynamics.

Of the three rate parameters, α, γ, and δ, the most important one affecting stability is α. This parameter relates the radicalization rate to the proportion of radicals in the total population, so it can be called "propensity for radicalization". It stands to reason that increasing α should make cycles more pronounced, while decreasing this parameter should eventually stabilize the dynamics, and that is indeed what the model does.

Fathers-and-Sons Cycles and Secular Waves: A Model with Multiple Feedbacks

Propensity to radicalize (parameter α in the model) offers us a way to connect the social contagion model to the Structural-Demographic Theory. It stands to reason that during the disintegrative phases of secular cycles, when structural-demographic conditions result in high social pressure for instability, radical ideas should fall on fertile soil and readily take root. In other words, during a disintegrative phase parameter α should be high. Conversely, during integrative phases, when popular and elite mobilization potentials are low, α should also be low. Roughly speaking, propensity to radicalize should be positively related to the Political Stress Index, $\alpha \sim \Psi$.

This argument suggests that one way to generate the complex dynamics of sociopolitical instability, characterized by two periodicities superimposed on each other, is to vary α cyclically. Figure 2.4 shows the resulting dynamics. When propensity to radicalize is high ("disintegrative phases") we observe a series of fathers-and-sons cycles, recurring roughly every 50 years. When α is low ("integrative phases"), father-and-sons cycles are suppressed.

The dynamics in Figure 2.4 share certain similarities with historical data on sociopolitical instability in real societies, in particular, the pattern of two cycles overlaid on each other (see Figure 1.1). However, the data in Figure 1.1 are sampled at 25-year intervals, which makes it hard to see what is happening on shorter (e.g., decadal) time-scales. A finer-resolution view is made available by a more detailed historical record for England (Turchin and Nefedov 2009: Chapter 2 and 3). These data are based on enumerating years with major incidents of sociopolitical instability (coups d'état, popular rebellions, and full-scale civil war). The binary (presence/absence) data is then smoothed to reveal the dynamics at two different time scales: decadal and semicentennial (see Turchin 2005 for details). The decadal time step reveals fathers-and-sons cycles, with periods between 40 and 60 years in the English data (Figure 2.5, thinner curve). The semicentennial scale smoothes over fathers-and-sons

dynamics and reveals longer secular cycles, with periods of 250–300 years
(Figure 2.5, thicker curve).

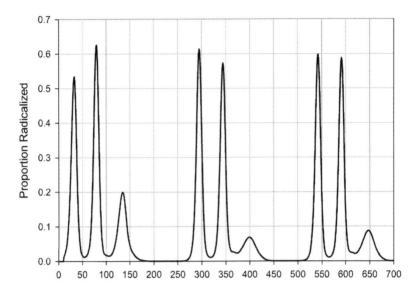

FIGURE 2.4 Dynamics of the age-structured social contagion model with
a periodically-changing propensity to radicalize. Same parameters as in
Figure 2.3 ($\gamma = 1$, $\delta = 0.5$, $\tau = 10$, $T = 35$), except α varies as a sine wave with
period = 250 years and amplitude between 0 and 0.4.

There are three secular disintegrative phases (early medieval: c. 1050–1150,
late medieval: c.1380–1500, and early modern: c. 1640–1700). These disintegrative phases tend to consist of two fathers-and-sons cycles. For example, the early modern disintegrative phase has two clusters of instability, one in 1639–1651
(the Bishops' War, Civil War I and II), and the second in 1685–1692 (Monmouth
and Argyll Rebellions, the Glorious Revolution, Williamite War in Ireland,
and the Jacobite Uprising in Scotland). During the integrative phases that followed the late medieval and early modern crises fathers-and-sons cycles were
suppressed. On the other hand, during the long medieval integrative phase
(c.1200–1350) shorter oscillations were not suppressed (these three clusters of
instability were due primarily to baronial rebellions against the Crown).

Thus, the real data are much "messier" than the dynamics predicted by
the model. This is not particularly surprising. First, political instability in
the historical society, England, was affected by a much more complex set of
factors than the ones included in the model. Second, the English state evolved
over the eight centuries from a rather chaotic medieval kingdom to much

more stable Renaissance and, especially, Enlightenment monarchies. Third, there is a theoretical reason why the model predicts behavior that is more regular than it should be.

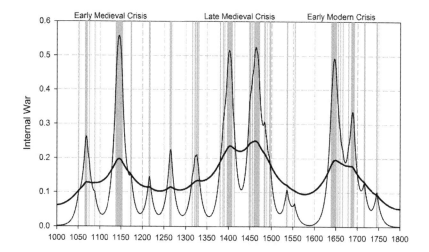

FIGURE 2.5 Complex dynamics of internal war (including rebellions, coups d'état, and civil war) in the Kingdom of England. Temporal patterns are shown at three time scales: yearly, decadal, and semicentennial. The gray vertical lines indicate years with internal war (present/absent). The thinner curve smoothes the presence-absence data with an exponential kernel regression using bandwidth h = 10 years. The thicker curve does the same with bandwidth h = 50 years. *Source of data:* (Turchin and Nefedov 2009: Tables 2.5 and 3.2)

The fathers-and-sons cycles in the model are generated by an endogenous mechanism, that is, one involving a nonlinear feedback loop (captured by equations 2.4–2.5). The longer "secular" cycle, on the other hand is imposed exogenously, simply by varying one of the model parameters periodically. However, according to the Structural-Demographic Theory, secular cycles are not exogenous. Instead, they arise as a result of endogenous mechanisms involving various feedback loops between the structural-demographic variables. Mathematical theory tells us that when a dynamical system has two kinds of nonlinear feedback loop with different periods, these two mechanisms are likely to interact nonlinearly and may generate erratic, unpredictable-looking behavior known as mathematical chaos (Gleick 1987). It is likely that if we model mechanisms for both types of cycles as endogenous, the resulting model output will not be simply two periodicities neatly superimposed on each other, but something much more complex and erratic (and looking more like the data).

Adding the structural-demographic machinery to the model of social contagion, however, would result in a very complicated model. Instead of going that route, I develop a very simple model that includes two types of dynamical feedbacks, one standing for fathers-and-sons dynamics, the other for structural-demographic dynamics—only that and nothing more. The question I am interested in is how the two types of feedback are likely to interact.

To keep the multiple feedbacks model simple, I formulate it in the discrete time framework, which explicitly assumes that there are distinct generations. As I discussed in the previous section (A Model of Social Contagion), human populations do not really have distinct generations. However, the model developed subsequently demonstrates that alternating radicalized/non-radicalized generations can arise naturally when age structure interacts with the dynamics of radicalization and moderation. The simpler discrete model, thus, captures this behavior phenomenologically, without going into mechanistic details of how it is generated. In other words, I follow here the modeling strategy outlined earlier in this chapter (Dynamical Feedbacks: An Overview): constructing dynamically complete models requires that we keep the number of dynamical feedbacks to an absolute minimum and drastically simplify how each link is modeled.

Let W_t stand for the degree of radicalization of generation indexed by time t (and since I use radicalization as a proxy for instability, W_t also stands for the intensity of internal war). Let X_t stand for the combined operation of all structural-demographic factors that are correlated with population and elite wellbeing. In other words, X_t is the net effect of structural-demographic factors that suppress instability (so it is an inverse function of Ψ; focusing on integrative factors leads to simpler and more intuitive functional forms in the model).

A general discrete-time formulation that captures dynamical feedbacks between W_t and X_t is

(2.6)
$$W_{t+1} = W_t \exp\left[f\left(W_t, X_t\right)\right]$$
$$X_{t+1} = X_t \exp\left[g\left(W_t, X_t\right)\right]$$

The reasons for using exponential forms are discussed in Turchin (2003a: 52–55).[5] The functions within the exponent, f and g, capture both direct effects of variables on itself and the interaction terms (how variables affect each other).

---

5   For example, the exponential form prevents the state variables from becoming negative.

Because I am interested in a simplest possible model, I assume a linear function for f, $f\left(W_t, X_t\right) = a - bW_t - cX_t$. This formulation says that the growth rate of W_t is negatively affected by a direct feedback of instability on itself (higher W_t means lower, or even negative, growth in the next time step). Additionally, it is suppressed by high values of X_t. Function g has an even simpler form: $g\left(W_t, X_t\right) = k(W_t - W_0)$. X_t declines for low values of W_t, grows otherwise. Parameter W_0 is the threshold value of W_t below which X_t starts declining. On the other hand, when W_t exceeds this threshold, X_t begins to grow. This eventually leads to X_t suppressing W_t, after which X_t declines itself. To sum the model assumptions, there are two kinds of negative feedback regulating W_t: a fast one involving itself (direct feedback), and a slow one involving X_t (indirect feedback).

Inserting definitions of the growth rate functions f and g into Eqn (2.6) and scaling the variables to get rid of extra parameters yields the following model:

$$W_{t+1} = W_t \exp\left[r(1 - W_t) - X_t\right]$$
$$X_{t+1} = X_t \exp\left[k(W_t - W_0)\right]$$

(2.7)

The model has only three parameters, but it can generate a variety of dynamical patterns, depending on the parameter values. One type of behavior is a cycle of alternating high and low W_t (Figure 2.6a). Because the time step in the model represents one generation, this pattern corresponds to pure fathers-and-sons cycles. Assuming a human generation length of 25 years, two-cycles correspond to the periodicity of 50 years.

For another set of parameters the model exhibits smooth longer-term cycles, which are usually referred to as "quasiperiodic" oscillations[6] (Figure 2.6b). The characteristic periods of quasiperiodic oscillations are between 6 and 12 time steps, or 150–300 years, corresponding to pure secular cycles. Whether the model predicts two-cycles or quasiperiodic oscillations depends on the relative strengths of the two dynamical feedbacks. If the direct feedback of W_t of itself dominates, we see two cycles. On the other hand, when the indirect feedback, mediated through X_t dominates, we observe quasiperiodic dynamics.

---

6   These oscillations are called quasiperiodic because they have irrational "periods" and never repeat themselves exactly (unlike limit cycles). This is a technical point, which has no practical relevance, because limit cycles and quasiperiodic oscillations are indistinguishable in the presence of dynamical noise, and in the real world dynamics are always affected by noise to a greater or lesser degree.

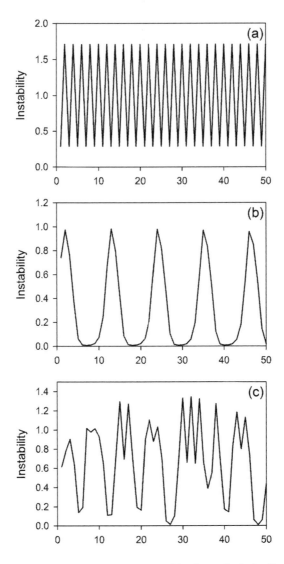

FIGURE 2.6 Dynamical patterns generated by the multiple feedback model
(2.7). (a) Two-point limit cycle, corresponding to pure fathers-and-sons oscillations (parameter values: $r = 2.5$, $k = 0$, $Wo = 0$). (b) Smooth long-term
oscillations, corresponding to pure secular cycles (parameter values: $r = 1.5$,
$k = 2$, $Wo = 0.3$). (c) Two-cycles superimposed on secular waves (parameter
values: $r = 2.1$, $k = 7$, $Wo = 0.7$).

Finally, for yet other parameter values, the model generates complex dynamics combining features of both two-cycles and quasiperiodic oscillations.
Typically, however, superposition of the two periodicities results in chaotic

behavior (Figure 2.6c). Most secular waves acquire "saw-toothed" peaks, with two or more fathers-and-sons cycles, but the degree to which these cycles are expressed in any particular secular disintegrative phase is quite variable. Additionally, the periods of oscillations also become much more variable than in the situation when only one feedback predominates.

In summary, the multiple feedbacks model demonstrates that two types of cycle, fathers-and-sons and secular, can be present simultaneously. However, they tend to interact dynamically, resulting in irregular, erratic-looking behavior known as mathematical chaos. In fact, the multiple feedbacks model produces output that looks very much like the dynamics of sociopolitical instability observed in real historical societies. This does not mean that *all* irregularities are due to endogenous chaos. We know perfectly well that human societies are complex systems that are affected by a multitude of exogenous influences. However, the simple model (2.7) raises the possibility that *some* of the irregularity observed in historical dynamics may be due to the nonlinear interaction between two dynamical feedbacks, one responsible for fathers-and-sons cycles and the other for secular waves. The mathematical model strongly implies that endogenous chaos is a generic result when both feedback loops are operating with similar strength.

PART TWO

Overview of Structural Demographic Variables: 1780–2010

Part II presents a systematic survey of time-series data on the overall dynamics of the fundamental variables of the structural-demographic model over the entire history of the United States. Parts III and IV then investigate in detail the secular cycle dynamics from the Revolution to the Great Depression (1780–1930) and from the Great Depression to the present (1930–2010).

As explained in Chapter 2, at the core of the Structural-Demographic Theory are three social subsystems and a process: population, elites, the state and sociopolitical instability (see Figure 2.1). Each of the next four chapters is devoted to one of those components. Chapter 3 deals with variables pertaining to the general population: demography and labor supply, economic and biological measures of wellbeing, and a proxy for social optimism. Chapter 4 focuses on the social structure and elite dynamics, with a particular emphasis on economic inequality and the numbers and consumption levels of the elites. Chapter 5 deals with the state: particularly its fiscal health, legitimacy, and, more generally, collective solidarity and levels of social cooperation. Finally, Chapter 6 documents the dynamics of sociopolitical instability over the long term. It also presents data on crime rates, with a particular focus on homicides.

3

Demography and Wellbeing

Labor Supply

In the nineteenth century two factors distinguished North American population dynamics from European (and, more broadly, Eurasian) dynamics: abundance of land sparsely settled by the Amerindians and massive immigration flows across the Atlantic. The importance of the first factor is that endogenous population growth did not necessarily lead to overpopulation, as long as the United States was able to prevail in Indian wars and open new territory for colonization. However, when local population growth was combined with the second factor, immigration, the result could be overpopulation (or, more accurately, oversupply of labor), especially in the Northeast, where the stocks of free land were exhausted first and where the great majority of European immigrants landed. Below, I review the dynamics of first the endogenous growth and then the exogenous inputs.

The trends in the US vital rates are depicted in Figure 3.1. The birth rate exhibited complex dynamics, resulting from the superposition of generation or bi-generation cycles on a long-term monotonic decline. The bi-generation, or Easterlin (1980) cycles, consisting of alternating baby busts and booms, are most obvious after 1920. The long-term pattern of change in the death rate will be discussed below, in the context of the dynamics of life expectancy. The net endogenous growth rate (births minus deaths, excluding immigration) was a very robust three percent per year in the eighteenth century and then gradually declined towards the 1930s. It increased again during the post-war baby boom and then declined towards the end of century (Figure 3.1).

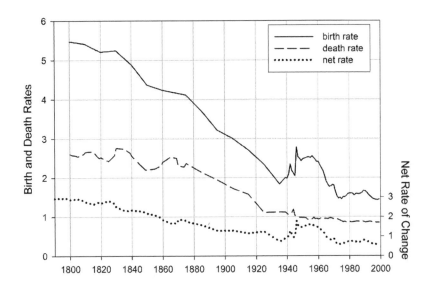

FIGURE 3.1 Vital population rates in the US, 1790–2000. The net rate of change is the difference between birth and death rates (thus, the overall population growth rate was higher due to immigration).

Apart from a very high starting point in the eighteenth century (due, without doubt, to large stocks of free land), dynamical patterns in American vital rates were not too different from the European patterns. With immigration, on the other hand, the story is very different (Figure 3.2a). During the early decades of the Republic the immigration rate was at a very low level, so that before the 1830s less than two percent of the population were born outside the country (Figure 3.2b). This changed dramatically around 1840. Repeated pulses of massive immigration arrived in America roughly every generation until the 1920s. The first peak c. 1850 nearly doubled the rate of population growth. As a result, between 1860 and 1920 the proportion of foreign-born Americans fluctuated around the level of nearly 15 percent. Following the Immigration Acts of 1921 and 1924, however, immigrant in-flows rapidly subsided, and during the 1930s the net flux briefly reversed its direction, with emigrants outnumbering immigrants.

The second period of high immigration began after World War II. Once the Immigration and Nationality Act of 1965 had abolished the National Origins Formula legislated in 1924, the proportion of foreign-born Americans began to increase again. Note that the curve in Fig. 3.2a and the solid line in Fig. 3.2b reflect only legal immigration. Including estimates of illegal immigration suggests that the proportion of population born outside the US had reached the levels of the late nineteenth century by 2005 (the broken line in Fig. 3.2b).

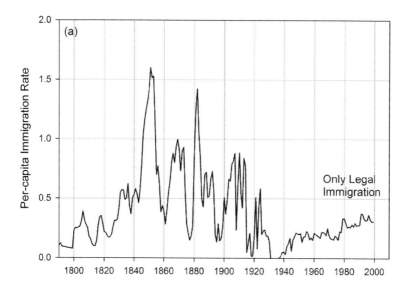

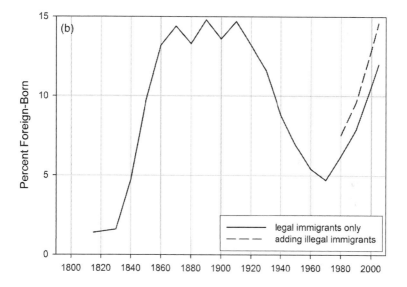

FIGURE 3.2 Immigration into the US. (a) Immigration rate per capita of population. (b) Proportion of population born outside the US. Based on data from the US Census Bureau.

Immigration, thus, has fluctuated dramatically, and in a cyclical fashion. The waxing and waning were due to the combined effect of both "push" and "pull" factors. The pull factors arose from a complex interplay between social structure and social mood dynamics within the US, and will be discussed in later chapters. The "push" factors, on the other hand, are easier to understand. Before the twentieth century, the east coast of North America received immigrants almost exclusively from Europe. As I discussed in Chapter 1, the European population went through periodic boom and bust cycles, recurring roughly every two or three centuries. Massive population growth in the eighteenth century, during the integrative phase of the last complete secular cycle (see Table 1.1), was succeeded by the disintegrative phase (c.1780–1870), also known as the Age of Revolution. During the first half of the nineteenth century overpopulation and political instability induced large numbers of people to look for better conditions in the New World. The most notable population flows into the US originated in Ireland as a result of the Great Potato Famine (during the 1840s), and in Germany after the revolution of 1848. When the Russian Empire started slipping into crisis towards the end of the nineteenth century (Turchin and Nefedov 2009: Chapter 9), eastern Europe became the major source of migrants to the US.

The second immigration wave was fueled by the global population explosion of the second half of the twentieth century. As a result, Europe ceased to be the dominant source, with people coming instead from all over the world. Mexico, being on the same continent, provided the great majority (and particularly, of illegal immigrants).

In summary, the period of 1780–2010 saw two (more precisely, one and a half) secular oscillations in the labor supply. The first wave began in the 1840s as a result of massive immigration supplemented by a very high rate of natural increase (between two and three percent per year). This wave ended when both immigration and population growth rates subsided after 1920. The second wave began with the baby boom of the 1950s and 1960s. After 1965, the main driver of change was again immigration. We are currently in the middle of this second wave.

Economic Wellbeing

Real Wages

What effect did these oscillations in labor supply have on the standard of living? The most common way to measure living standards is the real wage (nominal wage divided by the consumer price index). There are some problems with this measure, because it is sensitive to the composition of the basket of consumables, but it provides a logical starting-place for our investigation into popular wellbeing.

Although the general trend of the real wage over the 230 years was up, the rate at which it increased varied substantially, and in some periods it actually stagnated (Figure 3.3). During the first period of robust growth, between 1790 and 1850, the real wage increased by a factor of three (see the inset in Figure 3.3). The average annual rate of growth during this period was 1.8 percent. Between 1850 and 1880 the wage fluctuated considerably, but ended back at the starting level. The worst decline occurred during the Civil War, followed by another decline during the depression of the 1870s (Margo 2000:223). As a result, the growth rate over the 30-year period was a paltry 0.2 percent per year. After 1880 growth resumed: until 1930 the average annual rate of growth was 1.5 percent, while from 1930 to 1970 it was a remarkable 2.8 percent. The last period, 1970–2010, was the second period of stagnating wages.

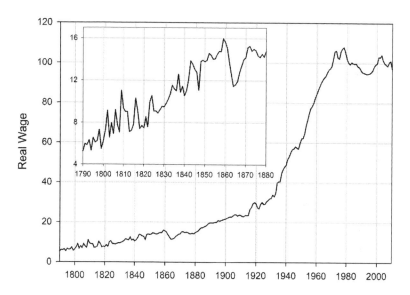

FIGURE 3.3 Real wages of unskilled labor in the United States, 1790–2010. The inset takes a closer look at the first century of the data series. Data source: MesuringWorth (for consumer price index see Officer 2007, Officer and Williamson 2009).

The pattern of real wage growth, then, was cyclic. In the first cycle, rapid growth to 1850 was followed by stagnation between 1850 and 1880, and in the second rapid growth to 1970 has been followed by stagnation up to the present.

Wages Relative to GDP per capita

The cyclic pattern in worker compensation is even more apparent when we consider how well wages did in comparison with GDP per capita (for a similar approach in the case of eighteenth-century England, see Angeles 2007). The question is, what proportion of economic growth translates into increased incomes for workers, and how does this quantity change with time? This question can be approached with an index constructed by dividing the annual wage by GDP per capita. In other words, instead of scaling nominal wages by the cost of the basket of consumables (which is affected by a variety of estimation biases, as will be discussed in the next section), we scale them by GDPpc. Both wages and GDP are expressed in nominal dollars (if expressed in real terms, we need to take care that we use the same GDP deflator, which will cancel out). I refer to this index as wages relative to GDPpc, or *relative wages* for short.

Using the annual GDP, however, introduces one problem. During deep recessions GDP can decline quite sharply. Wages, being "sticky" (that is, inertial, often taking several years to adjust to new economic conditions), decline more slowly, and the ratio of wages to GDP per capita will leap up. Thus, a deep recession will introduce a spurious upward "spurt" in the relative wage. One way of dealing with this problem is to divide wages not by actual GDP per capita, but by a smoothed GDP, also known as "potential" or "trend" level of output (Samuelson and Nordhaus 1998:376). I smoothed GDP with an exponential kernel smoother (Li and Racine 2006) using bandwidth $h = 4$ years, which removes short-term fluctuations of the business cycle.

Plotting the relative wages in Figure 3.4, we observe that this index of economic wellbeing increased to c.1830 and then declined and fluctuated at a lower level until c.1910. During the twentieth century, relative wages grew essentially continuously until 1960 and then went into another decline, which brought them to a level even lower than that around 1900 (Figure 3.4).

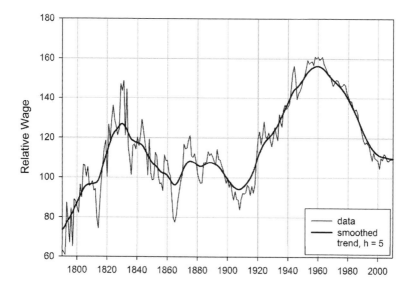

FIGURE 3.4 Dynamics of relative wages (wages relative to GDP per capita). Calculations by the author based on wages (production workers in manufacturing) and GDP data from MeasuringWorth (Johnston and Williamson 2013, Officer and Williamson 2013). The units of the y-axis are workers' annual compensation as percent of GDP per capita.

Other Wellbeing Proxies

A comparison between real and relative wages (Figures 3.3. and 3.4) highlights the problematic aspects of using the real wage as an index of wellbeing, especially for the nineteenth century. The curve in Figure 3.3 paints a rather cheerful picture of popular wellbeing then, with real wages marching ever upwards. Relative wages, on the other hand, show a cyclic movement, with a period of decline and stagnation after 1840. The critical issue is to have a good estimate of the consumer price index, and this is particularly difficult to do for changing economies, characterized by rapidly evolving baskets of consumables.

The United States rapidly industrialized and urbanized during the nineteenth century. An increasing proportion of the labor force moved to the cities where they had to rent living space. However, the David-Solar cost-of-living deflator, which provides the basis for reconstructing real wages in the US, uses house-construction costs as a proxy for rental price of housing

(Margo 1992:180, Williamson 1992:212). In an investigation focusing on New York metropolitan area between 1830 and 1860, Robert Margo found that housing prices increased very rapidly during this period (and, especially, in the 1850s). He concluded that "economic historians over-estimated real wage growth before the Civil War" (see also Fogel et al. 1992, Margo 1994).

In addition to experiencing a hefty increase in housing costs, migrants to cities were exposed to a greater chance of disease. Furthermore, although our data on the living conditions of poorer population strata are inadequate, it is likely that the quality of their diet declined during the nineteenth century (Walsh 1992). For example, as population density in the cities increased, the poor would have been less able to supplement their diet by growing vegetables in urban gardens.

More generally, even if impressionistically, the United States during the Gilded Age feels like a very different country from the one observed in the 1830s by Alexis de Tocqueville. In particular, images in *How the Other Half Lives: Studies Among the Tenements of New York*, published by Jacob Riis in 1890, clash with the rosy picture painted by a relentless upward trend of the estimated real wage in Figure 3.3.

These observations suggest that we need to look for additional quantitative proxies of wellbeing. One possible sign of growing desperation among the poorer classes is the rising incidence of infanticide in New England. The combined rate of neonate (up to a day old) and infant (from one day to one year old) murder in Vermont and New Hampshire rose from 5 per 100,000 in the period 1794–1827, to 11 in 1828–1847, to 19 in 1848–1865, and to 32 in 1866–1880 (Roth 2001).

For more geographically and temporally comprehensive proxies of wellbeing, I turn to physical stature (height) and life expectancy, extensively investigated by economic historians during the past two decades (Fogel 2004).

Average Stature

Average height is one of the most sensitive indicators of the biological wellbeing of a population (Komlos 1985, Fogel 1986, Steckel 1995). Physical stature is determined by the balance between nutritional intakes and demands made on the organism by the environment during the first 20 years of its life. The most important aspect of nutrition is the energy intake, but diet quality (availability of fresh vegetables, for example) also affects stature. Environmental demands include prevalence of disease (fighting off infection costs energy) and how much work children and adolescents have to do (again, heavy labor requires higher energy inputs). All factors determining stature are affected by the economic status of the family. Most obviously, greater income translates into greater quantity and quality of food. Income also buys better medical services, frees children from the necessity of performing heavy labor, and affects health in a multitude of other ways (eg, a beach vacation allows the organism to replenish its stocks of vitamin D). Thus, average height of a population provides a highly useful corrective to purely economic measures, such as the real wage.

In the eighteenth century, Americans were the tallest nation in the world (Komlos and Baur 2004). The average height of US-born Americans continued to increase until the cohort that was born in 1830. During the next 60 years, however, it declined by more than four centimeters (Figure 3.5). Because adult height is determined by environmental influences during the first 20 years, in order to estimate the timing of this turning point, we need to add 10 years (the midpoint) to the birth date. Thus, between approximately 1840 and 1900 the biological standard of living in the US was declining. After the turning point of 1900 and until 1970 (that is, before the cohort born in 1960), the trend was highly positive. During this period the average height increased by a remarkable nine centimeters. After 1970 steady and robust improvements in the biological wellbeing ceased (a detailed discussion of the post-1970 trends is deferred until Chapter 11).

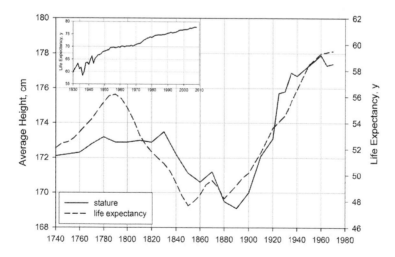

FIGURE 3.5 Biological proxies of wellbeing: average population height of US-born American men and life expectancy at 10 years of age. Both curves are plotted for cohorts by the year of birth. Data sources: Tables Bd653-687 and Ab704-911 in *Historical Statistics of the United States* (Carter et al. 2004) and (Fogel 1986). Inset: expectation of life at birth, 1930–2008. Source: *Historical Statistics of the United States* (Carter et al. 2004) and the US Census Bureau.

Life Expectancy

The dynamics of life expectancy confirm the pattern revealed by the stature data (Figure 3.5, broken line). This is not surprising, because at the individual level there is a strong positive correlation between life expectancy and stature, except at extreme heights (Fogel 2004). These two measures provide complementary views of biological wellbeing. Whereas height is affected by conditions during the first two decades, life expectancy averages over the whole duration of an individual life. For example, a man born in 1790 (the turning point for the life expectancy curve in Figure 3.5) could have had his life shortened by dying at the age of 59 in the great cholera epidemic of 1849, which carried away up to 10 percent of the American population (Kohn 2001:356). In order to compare the two curves directly, life expectancy needs to be shifted forward by some unknown period, which is probably related to half the life expectancy, or roughly 30 years. In other words, upward and downward trends in life expectancy are broadly consistent with the periodization suggested by the stature data. Unlike average height, however, life expectancy did not stagnate in the post-1970 period (see Figure 3.5 inset).

Age at First Marriage as a Proxy for Social Mood

The final variable we examine in this chapter is age at first marriage. This variable is not a direct proxy for economic or biological wellbeing; rather it is an index of the optimism/pessimism with which young adults regard their future economic prospects. If the future looks bright, people tend to marry earlier, and the proportion who never marry declines, compared with times when economic prospects are dim. Thus, the ease with which people enter matrimony is an indicator of optimistic social mood (Casti 2010).

Age at first marriage is only imperfectly correlated with social optimism, because it is also affected by other factors. For example, today people who are completely secure in their economic prospects tend to marry later than people in a similar position who lived two centuries ago. For a variety of reasons, as societies modernize, people tend to marry later. This means that we expect a long-term upward trend in marriage ages. The question is whether there are any cyclic movements superimposed on this trend. Additionally, it is important to note that delaying marriage in response to tough economic conditions is not a human universal (Hajnal 1965), but this pattern holds both for populations of northwestern Europe and for those of North America (Haines 1996).

The long-term marriage patterns paint a broadly consistent picture with other indicators of wellbeing (Figure 3.6). As expected, there is a long-term upward trend. However, this trend is by no means uniform. First, there is a dramatic rise in the age at first marriage towards the end of the nineteenth century. It is then followed by a decline between 1900 and 1960, and another period of increase after 1960. In other words, these data trace out the same one-and-a-half secular cycles that we have already observed in the dynamics of average stature and life expectancy. There are minor discrepancies (of the order of a decade) between the turning points observed in different trajectories, but these are probably due to different time lags affecting the responses of variables to worsening or improving economic conditions.

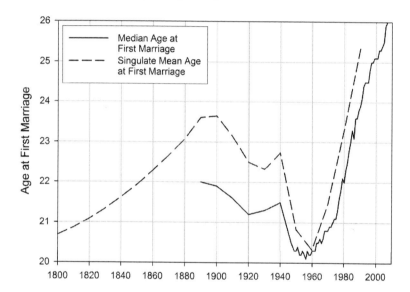

FIGURE 3.6 Two measures of age at first marriage for American females. Median age at first marriage (solid line) is from Table Ae481-488 in *Historical Statistics of the United States* (Carter et al. 2004), supplemented by data from the US Census Bureau for the period after 1999. Singulate mean age at marriage (defined as the average length of single life expressed in years among those who marry before age 50; think of it as simply another measure of how long people wait before marrying) is from Sanderson (1979) for the years 1800–1920 and Haines (1996) for 1880–1990. The Sanderson and Haines curves were spliced by upwardly adjusting the Sanderson data, as suggested by Haines (1996:35).

Synthesis

The primary goal of this chapter was to survey the long-term dynamics of demography and wellbeing over the whole period of the study. Additionally, the data patterns allow us to make a preliminary test of the first theoretical proposition, relating the supply of labor to popular wellbeing. To a first approximation we can use the magnitude of immigration influxes as a proxy for the oversupply of labor (in Chapters 9 and 12 I show that immigration is only one of the forces resulting in labor oversupply, but it also turns out that taking into account other processes affecting the supply and demand of labor does not change the qualitative picture presented below).

To investigate the possible dynamic interaction between the processes examined in this chapter, I plotted on the same graph standardized variables reflecting the fluctuations of labor supply (proxied by proportion of Americans born outside the US) and various measures of wellbeing (relative wage, average stature, life expectancy, and age at first marriage). "Standardized" means that all variables have been first smooth-interpolated (using the bandwidth = 5 years) so that they could be plotted at the same five-year intervals (quinquennia). Next, each variable was linearly detrended and scaled to mean = 0 and variance = 1. Finally, variables negatively correlated with wellbeing (labor oversupply and age at marriage) were plotted on an inverse scale, so that their dynamics could be directly compared with variables positively correlated with wellbeing (relative wage, average stature, and life expectancy).

The plot in Figure 3.7 shows that different variables reflecting popular wellbeing tend to go up and down together. This synchrony is statistically significant, but not perfect, and the timing of trend reversals for different variables may be separated by as long as two decades. The thick gray curve, an average of all five proxies, provides a basis for periodizing American history, from the point of view of structural-demographic variables reflecting popular wellbeing.

The data surveyed in this chapter suggest that the history of the United States since 1780 can be divided into four phases; two during which popular wellbeing increased, and two during which it declined. The transitions between different phases were gradual (and, as noted above, there was substantial variation between the timing of some trend reversals for different variables), so the dates given below are very approximate.

The first phase (1780–c.1830) was characterized by low immigration. During this period real wages tripled and the relative wage more than doubled, while the American population enjoyed tall (and increasing) stature and long life expectancy. The optimistic social mood prevailed and young adults married early.

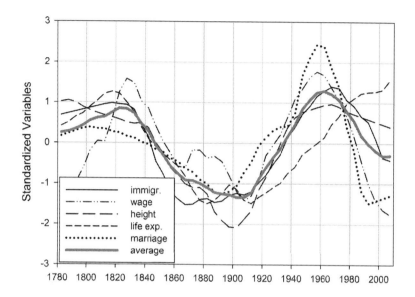

FIGURE 3.7 Summary of labor and wellbeing dynamics. This graph plots together standardized variables reflecting the fluctuations in labor supply and various proxies of wellbeing (see the text for the explanation). The gray curve is the average of the five proxies.

During the second phase (c.1830–c.1910), the United States experienced a massive immigration wave. Real wages stagnated (between 1840 and 1880), but more tellingly, the proportion of the GDP going to the wage labor declined from 1830 to 1910. During the second half of the nineteenth century average stature and life expectation declined, while the age at first marriage increased.

The third phase (c.1910–c.1960) was characterized by declining immigration (especially after 1920). Real wages increased dramatically (by a factor of 3.5). The average height and life expectancy also grew in a remarkable fashion, while the age at first marriage decreased (except during the 1930s).

The fourth phase (from c.1960 and continuing today) saw another wave of massive immigration. The GDP share to workers declined, and real wages stagnated (after the 1970s). The rate at which stature and life expectancy increased slowed down (and, for some population segments, even reversed, as will be discussed in Chapter 11), while the age at first marriage grew to levels never seen before.

In summary, this empirical survey suggests that between 1780 and 2010, the factors affecting labor oversupply and indicators of popular wellbeing generally moved cyclically and in opposite directions. This pattern was not perfect, and there could be substantial lags (up to two to three decades) between trend reversals in different variables. Nevertheless, overall there was a negative relationship between labor supply and indices of wellbeing, as predicted by the labor oversupply principle. I will return to this issue with more quantitative tools in Chapters 9 and 12.

4

Elite Dynamics

Approaches to Studying the US Elites

Defining the Elites

Because the study of elites is a somewhat contentious area in sociology, I begin this chapter with definitions. The elites are the (typically very small) fraction of the population in whom social power is concentrated; they are the "ruling class". Power, in turn, is defined in sociology as the ability to influence the behavior of other people. In an influential book, Michael Mann (1986) distinguishes four sources of social power: military, economic, political (or administrative), and ideological. Which of those dominate varies among different societies, but as a rule just one or two are significant in shaping the ruling class. For example, the most common source of power in premodern agrarian societies was military supplemented by economic (ownership of land). Today, some countries continue to be ruled by networks of military professionals (for example, Egypt), but this is unusual. Even more rare are societies that are ruled by networks of religious specialists (the Islamic Republic of Iran being, probably, the best example).

The most common source of power in large modern states is administrative. Such countries as China, Russia, and France are largely ruled by administrative networks (bureaucracies). The basis of power tends to be very conservative, and usually survives even times of political turbulence. For example, in Russia a group of newly wealthy bankers and industrialists (the so-called "oligarchs") attempted to gain control of the state during the 1990s, but was easily defeated by the bureaucratic class.

By contrast, in the United States the political power network does not reign supreme. In a series of influential publications, *Who Rules America?* (as of 2016, in the seventh edition) William Domhoff (2010a) has argued that the dominant power network in the US is the economic one (for a similar view, see also Dye and Zeigler 1970). According to this *class-domination theory*, at the top of the power pyramid is the corporate community, the owners and managers of large income-producing properties, such as corporations (including agri-businesses), banks, corporate law firms, and real estate. Not all sociologists agree with this conclusion, and other theories of how power functions in America exist, such as pluralism (Dahl 1961) and state-centric theory (Skocpol 1979).

It is important to note that according to Domhoff's theory, the corporate community rules indirectly. Its "structural economic power" allows it to dominate the political class through lobbying, campaign finance, and appointments to key government positions (Domhoff 2010b). In fact, at the top levels many politicians and senior bureaucrats are themselves members of the economic network, moving back and forth between government and industry positions in a "revolving door" fashion.

The corporate community also controls the ideological basis of power through ownership of mass media corporations and a policy-planning network made up of foundations, think tanks, and policy-discussion groups. The remaining source of social power, the military, has been thoroughly subordinated by the political network throughout American history.

In the rest of this book I use Domhoff's theory as a convenient framework for a structural-demographic analysis of power relations in the US, and refer the reader to Domhoff's publications (e.g., Domhoff 2010a, b) for the theoretical and empirical support of his thesis. However, while class-domination theory provides a useful starting point for the structural-demographic analysis, it also has some limitations. First, Domhoff's approach, in my opinion, has a tendency to be too static in its emphasis on corporate community domination of other power groups. By contrast, my primary interest is in the dynamic power shifts between various elite groups and their relations with the general population and the state. Second, Domhoff tends to focus on social ties among the wealth-holders (via, for example, "interlocking directorates") and on the policy-planning network as the main vehicles for generating and sustaining collective action. However, collective action in any large group is only possible if there is a mechanism to prevent free-riding. For this reason, I find Calavita's (1984) structural model of the capitalist state, which emphasizes the role of the state in managing the common affairs of the whole bourgeoisie, to be a valuable refinement of Domhoff's theory. Further discussion of this important topic is deferred to later chapters in which I will discuss specific shifts in the distribution of social power that took place at critical junctures in American history.

Quantifying the Elites

For a number of reasons, the American elites are particularly difficult to study using quantitative methods. First, since the elites in the US are defined by the possession of considerable wealth, there is no obvious way to divide the population into the elites and the commoners. In *ancien régime* societies of France and Russia the elites—the nobility—had a distinct legal status. But the curve of the distribution of wealth in the US grades smoothly and any distinction between the rich and the rest is bound to be arbitrary. We can rely on a measure, such as the Gini index, which quantifies the whole distribution of wealth, and trace its evolution through time. However, such measures are exceedingly abstract and difficult to interpret. An alternative approach is to calculate the proportion of total wealth controlled by the wealthiest fraction of the population, for example the top one percent.

Second, because the dominant ideology in the US emphasizes equality of opportunity and democratic values, the American upper class has effectively discouraged scrutiny by sociologists. Its members are reluctant to give interviews, and they are difficult to observe in their "natural environment", which is accessible only by other members of the class (Domhoff 2010b).

Third, the network structure of economic elites lacks easily identifiable hierarchies, such as those found in the army and in the bureaucracy. There is no obvious center for building consensus and for making or enforcing policy. Social scientists must use indirect methods, such as tracing corporate board interlocks and examining membership lists in exclusive clubs or attendance at private prep schools to infer the internal structure of the economic elite network.

For these reasons, the study of elite dynamics must rely even more on proxies and indirect indicators than is usually the case in structural-demographic analysis. I start by looking at the data on the dynamics of economic inequality. The elite overproduction principle predicts that labor oversupply not only depresses the living standards for the majority of population but also increases the numbers and consumption levels of the elites, resulting in increasing economic inequality. I will test this prediction by examining the proportion of total wealth owned by the richest one percent of the population. Next, I turn to more direct measures of the numbers of elites and elite aspirants. Finally, I look at some proxies of intraelite competition and fragmentation.

Dynamics of Economic Inequality

The dynamics of economic inequality since World War I are relatively well understood. Between 1920 and 1980 inequality declined. The decade of the

1940s, when the distribution of both wealth and income became much more evenly distributed, is sometimes referred to as the "Great Compression" (Goldin and Margo 1992). The share of the national wealth held by the richest one percent of households declined from a high of 44 percent in 1929 to a low of 20 percent in 1979 (Figure 4.1). In the last three decades, however, wealth inequality has been growing, although it has not yet reached the same level as during the early twentieth century (Figure 4.1).

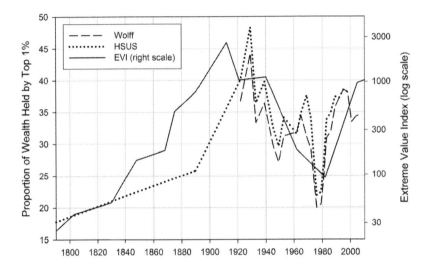

FIGURE 4.1 Dynamics of wealth inequality in the US. Broken line: the proportion of total wealth held by the top one percent (Wolff 1996, 2010). Dotted line: an alternative estimate of the proportion of total wealth held by the top one percent (HSUS). Solid line: the Extreme Value Index (the largest US fortune divided by the median annual wage; from Table 4.2).

Due to the lack of good national data on wealth distribution before World War I, the dynamics of wealth inequality cannot be traced with the same precision. European visitors, such as Alexis de Tocqueville (1984), stressed the equality of economic conditions among Americans. One estimate supporting this contention (Jones 1977: Table 8.1), puts the proportion of wealth owned by the top one percent in 1774 at 16.5 percent (see the dotted line in Figure 4.1). On the other hand, Edward Pessen (1973) argued that antebellum society was already highly inegalitarian. Much of this disagreement arises from questions of definition: how much inequality do you need before you call it "highly inegalitarian"? My interest, however, is not in the absolute level of inequality, but in its dynamics. Pessen's data exhibit a clear upward trend (Table 4.1), supporting the general view that the distribution of wealth was becoming more unequal with time. However, just when economic inequality began its rise during the nineteenth century is not known. Pessen's data are suggestive, but they are affected by two opposing biases. First, he had to exclude corporate assets from his calculations, because of difficulties with tracing ownership. This tends to reduce the degree of inequality. On the other hand, cities concentrate both the wealthiest and the poorest economic strata. Thus, the degree of inequality in the overall population had to be lower than that calculated for the cities in Pessen's sample.

TABLE 4.1 Proportion of noncorporate wealth held by the top one percent in some antebellum American cities (Pessen 1973).

year	city	proportion
1810	Brooklyn	22
1828	New York	29
1833	Boston	33
1841	Brooklyn	42
1845	New York	40
1848	Boston	37
1860	Philadelphia	50

In our previous work we have used the "method of extreme values" to trace the dynamics of inequality for periods for which detailed data on the distribution of wealth are not available (Turchin and Nefedov 2009). This approach works as follows: for each generation-long period (ideally 25 years or less) we identify the largest privately-held fortune (in other words, excluding wealth held by rulers). This kind of information is available for many periods ranging from Republican Rome to early modern France, because contemporaries usually had a good idea of who the wealthiest individual was, and roughly the size of his (or her) fortune. This estimate provides us with the location of the very tip of the wealth distribution. It next needs to be scaled with respect to some measure of the median wealth or better income, because in many historical societies, characterized by a very wealthy minority and destitute majority the median wealth was zero or even negative. For example, 84 percent of economically active inhabitants of New York City in 1856 owned no personal or real wealth (Beckert 2001:19). For this reason, we scale the largest fortune by the annual wage of some typical nonelite individual.

One possible objection to the EVI is that it relies on a single number, the size of the largest fortune, which could make this proxy overly sensitive to stochastic fluctuations. However, our primary focus is not on the precise number, but rather on the *scale of magnitude* of maximum fortunes (thus I will be graphing the logarithm of the EVI). For example, during the first decade of the 2000s the wealth held by Bill Gates was of the same order of magnitude as that by Warren Buffett; in fact, Buffett briefly occupied the number one position in 2008. Nevertheless, a check of the approach would be useful, and in the next section I will show that a more broadly-based measure of top wealth holders exhibits precisely the same dynamics as the EVI.

To calculate the EVI for the United States, I start with the list of the wealthiest American individuals, compiled by Kevin Phillips (2002) and scale it with the wage data of Officer and Williamson (2009) (see Table 4.1). Plotting the resulting EVI together with other measures of inequality (Figure 4.1) we observe that during the twentieth century it indicates the same pattern: decline towards 1980 followed by rapid increase. The difference between peaks (1912 and 1929) is due to the fact that the EVI misses 1929, when wealth inequality was greatly inflated due to the runaway growth of stock prices (which crashed in October of that year). Another difference is that the EVI smoothes out shorter-term fluctuations, which is not a problem for our purposes, because we are interested in long-term movements of inequality. Now that we have satisfied ourselves that the approach works reasonably well, we apply it to the pre-1900 period.

We observe that until 1830 the scale of the largest fortune grew at a rate that only slightly exceeded the growth rate of wages (Table 4.1). Over those four decades the EVI doubled. After 1840, however, wages largely stagnated, while the size of the top fortune exhibited a runaway growth. In particular, between 1830 and 1875 the Index grew tenfold and over the following four decades it quintupled again. In the early twentieth century, when top fortunes first reached a billion dollars, the trend changed. After 1912 it was the largest fortunes that were becalmed, at levels between one and two billion dollars, while wages increased by two orders of magnitude, so that by 1980 the Index had returned to the pre-1840s levels.

The dynamics of economic inequality as measured by the EVI, thus, conform to the predictions of Structural-Demographic Theory. Rises and falls in inequality followed those of labor oversupply (as proxied by the proportion foreign-born), but with a slight lag time of about a decade (Figure 4.2).

TABLE 4.2 Largest Fortunes in the U.S., 1790–2005. Source: (Phillips 2002), supplemented by *Forbes* magazine for 2010. Wage data are from (Officer and Williamson 2009). All data are in nominal dollars (not adjusted for inflation).

Year	Name	Largest Fortune	Annual Wage	Inequality Index (Ratio × 1000)
1790	Elias Derby	1 mln	40	25
1803	William Bingham	3 mln	80	38
1830	Stephen Girard	6 mln	120	50
1848	John J. Astor	20 mln	140	143
1868	Cornelius Vanderbilt	40 mln	220	182
1875	Cornelius Vanderbilt	105 mln	220	477
1890	William H. Vanderbilt	200 mln	260	769
1912	John D. Rockefeller	1 bln	380	2,632
1921	John D. Rockefeller	1 bln	960	1,042
1940	John D. Rockefeller	1.5 bln	1,340	1,119
1962	John Paul Getty	1 bln	5,420	185
1982	Daniel Ludwig	2 bln	21,600	93
1992	Sam Walton	8 bln	31,260	256
2005	William Gates III	46 bln	47,840	972
2010	William Gates III	54 bln	52,300	1,033

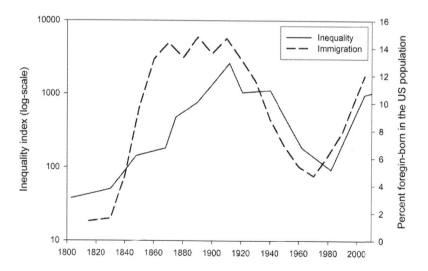

FIGURE 4.2 Dynamical relationship between immigration and economic inequality.

Numbers of Top Wealth-Holders

Is it possible to relate these inequality swings to quantitative estimates of elite numbers, which is one of the key variables in the Structural-Demographic Theory? We need to estimate how the proportion of individuals holding wealth greater than a certain threshold changed with time. However, any boundary distinguishing "elites" from "non-elites" is necessarily arbitrary. This problem can be solved by using a series of thresholds and checking whether the same pattern holds for different choices of cut-off point.

Such a calculation was performed by Edward Wolff (1996, 2010) for the period 1983–2007. This was the period of rapidly growing inequality (the EVI grew more than tenfold), so it is not surprising that the numbers of millionaires in all categories grew much faster than the general population (Table 4.3). In relative terms, the fraction of millionaires in the general population more than doubled (from 2.9 to 6.3 percent), while the proportion of deca-millionaires quintupled (from 0.08 to 0.40 percent). Thus, no matter what threshold we choose, the numbers of top wealth holders increased in relation to the general population. Additionally, the higher the cut-off point, the faster the growth in numbers with wealth above it.

TABLE 4.3 The count of millionaires and multimillionaires, 1983–2007 (Wolff 2010: Table 3). Net worth is calculated in constant 1995 dollars.

Year	Total number of households (×1000)	Number of households (×1000) with net worth exceeding:		
		1 mln	5 mln	10 mln
1983	83,893	2,411	247	66
1986	93,009	3,024	297	65
1992	95,462	3,104	277	42
1995	99,101	3,015	474	190
1998	102,547	4,783	756	239
2001	106,494	5,892	1,068	338
2004	112,107	6,466	1,120	345
2007	116,120	7,274	1,467	464

For the nineteenth century, unfortunately, we do not have such detailed data (except for the period 1850–1870—see below). However, we can look at what happened at the very top of the wealth pyramid, by analyzing the lists of wealthy American individuals compiled by the *Encyclopedia of American*

Wealth project (Shouter 2010). These lists are available at quarter-century intervals until 1950.

I used the *Encyclopedia* to calculate the number of millionaires (individuals with fortunes equal to or exceeding one million dollars, adjusting for inflation). The relative number of millionaires (per million of general population) increased dramatically during the nineteenth century (Table 4.4). Remarkably, between 1900 and 1950 the proportion of millionaires decreased (by a factor of 4.3). This is the same pattern that we have already observed in the dynamics of the Extreme Value Index, providing further support for the usefulness of the EVI as an index of economic inequality.

TABLE 4.4 The number of millionaires (in constant 1900 dollars) in the United States, 1800–1950 (data from Shouter 2010).

Year	Number of millionaires	US pop, mln	Millionaires per mln population
1800	6	5.3	1.1
1825	28	11.1	2.5
1850	100	23.3	4.3
1875	629	45.5	13.8
1900	1472	76.1	19.3
1925	1614	115.8	13.9
1950	889	152.3	5.8

As the author of the *Encyclopedia of American Wealth* emphasized, some estimates of individual fortunes and family estates may be inaccurate or not even close. A substantial proportion of wealthy individuals, especially in lower wealth categories, is missing from the lists. However, these are not serious problems and in no way invalidate the results of Table 4.4, because our primary interest, as ever, is in the dynamics—that is, in the relative change with time. As long as roughly the same proportion of individuals is missing from each list, the general result will be valid.

One way to test for any serious bias is to repeat the calculation for different wealth thresholds. It seems safe to assume that individuals at the very top of the wealth pyramid are far less likely to be missed out than those lower down the scale, and a bias (a temporally variable probability of being omitted from the list) will be noticeable when we compare the millionaire curves to those of, for example, decamillionaires. Figure 4.3 suggests that if any such bias is present it is not particularly strong, because curves calculated for different thresholds all move largely in parallel. Note that the steepest slopes—representing the fastest rates of increase in the numbers of top wealth holders—are for the period 1850–1875 (Figure 4.3).

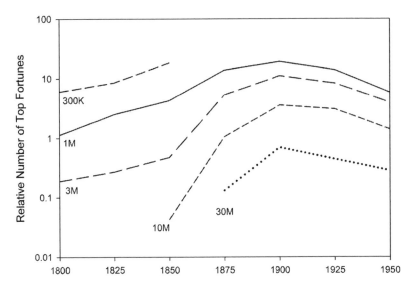

FIGURE 4.3 Relative numbers (in relation to general population) of top wealth holders, using a series of thresholds, from \$300,000 to \$30 million. Source calculations by the author based on data from (Shouter 2010).

Intraelite Competition Proxies

Law and Business Students

Structural-demographic theorists have argued that the most useful proxy for intraelite competition is the demand for advanced degrees (for a related argument, see Collins 1979, Goldstone 1991, Turchin and Nefedov 2009). The two degrees most relevant for individuals with ambitions to join the economic and political power networks in the US are, respectively, Master of Business Administration (MBA) and the Juris Doctor (JD) law degree. I will first discuss the latter, and then take a look at the MBA, which has relatively recently become popular with individuals aspiring to a business career.

The dynamics of those seeking and holding a law degree provide us with a perspective on the American elites different from that offered by the numbers of wealth-holders. The numbers in various high-wealth classes tell us what is happening with the established elites: these are the individuals who have "arrived". By contrast, law school students are not guaranteed entry into the elites. This is graphically demonstrated by the bimodal distribution of starting salaries of law school graduates (Figure 4.4). Graduates earning a starting salary of $160,000 (the peak on the right) are well on the way to joining the established elites. Those who start on between $40,000 and $60,000 per year (the larger hump on the left), on the other hand, are in trouble. Considering that the average debt of a law school graduate in 2011 was around $100,000 ($85,000 for public schools and $122,000 for private schools, data from the American Bar Association), few of these individuals will manage to enter the ranks of the elites.

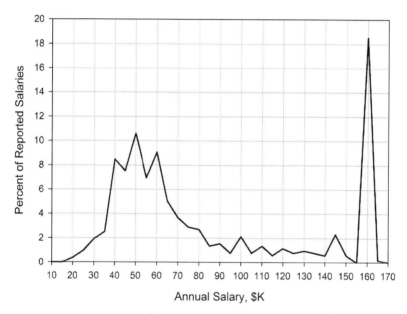

FIGURE 4.4 Frequency distribution of full-time salaries for all members of the Class of 2010 who reported income data to their law school. Source: (NALP 2010).

The bimodal distribution of starting salaries is a striking (and quite unusual) recent development. Later in this chapter I shall discuss how it evolved during the 1990s from a more typical Pareto-like distribution (*Elite Overproduction and Intraelite Inequality: Emergence of a Bimodal Distribution of Lawyer Salaries*).

Students in law schools, thus, are one of the most important types of elite aspirant. Some will become very wealthy (becoming, for example, a partner in a corporate law firm) or succeed in politics (historically, over a half of congressmen have had law degrees, and this proportion has been much higher in the Senate). This incentive motivates the student to seek arduous and expensive legal training, and after graduation accept positions with law firms that require 80–100-hour work weeks. However, a large proportion (and today, the majority) will become failed elite aspirants, earning in the range of $40,000–$60,000—something lots of people manage without three years of arduous training and $100,000 of debt.

Generally speaking, tougher competition for elite positions results in more importance being given to a degree that will offer a competitive advantage. The demand for legal education, thus, provides us with a good generalized proxy for intraelite competition in the US. However, in interpreting this index it is important to bear in mind that the normal functioning of American society today requires many more lawyers than two centuries ago. This process will result in an upwardly trending curve. As is often the case, we are interested in the oscillations that should reflect waxing and waning intraelite competition on top of the long-term trend.

The value of a law degree has fluctuated throughout the past two centuries. In the first half of the nineteenth century there was so little demand for legal education that fledgling law schools came and went with great rapidity (Stevens 1983, Clark 2003). For example, Princeton University made unsuccessful attempts to establish a law school in 1825 and 1835, and succeeded in 1846 only to abandon it in 1852 after producing a mere six graduates (Stevens 1983:8). Harvard was more successful in establishing a law school (in 1817). However, by 1869 the curriculum had been reduced, examinations abolished, and less than half of the students studying law possessed college degrees (Clark 2003:95).

The turning point came in 1870. The last 30 years of the nineteenth century saw the number of law schools rise from 31 to 102 and a tenfold increase in the number of law students (Clark 2003:96). This trend continued in the early twentieth century, and the *relative* number of law students (in relation to the total population) increased tenfold between 1870 and 1930 (Figure 4.5).

The next turning point was in 1930, after which the relative enrollment went through two bust cycles. Over these three decades the relative enrollment decreased by about one-third (Figure 4.5). The final turning point was the "1960s enrollment revolution" (Clark 2003). Although the boom-and-bust cycles with a period of about 20 years continued, the overall trend was up, and substantially so. Overall during the post-war period (1947–2008) the proportion of young adults going to the law school approximately doubled.

In summary, the data in Figure 4.5 suggest that the periods 1780–1870 and 1930–1960 were characterized by a stagnating demand for law degrees, whereas demand grew rapidly during the periods 1870–1930 and 1960 to the present.

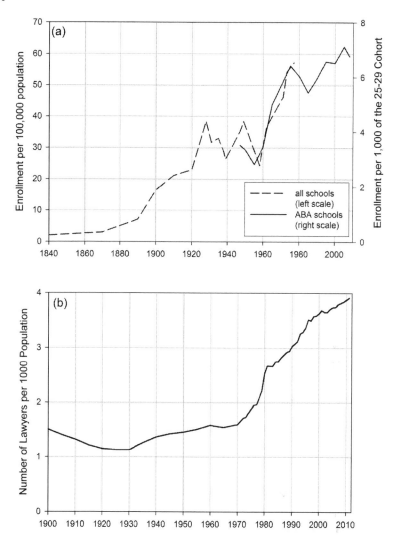

FIGURE 4.5 Legal profession in the US. (a) Dynamics of enrollments in American law schools. The solid curve shows the numbers enrolled in law schools with the ABA (American Bar Association) certification, scaled by the size of the cohort aged between 25 and 29 years. The broken curve shows enrollment in all law schools (both ABA and non-ABA). These numbers are scaled by the total population, because data on cohort sizes are not available for the nineteenth century. Data sources: the ABA and Stevens (1983). (b) Numbers of lawyers per 1000 population, 1900–2011. Source: American Bar Association, Legal Profession Statistics.

Lawyer numbers tell a qualitatively similar story. However, during the nineteenth century most practicing lawyers had no formal law education, so the post-1870 explosion in law school enrollments resulted in a much milder proportional increase in lawyer numbers.

Data in Table 4.5 show that until 1870 the relative numbers of lawyers stayed essentially constant at 1 lawyer per 1,000 population. In the single decade after 1870 it jumped by 30 percent, and by 1900 it had reached the peak at 1.5 lawyers per 1,000 population. After that peak, however, the growth in the size of the legal profession did not keep up with the growth of the overall population, and lawyer numbers declined to 1.13 per 1,000 population (Table 4.5).

The more-detailed data on lawyer numbers for the twentieth century are plotted in Figure 4.5b. We see that following a decline from 1900 to 1930, the relative numbers of lawyers grew mildly to 1970, at which point they essentially regained the 1900 level. Following 1970, however, the growth of the legal profession rapidly accelerated. Today there are nearly four lawyers per 1,000 population, 2.5 times more than 40 years ago.

TABLE 4.5 Absolute and relative numbers of lawyers in the US, 1850–1930. Sources: (Stevens 1983, Carter et al. 2004) and the American Bar Association.

Year	Lawyer numbers	U.S. pop. million	Lawyers per 1,000 pop
1850	23,939	23.3	1.03
1870	40,376	39.9	1.01
1880	64,137	50.3	1.28
1890	89,630	63.0	1.42
1900	114,460	76.0	1.50
1910	122,149	92.4	1.32
1920	122,519	106.4	1.15
1930	139,059	123.1	1.13

Finally, we can compare the trends in law students and lawyer numbers with the numbers earning the MBA. Demand for the MBA has grown even more rapidly than that for a law degree. Between 1971 and 2007 the numbers earning the MBA grew sixfold in absolute terms and almost fourfold in relative terms (Table 4.6).

TABLE 4.6 Numbers of individuals earning the MBA degree, and MBAs per 1,000 individuals aged 25–29 years. Source: US Dept of Education.

Year	MBAs	MBAs per 1,000
1971	26,490	1.9
1976	42,592	2.3
1981	57,888	2.9
1986	66,676	3.0
1991	78,255	3.7
1996	93,554	4.7
2001	115,602	6.1
2007	150,211	7.2

Cost of Advanced Education

Demand for education can be measured not only by the numbers of students, but also by the cost that they are willing to pay for it. Data regularly published by the American Bar Association indicate that over the past three decades the average law school tuition has increased 2.5-fold *in real terms* (Figure 4.6). The ABA did not provide data for pre-1985 tuition costs, but it appears that the rise in law school tuition parallels that for private universities (Figure 4.6). If this parallelism held before 1985, then we can infer that real cost of education was essentially flat before 1980, while rising linearly between 1980 and now. Thus, the rising demand for law degrees (and college degrees) was satisfied simply by expanding enrollments until 1980, while education costs kept pace with inflation. After 1980, costs of education in law schools (and universities) escalated. At the same time, the enrollments in law schools increased less rapidly than prior to 1980 (see Figure 4.5). However, because the curve in Figure 4.5 traces only students enrolled in the ABA-approved schools, it may underestimate the increase in the total number of law students. As costs of attending ABA law schools spiraled up, many students were forced to turn to non-ABA law schools.

Let us pursue the issue of education costs further. A university degree is certainly not a ticket to elite status today, when over half of high-school graduates go to college. However, a BA from a top private university, such as one of the Big Three (Harvard, Yale, and Princeton) does carry weight. Does the cost of attending such universities respond to the pressures of intraelite competition? We can answer this question because at least one of these universities made data on long-term dynamics of its tuition available (Pierson 1983, Waters 2001).

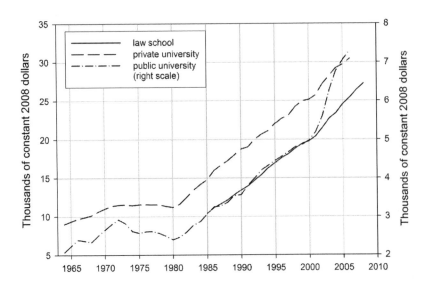

FIGURE 4.6 Solid curve: average annual tuition in the ABA law schools in constant 2008 dollars (a weighted mean of tuition at public and private schools; weighted by the number of schools in each category). Source: ABA. Dashed and dot-dashed curves: average tuition at private and public universities, respectively (in constant 2008 dollars). Source: the 2007 *Digest of Educational Statistics* (US Dept. of Education).

Between 1833 (when the time series starts) and 2009, the real cost of studying at Yale College increased about 40 times. This result shows that the CPI is not the correct deflator for these data, when used over such long intervals. During this period, real incomes of Americans also increased many-fold. Earlier, when calculating the magnitude of top fortunes, I used the annual income of a blue-collar worker as the scaling factor. This variable offers a much better deflator for the cost of education at a prestigious school such as Yale, because high prestige is a relative thing. If too many people can afford it, the value of a status indicator decreases. As most Americans became very wealthy (by the nineteenth century's standards), the cost of prestigious education had to grow even faster to maintain the exclusive status of the Yale diploma.

Scaling Yale tuition by annual blue-collar salaries removes the long-term trend, and results in stationary-looking oscillations around the mean of 0.4 yearly wage (Figure 4.7). The deviations from the mean are very informative. First, there are sharp downticks corresponding to most of the major wars in which the US was engaged during this period. In fact, in each of these cases the university temporarily decreased its tuition in nominal terms, sometimes quite dramatically. This observation suggests that the cost of attending Yale responded to short-term fluctuations in demand resulting from young males being drafted. This effect happened in all major conflicts except the Vietnam War, which did not produce a downtick because of exemptions and deferments available to college students.

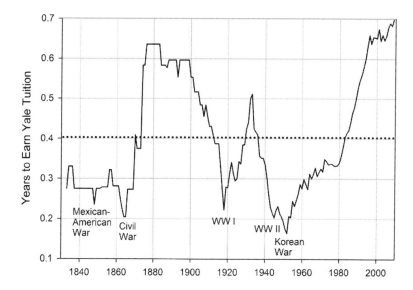

FIGURE 4.7 Annual tuition at Yale expressed in terms of manufacturing worker annual wage. The dotted line indicates the overall mean of oscillations. Data for Yale tuition: (Pierson 1983, Waters 2001), supplemented by the Office of Institutional Research, Yale University. Blue collar wage: (Officer 2010).

Longer-term oscillations suggest one cycle consisting of a period of low and declining demand for a Yale degree lasting until c.1870, was followed by a period of generally high demand until the 1930s. This trend was interrupted by a drop around 1920 which was due to the combined effects of World War I and rapid inflation during the 1910s. As prices doubled during this decade, the blue-collar wage tripled in nominal terms. Yale tuition eventually tripled, too, but more slowly. It took another decade (the 1920s) for tuition to catch up with salaries.

The second, incomplete, cycle began with a period of low demand from the 1930s until 1980, followed by a rapid increase and high demand to this day. It is startling to note that, according to this index, Yale education is less affordable today than it was during the Gilded Age.

Proxies for Elite Fragmentation

Usually, the process of elite fragmentation is difficult to study with quantitative methods. But, as luck would have it, the political scientists Nolan McCarty, Keith Poole, and Howard Rosenthal (McCarty et al. 2006) have recently published the results of their analysis of voting patterns in the US Congress, quantifying polarization among the American political elites.

The logic underlying the approach to quantifying political polarization, first proposed by Poole and Rosenthal (1984, 1997), can be explained as follows: each member of Congress is characterized by a distinct position on a liberal-conservative spectrum. The voting record of a very liberal senator, for example, will get high ratings from such liberal interest groups as the Americans for Democratic Action or the United Auto Workers. A very conservative senator, on the other hand, will score low in the ratings of those groups, but high with the American Conservative Union or the National Taxpayers Union (McCarty et al. 2006:4). Conservatives and liberals will occupy extreme positions on the political spectrum, and the space between them will be filled with moderates. A measure of political polarization, used by Poole and others, is the distance between the *average* scores of the Democrats and the Republicans, calculated for each Congress (that is, every two years). For early American history (before these two parties crystallized) we can use the distance between average scores of the two major parties that dominated Congress.

The analyses of McCarty et al (2006) focus on the results after 1879, but they have posted the raw data (DW-NOMINATE scores for the 1st to the 111th Congresses) on the Web and thus we can extend their time series to 1789. The dynamics of the Polarization Index for the House of Representatives and the Senate are very similar. However, the Senate trajectory, especially for the early period, when the estimates were based on a small number of senators, is much noisier and for that reason I shall focus on the House.

The House trajectory also shows great volatility for the early period (pre-Civil War). This is due in part to the smaller number of Representatives (overall, between the 1st and 111th Congresses, the sample size increases sevenfold), but also to instability in the party system. Thus, the transition periods from the First to the Second (the 1820s) and from the Second to the Third party systems (the 1850s) may introduce a degree of measurement noise in the trajectory.

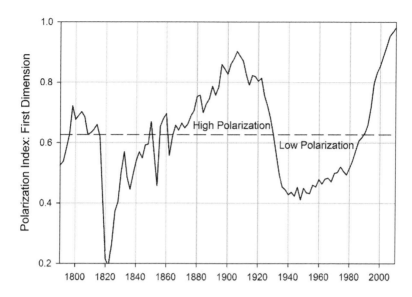

FIGURE 4.8 Political polarization in the US House of Representatives, 1789–2009. Raw data source: VoteView.com (http://voteview.com/downloads.asp, downloaded on Jan. 3, 2011).

Despite these potential complications, long-term dynamics of political polarization in the US are reasonably clear (Figure 4.8). Political polarization declined from moderately high levels around 1800 to a very low value in the 1820s. This decline in partisan acrimony is known as the Era of Good Feelings, roughly coinciding with the presidency of James Monroe (1816–24) (Howe 2008). After 1830 polarization increased, reaching a peak c.1910. This result suggests that the period between c.1850 and 1920 was characterized by a very high degree of fragmentation among the political elites (Figure 4.8). During the 1920s, however, the political elites pulled together, and during the New Deal and World War II the degree of polarization reached a minimum. The three post-war decades were also characterized by relatively consolidated elites. During this period there was a broad degree of overlap between the liberal-conservative scores of Democrats and Republicans in Congress (Poole and Rosenthal 1984: Figure 8). However, during the 1970s the overlap shrank, polarization surged, and by 2003 a large gap had developed between the Republican and Democratic distributions (McCarty et al. 2006: Figure 2.10). In summary, there have been two low polarization periods: 1815–1850 and 1930–1980, and two high polarization periods, 1850–1930 and 1980–the present (Figure 4.8).

In an attempt to explain the decline and surge of political polarization between 1879 and the present, McCarty et al (2006) examined a number of social and economic indicators. They discovered that the dynamics of polarization were correlated with the dynamics of inequality and immigration. Figure 4.9 illustrates this finding, except that I am using my own index of inequality, because the index of income inequality, used by McCarty et al, is available only for the period after 1913. Additionally, I have extended the period of interest back to 1800. The degree of correlation is generally good, with the exception of the early (and moderate) peak of polarization c.1800.

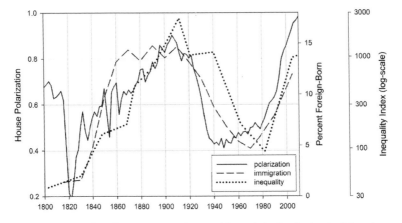

FIGURE 4.9 Elite fragmentation (proxied by political polarization) in relation to labor oversupply (proxied by percent foreign-born) and elite overproduction (proxied by the wealth inequality index).

Much of the book by McCarty, Pool, and Rosenthal is devoted to developing a theoretical explanation for the observed association between polarization, inequality, and immigration. After considering and dismissing several alternative explanations, they come to the conclusion that immigration results in a larger proportion of population who are both poor and cannot vote. This facilitates the move to the right and away from redistributive policies, which then causes income inequality to rise.

My explanation of the observed association is based on the Structural-Demographic Theory: (1) labor oversupply (proxied by immigration) leads to (2) elite overproduction (proxied by wealth inequality) and heightened intraelite competition that, in turn, results in (3) elite fragmentation (proxied by political polarization). Note that this explanation was not constructed *post hoc*, after observing the empirical associations between polarization, inequality, and immigration. Instead, each of these variables serves as a proxy for the movements of the structural forces postulated by the theory. In other words, the Structural-Demographic Theory provides a holistic explanation not only for these three particular variables, but for a host of others, some of which we have already examined, while others will be reviewed in the next two chapters. In my analysis, furthermore, I attempt wherever possible to find multiple proxies for the fundamental structural-demographic variables. Few proxies are a perfect reflection of the underlying fundamental variable; the influence of other factors tends to confuse the picture.

Synthesis

The overview of the structural-demographic variables describing elite dynamics in this chapter indicates that these variables tend to move up and down in a cyclic fashion. I now use the same approach as in Chapter 3 to summarize these dynamics. Figure 4.10a plots the three variables for which we have long-term data: economic inequality, a proxy for intraelite competition (Yale tuition scaled by manufacturing workers' annual wages), and a measure of intraelite fragmentation (political polarization). As before, the variables have been standardized (smooth-interpolated, linearly detrended, and scaled to mean = 0 and variance = 1).

Figure 4.10a shows that there is more variation between the timing when different variables reach their turning points, compared with what was observed for wellbeing proxies (Figure 3.7). The first troughs occurred during the period 1820–50, the peaks during 1880–1920, and the second troughs in the interval 1940–80. Thus, whereas for wellbeing variables we saw that the timing of trend reversals could be separated by as much as two decades, with elite-related proxies the lags can be twice that. This is partly due to the crudeness of the proxies that are available for this difficult-to-quantify process, but also probably because there are genuine time lags.

According to the Structural-Demographic Theory, the three variables plotted in Figure 4.10, inequality, intraelite competition, and intraelite fragmentation, should all be positively related to elite overproduction (the second general principle, see *Reformulating the Theory for Modern Societies* in Chapter 1). However, it does not mean that we expect all of these variables to be completely correlated and to experience trend reversals at the same time. For example, it appears that inequality tends to lag behind the other two variables by 20–30 years (especially clear in the last two trend reversals, see Figure 4.10a). One possible explanation for this pattern is that a changed economic conjuncture that makes it possible for employers to reduce wages may not immediately lead them to do so. Corporate managers may be constrained by prevailing social norms of fairness from taking advantage of a favorable economic conjuncture. Note in particular that the relative wage went through a peak around 1960 (Figure 3.4). Even though during the next two decades the proportion of GDP that went to workers was declining, inequality started increasing only 20 years later, after 1980. In Chapter 12 (*Looking for a Proxy for "Culture"*) I will show that cooperative norms that restrained the ability of managers to lower worker wages unraveled only during the 1970s. The runaway growth of top incomes and fortunes then followed, after 1980.

In summary, although variables related to elite overproduction should be generally going up and down together, there is no reason to expect that their turning points would be perfectly correlated. As a result, the thick gray curve that summarizes the three proxies in Figure 4.10a and that can be interpreted as a general proxy for elite overproduction, should be taken with a grain of salt. Nevertheless, despite these problematic aspects, the statistical analysis (see Chapter 7 and Figure 7.2) confirms that these elite-related variables do not simply fluctuate in a random manner. Their ups and downs are statistically significant, relative to the overall secular cycle.

The empirical survey in this chapter, thus, suggests that between 1780 and 2010 the factors reflecting elite overproduction moved cyclically and were positively (if imperfectly) correlated. What is particularly interesting is that the overall curve reflecting elite overproduction was *negatively* correlated with the average wellbeing curve. Over the course of American history elite overproduction and popular wellbeing have moved in opposite directions, tracing out a characteristic "double spiral" predicted by the Structural-Demographic Theory (Figure 4.10b).

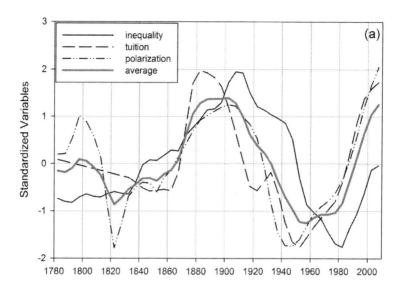

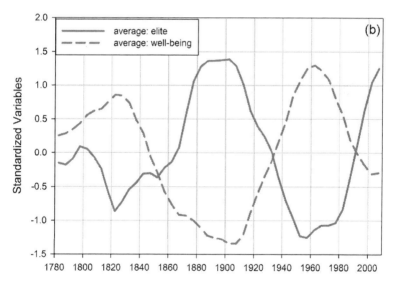

FIGURE 4.10 Summary of inequality and elite competition dynamics. (a) Standardized variables reflecting the fluctuations of the three elite prox-ies. The gray curve is the average of the three data series and a proxy for the general process of elite overproduction. (b) A comparison of elite over-production curve (from Figure 10.4a) to the average wellbeing curve (from Figure 3.7).

5

The State

Federal Government: Revenues and Debt

While all complex societies have elites (even though the boundary between the elites and the general population is usually fuzzy—as discussed in Chapter 4), the presence of state structures and how much autonomy they enjoy is a variable. At one extreme are societies such as the Roman Republic, in which the state had essentially no independence from the elites. Bureaucratic functions were performed by politically ambitious nobles serving without pay. In fact, holding office in Republican Rome was very expensive, so not only were magistrates unpaid, they subsidized government from their private fortunes. At the other extreme are societies such as the Tang China with a clearly distinct state bureaucracy complete with a civil service examination system.

The degree of power and autonomy of the American state has changed dramatically over the last 230 years. In the early Republic, the revenues of the Federal Government hovered around two percent of the GDP (Figure 5.1). The main function of the federal state was war. For example, in the first three decades of the Republic more than 80 percent of federal expenditures went to the army, the navy, veterans' pensions, and to servicing the debt incurred as a result of military actions (Wallis 2006).

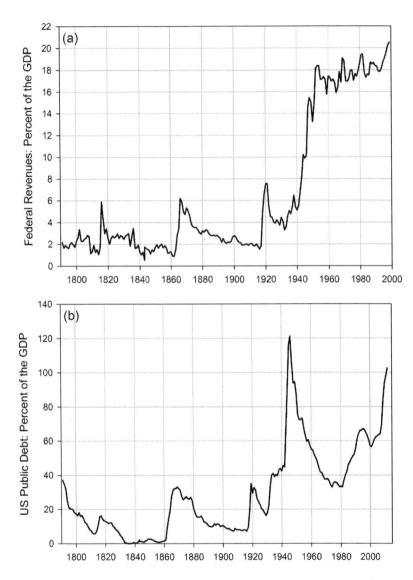

FIGURE 5.1 History of the US federal finances: (a) revenues as percent of the GDP, 1791–1999; (b) public debt as percent of the GDP, 1791–2012.

Because war was the main business of the federal government, major conflicts always resulted in a spike in expenditures, which was then followed by a revenue hump (Wallis 2006). This is the pattern that we see following the Revolutionary War, the War of 1812, the Civil War, and World Wars I and II.

The public debt, similarly, grew sharply during the wars and then was gradually paid off in post-war periods.

Before the New Deal, as the wartime debt was reduced federal revenues
also tended to decline to the level of roughly two percent (Figure 5.1a). During
this period, state and local taxes together usually generated more revenue
than federal taxes (Table 5.1). Even on the eve of the Great Depression, local governments collected more than half of all tax revenues in the United
States (Wallis 2006). Although the Federal Income Tax had been introduced
in 1913, the greatest source of revenue was property taxes (about 40 percent
of the total). During the New Deal and World War II the US financial system
experienced a radical change. The federal revenues increased by an order
of magnitude, jumping to 18 percent of the GDP by 1950, and then growing
more gradually to c.20 percent by the end of the century (Figure 5.1a).

TABLE 5.1 Government revenues, by level of government, as a percent of
gross national product (data source: Wallis 2006: Table Ea-A).

Year	Federal	State	Local
1840	1.7	1.0	1.4
1850	2.0	1.0	1.2
1860	2.5	1.3	1.6
1870	4.7	1.1	2.6
1880	2.8	0.7	2.2
1890	2.7	0.9	2.8
1900	2.6	1.0	3.6

The specific features of the pre-New Deal fiscal regime made the federal
government a minor player in structural-demographic dynamics. Simply put,
during this period (which was also the first secular cycle) the United States
lacked the pressures that typically drove the development of the state elsewhere. The only sustained threat during the nineteenth century came from
militarily weak and disunited American Indian tribes. The European Great
Powers tended to leave the US alone, with a few minor exceptions (such as a
brief war with Britain in 1812). Mexico was such a weak state that winning the
1846–1848 Mexican-American war required very few resources (note that the
rise in the public debt associated with that war is almost invisible in Figure
5.1b).

Additionally, during this period the largest source of federal revenue was
tariffs on imported goods. The primary goal of these tariffs was to protect
budding American industries, so any revenue generated was essentially a

side-effect. As a result of the minor role of the federal government and the abundant tariff revenues, fiscal insolvency of the state was not a factor that we need to take into account during the first secular cycle.

At the beginning of the second secular cycle the fiscal regime changed in ways that should make the central state an important factor in structural-demographic dynamics. First, as a result of legislation introduced during and following the New Deal, the US developed a welfare state that assumed increasing responsibility for the economic and social wellbeing of its citizens. Second, after World War II the US became a global superpower with huge military commitments in practically every region of the world. As a result, we expect that the financial health of the state should become susceptible to structural-demographic developments and, in turn, itself affect other parts of the system.

The fluctuations of the federal debt since 1945 appear to support this view. During World War II, the US public debt increased to 120 percent of the GDP (Figure 5.1b). There is nothing surprising about this development, because all governments are forced to borrow in order to survive a major war. After 1945 the debt started shrinking, partly because the government ran budget surpluses in some years, and partly as a result of the growth in gross national product. By the 1970s the public debt shrank to below 40 percent of the GDP. What came next, however, is unexpected. For the first time in the US history the debt started growing in the absence of any major war. This growth continued, with the exception of the Clinton presidency period, and in 2012 the size of the debt exceeded that of the GDP. As we know, runaway growth of the public debt is what usually happens during the stagflation phase of most secular cycles (but did not happen in the nineteenth century America, as was noted above, nor during Rome's Republican cycle, see Turchin and Nefedov 2009)

External Wars and Territorial Expansion

The geographic extent of the power and influence of the American state expanded in two great spurts. First, by the middle of the nineteenth century the US had become a continental great power. Second, after the end of World War II it became one of the two superpowers (and when the Soviet Union collapsed in 1991 the US achieved world hegemonic power unrivaled by any other state). These expansions were largely a result of external wars fought by the US against a variety of opponents (see Table 5.2).

TABLE 5.2 Major external wars of the US, 1785–present. "Major" is defined as resulting in at least 1,000 US total deaths (both combat and "other"). Source: Wikipedia

Conflict	Date	US deaths
Northwest Indian War	1785–1796	>1056
War of 1812	1812–1815	~15,000
Second Seminole War	1835–1842	1535
Mexican–American War	1846–1848	13,283
Spanish–American War	1898	2,446
Philippine–American War	1898–1913	4,196
World War I	1917–1918	116,516
World War II	1941–1945	405,399
Korean War	1950–1953	36,516
Vietnam War	1955–1975	58,209
Afghanistan	2001–present	2,229
Iraq War	2003–2011	4,488

I begin by briefly reviewing the US territorial expansion as a nation-state. The bulk of territorial growth of the United States (not counting its initial establishment as an independent state by winning the Revolutionary War) was accomplished between 1803 and 1848 (Table 5.3). By 1848 the area that would be later organized as the 48 contiguous states was acquired by treaties with European Great Powers and Mexico (although many Native Americans would dispute the legality of these arrangements). This was followed by the purchase of Alaska in 1867 and annexations of various Pacific islands (most notably, Hawaii in 1898). Continental expansion of the US involved four major conflicts, taking place between 1785 and 1848 (Table 5.2). These wars were fought against Native Americans, a European Great Power (Great Britain), and another North American state (Mexico). In addition to these major wars, the US was also involved in a number of other conflicts, primarily against Native Americans (see Table 8.1).

The second bout of expansion, the acquisition of an informal empire, occurred after World War II. This development is more difficult to quantify, because it did not result in a permanent gain of additional territory. At the end of World War II the United States occupied defeated Axis powers, such as Germany and Japan. This temporary military occupation phase was succeeded by a more permanent world-wide network of military bases. In addition to this military component of the global projection of power by the US, there was a political dimension, which took the form of a system of treaties, such as the North Atlantic Treaty Organization (NATO: 1949–present), the South East Asia Treaty Organization (SEATO: 1954–1977), and the Central Treaty Organization (CENTO: 1955–1979), supplemented by various bilateral treaties.

TABLE 5.3 Territorial growth of the United States (some minor acquisitions omitted). The size of area gained is in Mm2 (= 1,000,000 km2).

Year	Territory	Mm²	Notes
1783	Original 13 states	2.3	Cession by Great Britain (Treaty of Paris)
1803	Louisiana Purchase	2.1	Acquired from France
1810	West Florida Republic	<0.1	Annexed (by Pres. James Madison)
1818	Along Canadian border	<0.1	Cession by Great Britain (Webster-Ashburton Treaty)
1819	East Florida	0.2	Cession by Spain (Adams-Onís Treaty)
1845	Texas Republic	1.0	Annexed
1846	Oregon Territory	0.7	Cession by Great Britain (Oregon Treaty)
1848	Mexico Cession	1.4	Cession by Mexico (Treaty of Guadalupe Hidalgo)
1853	Gadsden Purchase	<0.1	Acquired from Mexico
1867	Alaska Purchase	1.8	Acquired from Russia
1898	Puerto Rico, Guam, Philippines	0.1	Cession by Spain (Treaty of Paris)
1898	Hawaii	0.1	Annexed
1899–1929	Samoa and other Pacific Islands	<0.1	Annexed
1919	Virgin Islands	<0.1	Purchased from Denmark
1947	Marshall Islands	<0.1	Occupied during World War II

One way of quantifying the waxing and waning global military reach of the US is by tracking changes in the numbers of US troops stationed abroad. Figure 5.2 shows how the American military presence overseas fluctuated between 1950 and 2011. There are three peaks associated with the major wars fought after the end of World War II (these are the Korean War, the Vietnam War, and the wars in Afghanistan and Iraq, see Table 5.2). Abstracting from these peaks, we see that non-war related level of military power projected overseas went through three phases. These dynamics are especially clear when we consider troops stationed in Europe, where the US has not fought a major war since 1945 (Figure 5.2, broken curve). The highest level of buildup was achieved in the first phase of the Cold War during the 1950s. Another, more gradual rise occurred during the "Second Cold War" (1979–1991). After the end of the Cold War in 1991, the number of troops stationed in Europe declined by a factor of three, and in East Asia by a factor of two.

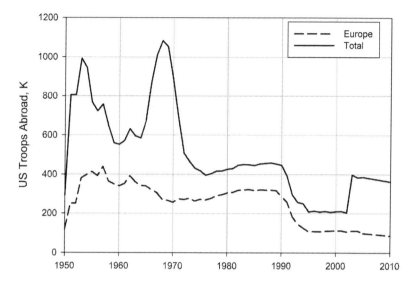

FIGURE 5.2 The number of US troops stationed abroad. Source: (Kane 2004, 2011).

Taking these numbers as a reasonable proxy for the extent of the America's informal empire, we observe that resources committed by the US to project-ing its global power peaked during the period encompassing World War II, the Korean War, and the active phase of the Vietnam War (1941–70). Since 1970 it has been declining, although with some fluctuations due to "hot wars". The overall pattern is the same, whether we focus on the total troops outside the US, which include those fighting hot wars, or only on those stationed abroad as part of cold war-style containment. The degree of decline would be even more clear if we expressed it in relative terms, scaled, for example, by the total American population (which more than doubled between 1940 and 2011), or by the real GDP (which grew by a factor of 11 in inflation-adjusted terms).

Commonwealth: State Legitimacy and Patriotism

It is interesting that the two periods of rapid expansion of the American polity, continental (1803–1848) and global (1941–1970), coincided with two peaks of wellbeing indicators (c.1830 and c.1960, see Figure 3.7). In fact, correlation between integrative phases and territorial expansion is a general pattern that is observed in many of the studied historical cases (Turchin and Nefedov 2009). Generally, while states tend to fight external wars continuously (or, at least, the probability of being involved in an external war appears to be independent of structural-demographic dynamics; and the US is no exception to this rule), *successful* wars resulting in territorial expansion occur disproportionately during the integrative phases of secular cycles. The reason is that success in war requires a high degree of cooperation within the society. At the very least, the elites have to pull together and bury their differences. In more significant conflicts the elites need to mobilize the rest of the population. Winning a major war requires that the elites and commoners be unified and equally willing to sacrifice blood and treasure for the sake of victory.

During the disintegrative phases, by contrast, it is very difficult to generate the cooperative action needed to win a major war. The elites are fragmented into interest groups feuding among themselves. High levels of inequality, which are characteristic of disintegrative phases, are destructive of cooperation. The prevailing "partisan" social mood (see Chapter 2) is not conducive to shared sacrifice. The wealthy segments of the population are primarily interested in reducing their taxes. The political elites do not send their children into the military. Impoverished commoners and frustrated elite aspirants, likewise, withdraw their cooperation by dodging the draft and avoiding taxes. The legitimacy of the state is low and patriotism is trumped by sectarian attitudes.

An example of the connection between integrative phases and territorial expansion is the Kingdom of France. Between 1150 and 1870 France went through three complete secular cycles: Capetian, Valois, and Bourbon (see Table 1.1). The three periods of sustained territorial expansion all happened during the integrative phases of these cycles (see Figure 4.1 of Turchin and Nefedov (2009)).

These observations suggest that it might be profitable to take a closer look at measures of state legitimacy, patriotism and, more generally, of cooperative social mood to find out whether they have oscillated as the theory suggests. Probably the most direct indicator of state legitimacy in America is provided by polls asking "How much of the time do you trust the government in Washington?" Figure 5.3 plots the combined proportions replying "just about always" or "most of the time". Faith in government peaked in 1965, reaching nearly 80 percent, dropped precipitously during the 1970s, and has continued to decline more slowly (but with fluctuations) ever since. In 2013 only 26 percent of the population had a high trust in government.

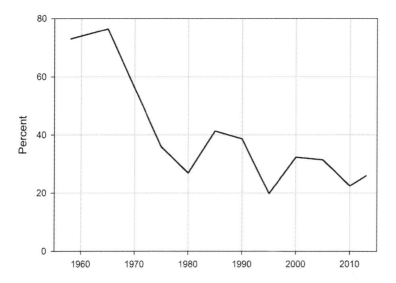

FIGURE 5.3 Public Trust in Government: 1958-2013 (moving average of multiple polls, plotted every five years). Source: Pew Research Center.

Such direct data on public trust, unfortunately, are available only from 1958 on. To probe the dynamics of changing social attitudes before 1958 we need to look to indirect proxies. In a recent investigation into the history of homicide in America, Randolph Roth proposed that rising and falling murder rates are strongly influenced by "the legitimacy of the government, the degree of unity and fellow-feeling in the nation" (Roth 2009:470); in other words, by cooperative social mood, a key structural-demographic variable. He further suggested that various measures of patriotism might serve as good indicators of the ups and downs in this social mood variable.

One proxy that Roth used was the trends in naming counties in the United States. More than two-thirds of American counties were named after a notable personage. During the colonial period most new counties were named after a British notable (eg, the eight Cumberland Counties, which were named after Prince William, Duke of Cumberland). During the early Republic the tendency was to name counties after national figures (Washington, Jefferson,

Franklin, etc). This "patriot-hero syndrome" reached a maximum during the years 1810–1830 (Figure 5.4). "More than coincidentally, this is the same period many historians regard as climactic in terms of spontaneous national sentiment" (Zelinsky 1988:122). However, after 1830 the tendency was reversed, and many more counties were named after local personages. This particularistic tendency reached a peak between 1870 and 1890 (Figure 5.4).

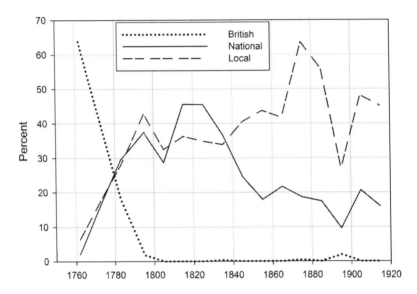

FIGURE 5.4 Proportion of new American counties named after British, American, and local notables, 1750–1920 (Zelinsky 1988: Table 4.1).

County names work well as a proxy for national versus particularistic social mood until 1920, when all decades but one have more than 100 new county names. After 1920, however, the number of new names drops to about 10 per decade, and therefore we need to look for other proxies of nationalism. In *Nation into State* Wilbur Zelinsky (1988) reported the number of visitors to nationalistically significant sites. Focusing on the Group I sites (for which data are available for the longest period), we see that the visitor numbers, scaled by the total US population, grew during the post-war years and reached a peak in the late 1960s (Figure 5.5). During the 1970s, however, this indicator declined.

For one of the historical sites included in this tally, Mount Vernon (the home of George Washington), we can extend the curve back into the nineteenth century. These data show a more gradual period of increase, which accelerated following 1920. The peak and the start of decline are also somewhat earlier than for aggregate data (Figure 5.5). The number of visitors to Mount Vernon peaked during the 1960s, with more than 1.2 million per year. In recent years the number of visitors has stayed at the same level (over 1 million), but since the US population grew by more than 50 percent, the proportion of the American population who visit has apparently continued to decline.

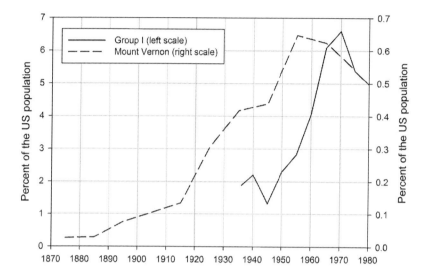

FIGURE 5.5 Number of visitors to nationalistically significant historical parks and sites in the United States. Solid curve: annual number of visitors to Group I sites (Lincoln's Birthplace, Colonial National Historical Park, Washington Birthplace, Statue of Liberty, Washington Monument, Monticello, and Mount Vernon), 1936–1980 (Zelinsky 1988: Table 3.3). Broken curve: annual number of visitors to Mount Vernon, 1870–1980 (Zelinsky 1988: Table 3.1). In both cases, visitor numbers are expressed as a proportion of the total US population.

In summary, a variety of proxies for cooperative social mood—high trust in government, county naming patterns, and visitors to nationalistically significant monuments—suggest that there were two peaks in American nationalism, the first in 1820 and the second in 1960 (both dates are approximate). These two peaks coincide with the periods of American expansionism (and periods of high popular wellbeing, as well as low economic inequality).

I argued above that a social mood of national consolidation and broad-based cooperation, which typically takes hold during the integrative phases of secular cycles, is usually necessary to generate concerted collective action that is translated into successful state expansion. The specific mechanisms translating the socially cooperative mood into action are a willingness among the wealthy elites to tax themselves and among the general population to supply recruits to the army. We have direct evidence that both of these mechanisms were operating during the integrative phase of the second secular cycle.

First, we can look at the curve tracing the evolution of the federal tax rate on top incomes between 1913 (when federal income taxes were first introduced) and the present. Because the American state is dominated by economic elites and most (all) major decisions can be taken only with their collective approval (see Chapter 3), this curve corresponds very closely to the willingness of the elites to tax themselves; in other words, to sacrifice for the common benefit. The curve shows two peaks, corresponding to World Wars I and II (Figure 5.6). The most interesting dynamics, however, are its behavior during the peaceful periods. We see that, apart from war periods, the peak occurred between 1950 and 1963, when the taxation rate on incomes greater than $400,000 was 91 percent, a level that is unimaginable in today's political climate.

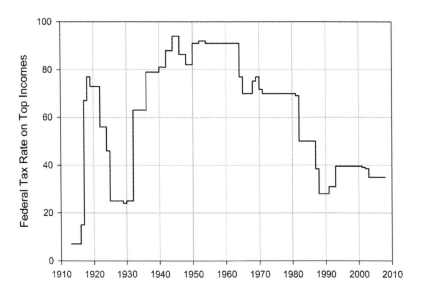

FIGURE 5.6 Federal tax rate on top incomes, 1913–2008.

Second, a proxy for the willingness of the general population to serve in the military is indicated by the institution of conscription, coupled with (positive) popular attitudes to it. This proxy works well for the United States because for most of its history it has relied on volunteers to fill the military ranks. War-time conscription was introduced during the American Civil

War (1862–65) and World War I (1917–18). However, especially during the Civil War, the draft was met with stiff popular resistance (and was the chief cause of the 1863 Anti-Draft Riot in New York City, the bloodiest riot in US history, see the next chapter).

The first peace-time draft in the US was introduced in 1940, and renewed in 1948. It was in operation until 1973, when the US Army switched to an all-volunteer military force. The period between 1940 and 1973 saw three major hot wars and the most intense phase of the Cold War (sometimes known as Cold War I). At least initially, there was a high degree of acceptance of the draft. According to polls conducted in 1940 and again in 1942, around 70 percent of Americans supported compulsory military training for all young men.[7] By the late 1960s, however, the support for conscription waned, and during the 1968 presidential election, Richard Nixon campaigned on a promise to end the draft. Again, however, we see that the integrative phase of the second secular cycle was characterized by a willingness in the general population to serve in the army, and that this willingness unraveled during the 1960s.

Synthesis

The history of the American state in the *longue durée* is characterized by two trends. The first was the shift from a minimalist role of the state that prevailed in the nineteenth century to a more activist state of today. The second trend was a cyclic one that conforms quite well with the pattern predicted the Structural-Demographic Theory. Integrative periods (with peaks in 1820 and 1960) were periods of national consolidation and patriotism, territorial expansion, and high state legitimacy. In contrast, disintegrative periods—or Ages of Discord—were characterized by particularistic mood, an inward rather than expansionist focus, and low state legitimacy.

---

7   "What the U.S.A. Thinks." *Life* (July 7, 1940), p. 20. "Survey Shows What Youth is Thinking." *Life* (November 30, 1942), p. 110.

6

Dynamics of Sociopolitical Instability

Approaches to the Study of American Political Violence

Political instability is violent, group-level conflict within a state. Because it occupies the middle ground between interstate warfare and individual violence/crime, its boundaries are, of necessity, somewhat imprecise. Instability events vary in scale from an intense and prolonged civil war claiming thousands (sometimes even millions) of human lives to a one-day urban riot with a handful of deaths, or even a violent demonstration with none. However, I will focus only on *lethal* events, those that have caused loss of life. Such a conservative approach excludes a number of legitimate instability events, but it has two advantages. First, it clearly demarcates political violence from peaceful demonstrations and non-violent labor strikes. Second, and even more important, events that involve loss of life are much more likely to be reported in the media. Thus, focusing on lethal events reduces the effect of various reporting biases and allows us more faithfully to reconstruct the temporal dynamics of political violence.

Apart from lethality, instability events also need to be distinguished from external warfare, on one hand, and interpersonal violence, on the other (later in this chapter I will survey crime patterns, focusing on homicides). For the United States, the boundary between internal and external warfare is usually noncontroversial, except possibly in the case of the Indian wars. I treat conflicts between the Native Americans and the settlers of European origin as external warfare prior to 1890, the official date of the closing of the American frontier (Turner 1921) and as political instability thereafter.

Political instability in the US has been examined by a number of authors. One such study is the database of political violence events in the United States between 1819 and 1968, compiled by the Inter-University Consortium for Political and Social Research (ICPSR) (Levy 1991). This team of investigators located violent events by searching a random subset of *Washington National Intelligence* from 1819 to 1850, and *The New York Times* from 1851 to 1968. Political-violence events were defined as those (1) involving an attack on an official or officials, and (2) an attack on an individual or group for political and social reasons (Levy 1969: 86).

A more recent database was compiled by the historian Paul Gilje for his book on American riots (Gilje 1996). Unlike the approach used in constructing the ICSPR database (Levy 1991), it was not Gilje's intent to search for riots in a systematic manner. Also, for a variety of reasons, his list becomes less comprehensive as one moves towards the present. However, the great advantage of this database is its sheer size: more than 4,000 events, of which 1,060 fit my definition of political violence.

In a recent paper (Turchin 2012), I described a computerized database on the dynamics of sociopolitical instability in the US between 1780 and 2009. This database was constructed by digitizing data collected by previous researchers, most notably Gilje and the ICSPR team, and supplemented by systematic searches of electronic media archives (to check for potential biases). It includes 1,590 political violence events such as riots, lynchings, and terrorism. The following is based on the analyses of the US Political Violence (USPV) database.

Classes of Instability Events

Incidents of political violence can be roughly classified by whether both opposing sides are substantial groups of people (eg, more than 12 individuals), or whether one side is a group, and the other is one or few (under 12) individuals. The boundary of 12 between "few" and "many" is arbitrary: it simply follows the precedent established by Gilje (1996). However, the proportion of borderline cases, in which it is difficult to decide whether we are dealing with a group or not, is in any case tiny.

The generic term for group-on-group violence used both in scientific literature (Gilje 1996, Grimstead 1998) and in American newspaper reports is *riot*. Gilje defines a riot as "any group of 12 or more people attempting to assert their will immediately through the use of force outside the normal bounds of law" (Gilje 1996:4). I modify this basic definition in two ways. First, I distinguish between group-on-group violence (proper riots) and group-on-individual violence (termed lynchings, see below). Second, for the reasons stated earlier I included in the database only riots that actually led to at least one death.

There are many different kinds of riot. One useful way to distinguish them is by the motivations/issues involved. The most common issues are (1) race or ethnicity, (2) labor-management conflicts, and (3) politics, including election disputes and sectional conflicts before the Civil War. Some riots have mixed motivations (for example, race and politics in the South during the Reconstruction Era, or labor and ethnicity in many violent strikes), and the USPV database uses more than one code where appropriate.

If a riot is a conflict between groups of people, a *lynching* is lethal violence perpetrated by many on one or a few individuals. The most common issue leading to a lynching in the USPV database was race or ethnicity. The next common class of lynchings can be termed "extralegal", when a group of citizens executes a person (or persons) accused of serious crimes such as murder or rape. In many cases, race and extralegal motives are intermixed, and database coding reflects this fact. Finally, there are also some examples of lynchings following labor or political disputes, but these are relatively rare.

Violence perpetrated by one/few on many is more difficult to categorize. This class of events includes, first and most obviously, terrorism, such as the bombing of the *Los Angeles Times* by Italian anarchists in 1910, or the Oklahoma City bombing in 1995. Terrorism is generally directed against some social or political institution, or society as a whole. An important class of political violence—*assassination*—is the one in which an individual is targeted not as a private person, but as a representative or an embodiment of some social group or political institution. The most common issue motivating assassinations is politics, in which the victim is a government official or an elected representative. Other subtypes include assassinations motivated by religious, ethnic, or racial hatred.

Finally, there is *indiscriminate mass murder*, most often taking the form of a shooting rampage, because firearms are so readily available in America. This is a relatively new type of violence that has become common in the US only in the past three or four decades. Whether rampages are really instances of sociopolitical instability is controversial. News reports tend to dismiss them as incidents of senseless mass murder by mentally disturbed individuals who, for no apparent reason, "snap" (Ames 2005, this tendency is sometimes referred to as "medicalizing mass murder", see Krauthammer 2009). They give the appearance of senseless, random violence because the great majority of shooting rampages do not target specific individuals. Social science research, however, suggests that such attacks are not "random". For example, school shootings are typically aimed at the entire school as an institution (Newman 2004:261), whereas workplace rampages attack the company, or the corporate culture (Ames 2005:19). As Mark Ames (2005:19) noted, "… there are no 'random' victims – everyone in the targeted company is guilty by association, or they are collateral damage. The goal is to destroy the company itself…" After 2000 an increasing number of rampages have been directed against the state institutions—most frequently, the police and the courts, but sometimes at such prominent symbols of the government as the Pentagon and the Capitol.

These considerations suggest that indiscriminate mass murder is a form of terrorism—*suicide terrorism*—because in a large proportion of mass shootings the perpetrators are killed by the police, or shoot themselves. Those who do survive are invariably apprehended (or turn themselves in), and are imprisoned for life. As a result, killing rampages result in either physical or social death for the shooter. The only difference between a rampage shooter and a suicide bomber is in the weapon used to inflict damage (in fact, indiscriminate mass murderers use not only guns, but knives, vehicles, and indeed explosives). Both aim not at individual people but at groups, social or political institutions, or entire societies. The "random" or "senseless" appearance of this type of violence arises from the application of the "principle of social substitutability" (Kelly 2000: 5) or "fungibility of the victim" (Blee 2005: 607). A soldier on the battlefield is expected to try to kill another person simply because the other is wearing enemy uniform. Enemy soldiers are "socially substitutable". And so are victims of a shooting rampage. In other words, the principle of social substitutability helps us to distinguish between individual-on-individual crime and collective violence. According to this criterion, indiscriminate mass murder is a form of political violence.

Data Reliability Issues

The USPV database includes c.1,600 unique instability events. Note that the database contains only a sample of all instability events, because its primary purpose is to detect *relative* changes in the incidence of political violence with time. Using mark-recapture methods, I estimated that the probability of detection (an event making it into the database) can be estimated at roughly 50 percent. The probability of detection increases with the number of fatalities. For example, the estimated probability of detection for a riot claiming three or more lives is over 70 percent (Turchin 2012).

I also investigated whether there are any systematic biases affecting the sampling process that would distort temporal dynamics. The probability of an event being reported in a newspaper, such as the *Hartford Courant* (which was one of the newspapers I searched systematically for incidents of political violence), apparently increased between 1780 and the present. The long-term increase in communications and a general increase in the amount of news reported by the media (as quantified by the average number of pages per newspaper, Levy 1969), means that an instability incident is more likely to be reported today than in the nineteenth century. Additionally, because there is a long-term trend of decreasing interpersonal violence in human history (Eisner 2003), a death-causing event now probably has a better chance of being deemed newsworthy. This long-term bias is present in the database, and it must be kept in mind when interpreting the analysis results. On shorter timescales, various samples indicate very similar dynamics. Thus, the empirical results on the dynamics of rioting appear to be robust.

The situation is somewhat different when we deal with lynchings. Several considerations suggest that the number of lynchings in the database seriously under-reports the actual one (this was also noted by Gilje 1996:183). The problem is that lethal violence against blacks (and certain categories of whites) in the South was so common and routine that newspapers, especially in the Northeast, simply did not bother to report most of these incidents. On the other hand, the relative dynamics in the *Historical Statistics* data and the USPV database are the same: a peak in the early twentieth century and a rapid decline after 1920. The under-reporting bias in the database is highest in the early decades after 1882, and progressively decreases towards 1964.

Dynamical Patterns of Political Instability

The 1,600 instability events in the USPV database are distributed highly unevenly through time (Figure 6.1a). The period between 1780 and 1825 was characterized by a declining trend in political violence. While the post-revolutionary era saw several significant incidents (Pennamite-Yankee War, Shays' and Whiskey rebellions), these aftershocks of the Revolutionary War had died out by 1800, and the first quarter of the nineteenth century was a remarkably peaceful period in American history. The second quarter of the century, on the other hand, was a period of rising political turbulence. The first spurt occurred during the 1830s, but the highest level of political violence was reached during the 1860s.

From 1860 to 1920, the level of violence fluctuated around a very high level, with another spurt during the 1910s. The period between 1920 and 1960, however, saw another declining trend in instability. The 1940s and 1950s were the second peaceful period in domestic American history. After 1960 the level of political violence began rising again.

Spectral analysis suggests that there are two major rhythms underlying the dynamics shown in Figure 6.1 (Turchin 2012). The first peak in the spectrum indicates a long-term, or secular cycle. One complete oscillation was observed between the troughs of 1820 and 1950, and the rising trend after 1960 may indicate the beginning of the next secular cycle. The second peak in the spectrum is associated with a period of 50 years. These are the prominent spikes observed around 1870, 1920, and 1970. The smaller spurt during the 1830s may or may not be part of this pattern. Interestingly, the American Revolution (1775–83) appears to fit this sequence (as a "prequel" to the subsequent history). As was discussed in Chapter 2 (*Wheels within Wheels*), this pattern of two periodicities, superimposed on each other, is typical of instability dynamics in historical societies.

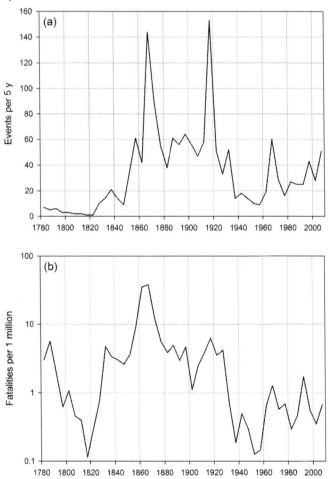

FIGURE 6.1. Temporal dynamics of sociopolitical instability in the United States, 1780–2010. (a) Fluctuations in the number of instability events per five-year interval. (b) The number of people killed in instability events per 1 million population per five years.

An alternative method for visualizing the dynamics of instability is to focus not on the number of political-violence events, but on the number of people killed in them, scaled by the total population of the United States (Figure 6.1b). This view of data shares many similarities with the trajectory of event counts, but it emphasizes the secular cycle. In particular, it shows the magnitude of the instability wave of the second half of the nineteenth century. Thus, the per capita fatality rate increased between 1820 and 1860 more than 100-fold (note that because the database reports only a sample of instability events, the absolute numbers of deaths per million of population are meaningless; what is important is the relative change from one time period to another). The decline from 1920 to 1950 was of similar magnitude, roughly 50-fold.

The 50-year cycle, on the other hand appears less prominently in the trajectory of per capita fatalities. The fatalities spectrum still contains the peak for the 50-year periodicity, but its height is greatly diminished compared with the event-count spectrum. The reason for this is not hard to fathom. Shorter-term dynamics appear to be "drowned" in random noise because of the statistical properties of the variable that is being averaged, the number of deaths per instability event. This variable is characterized by approximate scale invariance in which the frequency scales as an inverse power of the severity (Turchin 2012: Figure 2). Thus, although the most common fatality rate per event was one (48 percent of cases), on rare occasions the "butcher's bill" could run into hundreds (in less than one percent of events were 100 or more lives lost). As a result, rare-but-bloody has a disproportionate effect on the trajectory. This sensitivity makes the number of deaths a less useful quantity for the analysis than simply counting the number of events, and the following analysis focuses on event numbers.

Evolution of Political Violence: Forms and Issues

For 200 years between 1780 and 1980, the most common manifestation of sociopolitical violence was the riot (Figure 3). Overall, riots account for 56 percent of all violent events in the database. Therefore, it is not surprising that the trajectory of riot counts traces out both the secular wave of the second half of the nineteenth century, and the peaks of 1870, 1920, and 1970.

The second most common type of violence was the lynching, which accounts for 28 percent of events in the database (however, this is likely to be a serious underestimate, as discussed above). The number of lynchings per five-year period also exhibits the secular instability wave and two of the three peaks (around 1870 and 1920). After 1930, however, the incidence of lynchings rapidly declined. In more recent times this form of political violence has become rare.

The third form of political violence, terrorism in the broad sense (which also includes assassinations and shooting rampages) shows a somewhat different pattern. There is a peak around 1870, primarily associated with the wave of assassinations targeting both black and white Republican politicians during the Reconstruction Era (post-Civil War period). The next peak around 1970 is associated with assassinations of political leaders and the first mass appearance of the shooting rampage. The post-1980 rise is mainly a result of the current wave of shooting rampages, although traditional forms of terrorism also increased during this period.

As to the issues motivating political violence, the most common is race or ethnicity, followed by labor and politics (for details, see Turchin 2012: Figure 4). Race/ethnicity has been an important issue throughout American history, and was the common motive of riots, lynchings, and assassinations during the peaks of 1870, 1920, and 1970. The importance of other issues, however, has waxed and waned. Thus, politics was an important issue in c.1870 (election riots and sectional violence) and again in c.1970 (the civil rights and anti-war movements). By contrast, labor issues (in the form of violent and increasingly lethal strikes) reached their peak c.1920. What is interesting is that despite evolution of forms of political violence and the changing landscape of issues motivating it, none of the periods of enhanced instability (1870, 1920, and 1970) was dominated by either a single form or a single issue.

Dynamics of Homicides

The incidence of homicide, unlike political instability, is not a fundamental variable in Structural-Demographic Theory (it is not part of the feedback loops that drive structural-demographic dynamics). However, dynamics of the homicide rate may serve as a useful proxy for variables that are of primary interest. In particular, Randolph Roth (2009: 18) recently argued that over the long term, changes in homicide rates correlated with the level of trust in government and government officials, patriotism and empathy for fellow citizens, and the belief that government is stable and that social hierarchy is legitimate. In other words, murder rates should rise in periods of high sociopolitical instability and decline when the state authority is strong and perceived to be legitimate. This correlation has been found to hold for the United States and Western Europe over the past four centuries (Roth 2009:17). Additional support comes from our investigation of secular cycles in medieval England, and in nineteenth-century Russia (Turchin and Nefedov 2009: Chapters 2 and 9).

Despite these results, generally high positive correlations between high incidence of crime and political instability, homicide rates are not a very useful proxy for movements of political instability in the short run, because they are affected by a host of other factors (this is the point that Roth also makes). For example, improvements in health care and emergency services (motivated partly by medical advances in treating casualties in the Vietnam War) have lowered the death rate from serious wounds by about a fifth since 1960 (Roth 2009: 9). Such medical advances brought the homicide rate down by more than 1 per 100,000 persons per year during the 1990s and contributed to the much-commented-upon decline in murder rates during that decade.

Another factor that may affect the frequency of homicides is the incarceration rate. For example, Blumstein and Rosenfeld (1998: 1216) concluded that much of the decline in the homicide rate was associated with the doubling of the imprisonment rate between 1985 and 1995, although "that effect shows itself only in reduction in older individuals, since young people are only rarely candidates for incarceration". On the other hand, Michael Lynch (2007) more recently argued that the incarceration rate has only a slight effect on the homicide rate. In general, medical advances in treating wounds, the proportion of population in prisons, and fluctuations in the age structure of the population may all affect the recorded homicide rates. These caveats should be kept in mind when considering the patterns described below.

Reasonably detailed data on the US homicide rate are available from the beginning of the twentieth century (Figure 6.2). Murder rates during the Progressive Era were high and increasing, reaching a peak during the Great Depression (see Eckberg 1995 for complexities associated with reconstructing the homicide rate before 1933). However, the New Deal saw a dramatic (and well-documented) decline in the murder rate. By the 1950s the homicide rate declined to 4.5 per 100,000 persons per year—to less than half of the level observed in the early 1930s.

The crime wave of the second half of the twentieth century began in the late 1960s. At its peak in 1980 the homicide rate exceeded 10 per 100,000 per year before declining sharply during the 1990s (Figure 6.2). Interestingly, the two crime waves of the twentieth century tended to lag behind the instability peaks by about 10 years (compare with Figure 6.1).

US-wide homicide statistics do not exist prior to 1900 and therefore we need to look to regional studies to infer murder rate dynamics during the nineteenth century. One of the most detailed datasets was collected by Eric Monkkonen (2001) for New York City. Other regional data collected by Randolph Roth (2009: Figures 4.1–4.2, 5.1–5.8) show the same general pattern with minor variations. The pattern is a gradual decline during the first third of the century (Figure 6.3), an increase towards a peak during the late 1860s, and then another decline to the end of the century. The oscillations of the homicide rate were thus generally in step with instability dynamics (compare with Figure 6.1), but the amplitude of oscillations, between three and nine homicides per 100,000 people per year) was much less than the amplitude of instability (two orders of magnitude).

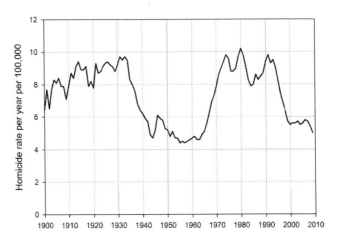

FIGURE 6.2 US homicide rates (per 100,000 people per year), 1900–2009. Data for 1900–1960 from (Eckberg 1995); for 1961–2009 from (Maguire 2010).

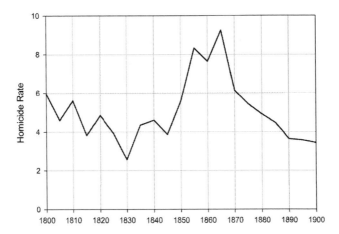

FIGURE 6.3 Homicides per 100,000 people per year in New York City, 1797–1898 (the borough of Manhattan). Data were averaged per five-year periods. Source: (Monkkonen 2001).

Synthesis

The main conclusion is that incidence of both political violence and homicides fluctuated dramatically in the US between 1780 and 2009. The dynamical pattern revealed by the instability data was a secular wave with 50-year (bi-generational) cycles superimposed on it.

During the second half of the nineteenth century the United States experienced a massive wave of sociopolitical instability: a more than 100-fold increase between 1820 and 1860 in the estimated number of deaths due to political violence, scaled by the total population. Between 1920 and 1950 this variable declined by a similar order of magnitude, 50-fold. Note that this estimate does not even take into account the mortality resulting from the American Civil War. Adding Civil War deaths would produce an even more striking pattern of rise and decline in political instability. The fluctuations in the homicide rate were not as dramatic, but still substantial. Between 1830 and 1860 murder rates increased roughly threefold, while between 1933 and 1950 they were halved.

In addition to this secular wave, the dynamics of instability exhibited shorter-term peaks, recurring with a period of approximately 50 years. These instability peaks were not dominated by a single issue, and the violence took several forms, suggesting that they were caused by fundamental social forces affecting the American polity. For example, political violence in antebellum America included a slave rebellion, a massive wave of urban riots, a prelude to the Civil War in Kansas ("Bleeding Kansas"), and even a religious war (against the Mormons). This explosion of political violence crested with the Civil War, the bloodiest war in the history of the US, which was followed by racial and political conflicts in the South and vigilante violence in the West.

Political violence in the years around 1920 similarly took many forms, and was motivated by diverse issues. During the Red Summer of 1919 there were no fewer than 26 major race riots that collectively caused more than 1,000 fatalities. This was also a period of intense class warfare, with labor strikes becoming increasingly more violent. To give just one example, the Battle of Blair Mountain in West Virginia in 1921 was the largest organized armed uprising in American labor history. Elite insecurity was further aroused by the terror campaign conducted by Italian anarchists and electoral challenges from the populists and socialists. The widespread belief among the elites during the Red Scare of 1917–21 that the country was on the brink of revolution was not just paranoia. The incidence of political violence events more than doubled during this period even above the already elevated level characterizing the secular instability wave (Figure 6.1a).

The last clearly defined peak around 1970 was also due to a variety of incidents: urban riots and violent campus demonstrations, political assassinations and terrorism. However, the level of violence achieved during this peak was much milder than that during the previous peaks.

The homicide rate also waxed and waned in waves. There was one crime wave during the American Revolution (Roth 2009:91), followed by three waves that peaked in the 1860s, 1933, and 1980. Thus, there is a rough correspondence—within a decade or so—between crime peaks and instability peaks. However, the magnitude of changes was quite different; this, together with the lack of precise match between the peaks suggests that factors other than political instability (as discussed earlier in the chapter) are of importance in determining the movements of the homicide rate.

PART THREE

A Complete Secular Cycle: from the Revolution to the Great Depression, c.1780–1930

7

Long-Term Trends, 1780–1930: a Synthesis

Goals of Part III

The empirical survey of structural-demographic dynamics in Part II suggests that between c.1780 and c.1930 the United States went through a complete secular cycle. As Chapters 3 to 6 documented, demographic, economic, social, and political variables during this period moved in a cyclic fashion. My approach so far has been to look at each variable, or group of variables, separately. However, the Structural-Demographic Theory posits that these variables are interconnected by a set of feedback loops; in other words, they are part of an integrated social system. The main goal of Part III will be to trace these feedback loops for the secular cycle of 1780–1930. Of particular interest are periods in American history when structural-demographic variables exhibit "trend-reversals", which as we have seen in Part II, tend to happen at approximately the same time (within a decade or two) for very different kinds of variables (demographic, economic, political, and others). Explaining such trend reversals from the perspective of the Structural-Demographic Theory is, thus, a major goal of this part.

Accordingly, instead of describing the long-term dynamics of each variable, I now focus on how variables have affected each other in each historical period. Additionally, it was not always possible to obtain quantitative estimates of all variables of interest (of interest, that is, from the theoretical point of view). Thus, the second goal of Part III is to fill in the gaps with a more qualitative, narrative-based approach. Finally, social scientists have advanced a number of explanations for various turning points in American history—such as the Civil War and the New Deal, to name two of the most important milestones—and the third goal here will be to engage these theories and compare their answers with those offered by the structural-demographic model.

This chapter presents a summary of empirical trends during this secular cycle. The two trend reversals that define the cycle are discussed in a narrative manner in Chapters 8 and 10, respectively. Chapter 9 develops a quantitative model (using the conceptual framework developed in Chapter 2) that traces out the feedback loops connecting the population and elite variables.

Dynamic Interrelations
Between Structural-Demographic Variables

The Structural-Demographic Theory assumes that such variables as popular wellbeing, elite overproduction, and political instability are part of a dynamical system. "Systemness" implies that changes in one variable affect the dynamics of others through feedback loops. The dynamics predicted by the theory are long-term *secular cycles*, during which different variables change in recurrent and, to a certain degree, predictable ways. More specifically, for the variables/proxies considered in Part II, theory predicts that oscillations in political instability should be positively correlated with labor oversupply, elite overproduction, and intraelite polarization, and negatively correlated with various measures of wellbeing. Measurement errors and process noise mean we should not expect a perfect correlation. Additionally, because feedbacks from one variable to another can act with time lags, trend reversals in different variables need not occur at the same moment. Nevertheless, if the feedbacks postulated by the theory are strong enough, we expect to find statistically significant correlations with correct signs.

To test this prediction, I employed the standardized variables (those shown in Figure 3.7 and the other proxies assembled in Part II) and compared them with the response variable, sociopolitical instability, proxied by the log-transformed number of political violence events per five-year interval. The other structural-demographic variables and their proxies are listed in Table 7.1.

Figure 7.1 plots the scaled variables together (for those measures of wellbeing that are predicted to correlate with instability negatively, wage/GDP and health variables, the figure uses the *inverse* scale). Visual inspection of the graph suggests that these variables are part of a single dynamical complex inasmuch as they tend to wax and wane together. A more formal analysis with cross-correlation functions confirms this (Figure 7.2). All cross-correlations between instability and the other eight variables at lag 0 are of the correct sign and statistically significant. However, cross-correlation functions (CCFs) also suggest that there are significant lags characterizing the relationship between the eight variables and instability. Because the time step in the data is five years, CCFs peaking at lags 1–4 suggest that time delays are on the order of 5–20 years.

TABLE 7.1 Summary of the dynamics of structural variables. The two columns labeled "Trend Reversals" indicate approximate dates of the trend reversals during the 1780–1930 cycle. The last column provides a reference to the figure summarizing the long-term trend of the variable. The years in parenthesis correspond to dates of trend accelerations.

Structural variable	Proxy	Trend Reversals		Figure
		c.1830**	c.1910**	
Labor oversupply	Immigration	1830	1910	3.7
Wellbeing, economic	Relative wage	1830	1910	3.7
Wellbeing, health	Average stature	1790 (1840)	1900	3.7
Wellbeing, health	Life expectancy	1820	1910	3.7
Wellbeing, optimism	Marriage age (–)*	1810	1890	3.7
Wellbeing, aggregate		**1830**	**1910**	3.7
Inequality, economic	EVI	none (1830)	1910	4.10
Intraelite competition	Yale tuition	1840 (1860)	1890	4.10
Intraelite fragmentation	Polarization	1820	1910	4.10
Elite variables, aggregate		**1820**	**1900**	4.10
Sociopolitical instability	USPV events per 5y	**1820**	**1920**	6.1

*The minus sign indicates that this proxy correlates negatively with the structural variable.

** c.1830 refers to 1820–1840, and c.1910 to 1900–1920.

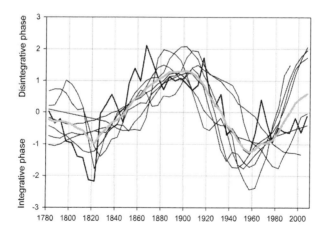

FIGURE 7.1 Dynamics of main structural-demographic variables in the US. The response variable, instability, is indicated with a thick black line, other structural variables are thin black lines, and the average of all time-series is indicated with the gray curve.

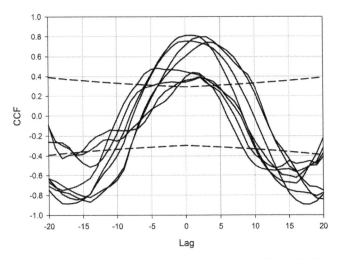

FIGURE 7.2 Cross-correlation functions between instability and eight other structural-demographic variables. The unit of time lag is five years; thus, a lag of 15 corresponds to 75 years. The broken curves are the 95 percent confidence intervals.

The Timing of Trend Reversals

The overall dynamical pattern in Figure 7.1, as depicted by the curve averaging the nine structural-demographic variables (or proxies), is that of alternating up and down trends separated by three trend reversals. Individual variables generally follow the same pattern, but in a much noisier fashion, with short-term fluctuations superimposed on the overall trends.

Additionally, some variables miss the first trend reversal (see Table 7.1). For example, the index of economic inequality increased throughout the nineteenth century (although it accelerated around 1830). Finally, as noted above, there is much variation about the specific dates when different variables experience trend-reversals. Nevertheless, the curve averaging these nine variables suggests that the first two reversals occurred approximately in 1830 (1820–40) and in 1910 (1900–20) (Figure 7.1; the third reversal will be discussed in Part IV, where I will use additional data to refine the estimate of its timing).

The Puzzle of the Civil War

Nineteenth century American history is dominated by one particularly traumatic, and at the same time deeply puzzling event: the American Civil War (1861–65). The causes of the Civil War are one the most controversial subjects in American History (Foner 1997, Burton 2006). I believe that the Structural-Demographic Theory can add much to this debate. However, it is important to acknowledge the limits to any insight that a general theory can bring to an explanation of a particular event, even one of such magnitude as the Civil War. Any particular event will have many "causes"—conditions that all need to obtain in order for the event to happen. General theory, thus, cannot explain a specific event with all of its peculiarities and special conditions. Rather the purpose of theory is to explain generic features of a class of events. The Civil War did not occur in isolation. It was a part—a very significant one, but still a part—of the instability wave in the US that began in the 1830s and crested in the 1860s. Because explaining the long-term dynamics of socio-political instability is a central issue in the Structural-Demographic Theory, it can offer insights into the causes and timing of this outbreak of political violence. Thus the goal in Part III is to dissect the mechanisms responsible for growing instability during the Antebellum period. Understanding these mechanisms, in turn, will clarify the structural causes of the Civil War.

8

The Antebellum Era

The Era of Good Feelings

The pre-Civil War period (c.1780–1860) was a particularly dynamic one in American history (Howe 2008). Many of the changes were directional, monotonic trends. The territory of the US grew more than threefold, and the population tenfold. The production of coal increased more than 200-fold, and the total length of railroads went from none to 30,000 miles. The social and economic mechanisms responsible for these transformations are reasonably well understood. On the other hand, causes of the trend reversal during the middle of the Antebellum Era are more difficult to understand within the framework of traditional historiography.

The first half of the period (to c.1820) involved progressive consolidation of the elites and the general population. After the turbulent decade following the end of the Revolutionary War, which saw two popular rebellions, sociopolitical instability declined to a very low level around 1820 (Figure 6.1b). Intraelite divisions and partisan conflicts similarly declined and the years around 1820 became known as the "Era of Good Feelings". The index of political polarization reached an all-time low (Figure 4.8). This was the America that Alexis de Tocqueville wrote about in his *Democracy in America* (based on his observations during a visit in 1831).

The reasons for the social cohesion and political consolidation in the mid-Antebellum Era can be understood by using the conceptual framework of Chapter 2 (see *Explaining Trend Reversals*). Essentially all cultural-evolutionary factors aligned to increase social cooperation. Within-elite competition was somewhat abated by forced emigration of well-to-do Loyalists. More important, successful territorial expansion at the expense of American Indians opened up vast new lands for settlement. Political expansion (via adding more states) and economic growth continuously created new power positions for political and economic elites, which further decreased intraelite competition.

Territorial expansion was fueled by success in external wars (see Chapter 5), the great majority of which during this period were against American

Indians (Table 8.1). Patrick Griffin (2007) argues that this conflict played a key role in the rise of the "American Leviathan". Settlers quickly realized that they could prevail against the Indians only by cooperating with the American state, which also meant acquiescing in taxation.

Finally, before the nineteenth-century immigration wave, white Americans were a remarkably homogeneous group, originating almost exclusively from northwestern Europe with most groups practicing protestant religion. These Americans were in conflict with "heathen savages". As I discussed in Chapter 2 (*A Cultural Multilevel Selection Framework for Trend Reversals*), cultural similarity within a group (the settlers) and intense conflict with others (the natives) tends to increase the capacity for within-group social cooperation. In my previous publications (Turchin 2006b:48–52, 2011) I provide additional details on how frontier warfare played a formative role in the spread of certain cultural forms of cooperation, such as Americans' "exceptional ability for voluntary organization" (Tocqueville 1984).

A particularly interesting case is eighteenth-century Pennsylvania (the following discussion follows closely the text in Turchin 2011:30–31). Initially, European settlers were divided by a number of ethnic and religious boundaries (Silver 2008). The English found it difficult to cooperate with the Germans and the Irish, and each ethnic group was further divided into feuding sectarian groups: Quakers against Anglicans, German Lutherans against Moravians and Mennonites. Yet, by the end of the eighteenth century the European settlers had forged a common identity ("white people") in opposition to the natives. As Nancy Shoemaker (2004) showed, these "metaethnic" labels (the Whites versus the Reds) were not evoked as soon as settlers and natives came into contact. Rather, during the course of the eighteenth century Europeans and Indians gradually abandoned an initial willingness to recognize in each other a common humanity. Instead, both sides developed new stereotypes of the Other, rooted in the conviction that they were peoples fundamentally at odds, by custom and even by nature (Shoemaker 2004).

The evolution of civic organizations reflected this expanding definition of common identity. Clubs with ethnic and denominational membership criteria appeared in Pennsylvania during the 1740s (Silver 2008). These associations represented what Putnam (2000) terms "bonding", rather than "bridging", social capital. For example, the St Andrew's Society was narrowly focused on helping the Scots, while Deutsche Gesellschaft did the same for the Germans. However, as settler-native warfare intensified, especially during the second half of the eighteenth century, the focus of civic associations gradually shifted to charity for any victims of Indian attacks, without regard for their ethnicity or religious denomination (Silver 2008). The social scale of cooperation took a step up. Of course, there were definite limits to this new "bridging" social capital: the Indians were most emphatically excluded; in fact, the integration of "white people" developed explicitly in opposition to the Indians.

TABLE 8.1 External Wars during the Antebellum Era, 1785–1860 (Source: Wikipedia)

years	war
1776–1794	Chickamauga Wars
1785–1795	Northwest Indian War
1798–1800	"Quasi-War" (undeclared Franco-American war)
1801–1805	First Barbary War
1811	Tecumseh's War
1812–1815	War of 1812
1815	Second Barbary War
1817–1818	First Seminole War
1823	Arikara War
1827	Winnebago War
1832	Black Hawk War
1835–1842	Second Seminole War
1836	Creek War
1846	Mexican-American War
1847–1855	Cayuse War
1854	Bombardment of San Juan del Norte (Nicaragua)
1855–1856	Puget Sound and Rogue River Wars
1855–1858	Yakima War
1855–1858	Third Seminole War
1858–1866	Navajo Wars
1860	Paiute War

Although the above description applies to pre-revolutionary Pennsylvania, a very similar dynamic obtained on the Northwestern frontier in Ohio after the Revolution (Griffin 2007). As Griffin (2007: 193) notes, for white Americans "Indians existed as cultural glue, since the hatred of them was fast becoming a basis for order".

In summary, growing social cohesion and political consolidation of the young American republic during the first half century of its existence was due to decreasing within-polity competition (both among the elites and among the common citizens) and high levels of interstate competition (against the British Empire and a multitude of Amerindian polities), which continued uninterrupted after the Revolution. Additionally, cultural distance between the Americans and their Indian enemies dwarfed the cultural distinctions between largely Protestant whites with ethnic roots in northwest Europe. Thus, all cultural evolutionary factors aligned to promote a more cooperative social mood.

The Jackson Era Trend Reversal

The remarkable period of national consolidation of the early nineteenth century did not last long. In the decades after 1820 both political polarization and instability began to accelerate, eventually culminating in the disaster of the Civil War.

As the survey of structural-demographic dynamics in Part II shows, sociopolitical instability was not the only variable that experienced a trend reversal during the 1820s (see Figure 8.1). Figure 8.1 focuses on three standardized indices of wellbeing (in other words, it inverts the scale used in Figure 7.1): economic, political, and stability. Apart from minor fluctuations, the trends were up before 1820 and down after 1830. Other SD indices, omitted from Figure 8.1 in order not to clutter it, behaved in a similar manner (see Figure 7.1, but because of the inverted scale, the trough in Figure 7.1 corresponds to the peak in Figure 8.1). There seems no doubt that the decades 1820s–1830s experienced a genuine structural-demographic trend reversal event.

The period of American history that followed the Era of Good Feelings is sometimes known as the Age of Jackson, referring to Andrew Jackson, the seventh President of the United States. In his first run for president in 1824 he won a plurality but not a majority of the popular vote, and was then defeated in the House of Representatives. His next and successful bid for the presidency was in 1828. Jackson is generally thought of as one of the more significant US presidents, as one of the principle architects of the "Jacksonian Democracy" (which broadened the participation of the public in government and promoted the strength of the executive branch at the expense of Congress). His years of active political life during the 1820s and 1830s coincided with the period when the majority of structural-demographic variables experienced trend reversals, hence my choice of the term "Jackson Era Trend Reversal" for the first turning point of the 1780–1930 secular cycle.

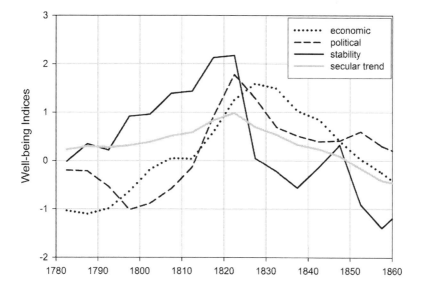

FIGURE 8.1 Dynamics of three standardized indices of wellbeing between 1780 and 1860: economic (relative wage, proportion of GDP going to workers), political (political consolidation, an inverse of political polarization), and stability (inversed log-transformed probability of being killed in an instability event). For data sources and details of analysis, see Chapter 7 and Figure 7.1.

How does the Structural-Demographic Theory account for these dynamics? The causal chain begins with demographic variables. As mentioned above, between 1780 and 1860 the US population expanded tenfold, from roughly three million to thirty million. Before 1830 this enormous growth rate was due to very high rates of natural increase—three percent per year—resulting from high fertility and low mortality. After 1830 population growth was further accelerated by massive influxes of immigrants (see Chapter 2), with the total rate of increase peaking at 3.75 percent per year in 1851. Although the United States acquired huge and sparsely populated territories, the majority of its population continued to live in the old eastern seaboard states. In this region, population density increased from nine persons per square mile in 1790 to 20 in 1820 and 42 in 1860 (Klein 2004: 80).

The US was still a predominantly agrarian society (over 80 percent of the population was rural as late as 1860) and, therefore, such massive population growth had standard Malthusian consequences. In particular, land became scarce on the eastern seaboard. In states such as Connecticut and Massachusetts, nearly all cultivable land was put to the plough, along with many marginal plots. The rural population reached its carrying capacity and the excess had to migrate to cities or out of state. These dynamics are illustrated in Figure 8.2 for the case of Massachusetts. By 1860 the rural population was at saturation point (in fact, it declined during the second half of the century). The urban population, on the other hand, had been surging, especially after 1820, and by 1850 it had exceeded the rural population (I will model the causes of this dynamic in Chapter 9). In other states the parity point was passed later (for example, 1870 in New York, 1880 in New Jersey, and 1890 in Connecticut), but the stagnation of the rural population and explosive growth of cities was the rule everywhere in the old Northeast.

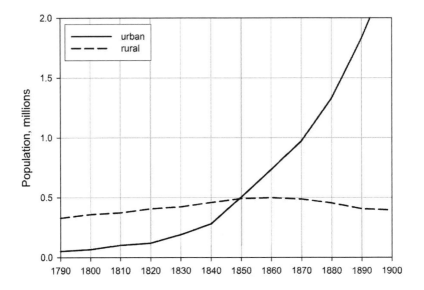

FIGURE 8.2 Divergent trends of population growth in Massachusetts: rural versus urban population (source: Carter et al. 2004).

Overpopulation on the eastern seaboard resulted in declining indices of health (average stature and life expectancy, see Chapter 2). Additionally, it began to depress birth rates (Easterlin 1976, Schapiro 1982), so that the annual rate of natural population growth declined from three percent to less than two percent. The consensus among demographers is that birth rates declined before 1860 as a result of Malthusian, rather than demographic-transition mechanisms (see Klein 2004: 80–82 for review of relevant literature).

Influxes of population from the countryside and from overseas into the Eastern cities created vast pools of labor, and depressed its cost. As economic power shifted in favor of employers, they began to profit disproportionately from the fruits of economic growth. The trend reversal in the relative wage, which occurred in the 1820s, was a result of this shift. Growing popular immiseration after 1820 resulted in greater incidence of urban riots and other instability events. It was also responsible for a rise in crime (for example, the homicide rate in New York City began increasing after 1830, see Figure 7.3).

The Pre-Crisis Period

Rise of the Elites

One result of favorable economic conjuncture for employers was that elite numbers and consumption levels began to increase. This process operated throughout the whole period, but greatly accelerated after 1850 (see Table 3.4 and Figure 3.3). Studies focusing on specific locations can flesh out the details of this process. For example, the number of New Yorkers with fortunes assessed at $100,000 or more increased from 59 in 1828 to 440 in 1856 (Jaher 1982:203). Similarly, the number of Bostonians worth at least $100,000 increased from 79 in 1835 to 342 in 1860 (Jaher 1982:71).

We are fortunate that during the critical 1850–1870 period we have census data on wealth distribution among Americans. In 1850, 1860, and 1870 each individual was asked to report the value of real estate that he or she owned. In addition, in 1860 and 1870 individuals were asked to quantify their personal estates.

Using a sample of these data, Lee Soltow (1975) estimated that there were 41 millionaires in 1860 and 545 millionaires in 1870 (wealth was estimated by adding together real estate and personal estate). Although these estimates are subject to wide sampling error (Soltow 1975:112), they confirm the dramatic increase in the number of millionaires discussed in Chapter 4. Furthermore, Lee's analysis yielded estimates for how the numbers of lesser wealth-holders increased during this period.

Because information about personal estate is unavailable for 1850, I focus here on the real estate. Of particular interest is the group of Americans with real estate equal to, or greater than $10,000. These individuals roughly correspond to the New York "bourgeoisie" studied by Sven Beckert (2001). According to Beckert's definition, the bourgeoisie included individuals owning assets of more than $10,000 in 1856 and $15,000 in 1873 (however, assets included both real and personal estate). This sum provided their possessors "well-furnished living quarters and the help of servants, and thus the essential attributes of respectability" (Beckert 2001:19).

According to the census data, individuals with wealth of at least $10,000 belonged to a rather select group of Americans: in 1850 they constituted an estimated 1.7 percent of the population (Table 4.5). During the next two decades they increased very rapidly. Between 1850 and 1860 alone, their numbers more than doubled (Table 4.5) and this was not due to inflation (over the decade the CPI rose only by eight percent). The same dynamic was observed for other wealth classes, defined by the cut-off points of $20,000 and $100,000 (Table 8.1). Overall, the proportion of Americans in all three wealth classes more than doubled between 1850 and 1870 (however, the increase from 1860 to 1870 was partly due to inflation; over that decade prices rose by 57 percent).

TABLE 8.1 Estimated numbers of adult American males in various wealth classes (free males in 1850 and 1860, white males in 1870). Source: (Soltow 1975: Table A4).

Year	>$10K		>$20K		>$100K	
	Number	%	Number	%	Number	%
1850	85,000	1.7	28,000	0.55	1,700	.034
1860	220,000	3.1	78,000	1.1	3,500	.049
1870	365,000	4.2	122,000	1.4	6,000	.069

Elite Fragmentation, 1845–1860

Major theories of why American politics "sectionalized", that is, why the American elites fractured along the sectional lines between the North and the South (eg, Ashworth 1997), do not even mention the massive expansion of the elite strata as a possible explanation. By contrast, in the Structural-Demographic Theory elite overproduction is the most important driver of increased political instability. The key link in this causal chain, which I examine in this section, is how elite overproduction breeds political fragmentation and intraelite conflict.

Before the Civil War, the United States was ruled by an economic elite dominated by the Southern slaveholders in collaboration with Northeastern merchants and bankers. The economic basis of this alliance was the agricultural commodities grown on Southern plantations with slave labor, first and foremost cotton. For example, trade in cotton was the most important business of the merchant elites in New York. Seventy percent of the wealthiest 300 New Yorkers in 1845 were merchants, auctioneers, brokers, and agents

(Beckert 2001:20). They exported Southern-grown commodities and imported European manufactured goods. An additional segment of the economic elites (especially in Massachusetts) used Southern cotton to produce textiles.

The domination of the early Republic by the Southern slaveholders is well documented. First, the votes of Southern whites had a greater weight due to the infamous "Three-Fifths" compromise of 1787, which counted three-fifths of the population of slaves in apportioning Representatives and Presidential electors. Second, the Southerners controlled half of the Senate, although the free population of the North was almost twice that of the South. Even more importantly, two-thirds of the wealthiest people in the US lived in the South—4,500 out of 7,000 Americans with wealth of $110,000 or more (Soltow 1975). Wealth-holders had the resources and leisure to pursue elected offices and careers in government, and to influence elections, and there were simply more of them in the South, compared with the North.

As a result, from 1789 to 1861 Southerners dominated the top government offices: presidents and vice-presidents, cabinet ministers, senators, and chief justices (Huston 2003:83). The Southerners held more than half of the top government posts (Richards 2000:92). Even under the Northern president, John Adams, 51 percent of high government officials were from the slave states.

The use of "Southerners" here is somewhat misleading, because the distribution of power within the South was highly concentrated in the hands of a few families. The slaves, obviously, had no political power, but the majority of the free population had neither resources, nor much interest in government. The planter class (individuals who owned 20 or more slaves) numbered less than 50,000 but "they dominated state senates and controlled virtually all southern United States senators as well as a majority of the region's governors" (Huston 2003:36–37).

In the North, similarly, political power was concentrated in the hands of relatively few wealth-holders. For example, between 1825 and 1850 three-fifths of Boston mayors were merchants, and an additional one-third were lawyers (Jaher 1982:54). Since the legal profession was thoroughly dominated by the patriciate (Jaher 1982:29, 223), the Brahmins essentially controlled local government. The situation was similar in other major cities in the Northeast during the second quarter of the nineteenth century: 92 percent of New York mayors and 100 percent of Philadelphia mayors were merchants or lawyers (Pessen 1973: Table 13.1).

The degree of political consolidation among the urban elites in the early Republic was remarkable. During the era of the First Party System (1792–1824, when politics were dominated by the Federalist Party and the

Democratic-Republican Party), the Bostonian patriciate overwhelmingly supported the Federalist Party, achieving "an almost comprehensive degree of political consolidation" (Jaher 1982:29). New York, similarly, was "a Federalist stronghold" (Jaher 1982:212). When the Second Party System formed (1828–1854, with the two dominant parties being the Whigs and the Democrats), economic elites in Boston and New York became Whigs. In Boston, for example, 86 percent of those worth at least $100,000 and 96 percent of millionaires between 1836 and 1848 voted Whig (Jaher 1982:55).

High consolidation among the elites was made possible by a relatively low rate of growth in their numbers before 1840. Even more importantly, the size of the political pie expanded fast enough to satisfy this modest growth of the elite strata. Thus, the number of states (and therefore senators, state legislators, etc) doubled between 1790 and 1837. At the same time, the number of representatives in the House almost quadrupled (Figure 8.3). Furthermore, the number of federal employees, an important source of patronage, expanded faster than the general population: from 0.57 per thousand in 1816 to 1.02 per thousand in 1841 (Carter et al. 2004: Table Ea894-903). Between 1837 and 1860, however, only seven more states were added, while the size of the House of Representatives slightly declined (from 242 to 237). The rate of growth of federal government also slowed: there were 1.09 and 1.14 federal employees per one thousand of population in 1851 and 1861, respectively.

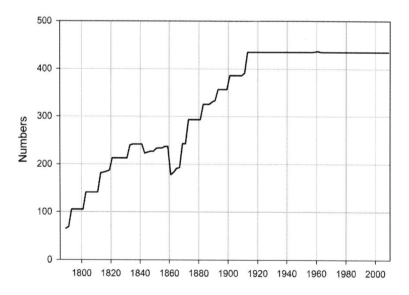

FIGURE 8.3 Growth in the size of the US House of Representatives.

As we saw earlier in the chapter, the numbers of wealthy New Yorkers and Bostonians (with fortunes assessed at at least $100,000) exploded during the Antebellum Era (New York: from 59 in 1828 to 440 in 1856; Boston: from 79 in 1835 to 342 in 1860). This dramatic expansion of the elite numbers destroyed the equilibrium between the demand and supply of government posts. As a result, competition for political power intensified at both the federal and local levels. Some wealth-holders ran for office themselves, while others threw their resources behind rival politicians. Additionally, the sons of merchant families often chose to go into professions, in particular becoming attorneys (Beckert 2001:36). Obtaining legal training was, and still is, the chief route to political office in the United States and, as I argued in Chapter 3, the surging numbers of lawyers is a good proxy for elite overproduction.

The gains from political power were dramatically increased by the introduction of the Spoils system by Andrew Jackson in 1829. Prior to Jackson's administration all presidents had made appointments to office from among their supporters, but generally waited for a position to become vacant through attrition—when the incumbent retired (Howe 2008:332). Jackson's "innovation" was to remove officials and replace them with his appointees. It is estimated that during his first year he removed about 10 percent of all government officials (Howe 2008:333). The stakes were very significant: in 1851, for example, federal employees numbered 26,274 (so that there were 1.09 federal employees per thousand of population, as noted earlier). Despite the increase in government posts, the supply was overwhelmed by demand for such positions. A horde of office-seekers nearly turned Jackson's inauguration into a riot (Howe 2008:331). Abraham Lincoln once said, "Were it believed that vacant places could be had at the North Pole, the road there would be lined with dead Virginians" (quoted in Potter 1976:432). And, most dramatically (although in a later period), President James Garfield was assassinated by a rejected office-seeker in 1881.

Divisive Issues: Economic Policy, Slavery, and Nativism

At the same time as the numbers of elite aspirants dangerously exceeded the number of positions available for them, politics at the national level provided several divisive issues that could be seized upon by politically ambitious individuals. There was a great degree of divergence between the economic interests of the established elites and those of the elite aspirants. Most importantly, the new elites, who made their money in manufacturing, favored high tariffs to protect budding American industries and state support for "internal improvements" (turnpike, canal, and railroad construction). The established elites, who grew and exported cotton, and imported manufactured goods, naturally favored low tariffs. They also were against using state funds for internal improvements, because they shipped their products by river and sea to the world market (Potter 1976:32).

The new economic elites favored domestic industrialization, import substitution, and the export of agricultural commodities produced by free labor, such as wheat (Beckert 2001: 90). These businessmen began to argue that the stranglehold of the Southern slaveholders over the federal government prevented the necessary reforms in the banking and transportation systems and, thus, threatened their own economic wellbeing (Beckert 2001:91). Differences over economic policy and the competition for office generated powerful incentives to break the Southern domination of the federal government.

These economic and political motivations were strengthened by ideological ones. By 1860 the majority of Northerners felt that slavery was morally wrong. However, only a tiny minority, the Northern abolitionists, felt strongly enough to make this issue central to their political program. In the South, on the other hand, the "peculiar institution" was so lucrative for the great majority of the whites (since most either owned slaves or aspired to own them) that they were compelled to defend it. Most of the Northern whites were not strongly motivated by the plight of enslaved Negroes (Potter 1976:37), certainly not enough to fight and die over it. However, as slavery provided the economic basis for Southern dominance, a political attack on the slaveholders could be strengthened by an ideological attack on slavery. As is well documented, only a small minority, the Abolitionists, pressed the argument that slavery was morally wrong. The majority of Northerners railed against the "slave power"—the wealthy and aristocratic Southerners—and their domination of national politics (Richards 2000).

The divergence of economic interests and differences over the morality of slavery were not new issues on the eve of the Civil War; they divided the American elites from the establishment of the Republic. Traditional historiography does not provide a good answer to the question of why sectionalization of American politics greatly intensified after 1845 and resulted in armed conflict in 1861: "explanation of the uncontrolled growth of sectionalism during the 1850s has been one of the major problems of American historical scholarship" (Potter 1976: 30). The Structural-Demographic Theory provides the missing link. Explosive growth of economic elites after the 1820s, especially in the North, led to an expansion in the cohort of elite aspirants vying for political power. Intensifying intraelite competition after 1845 fractured the ruling class by reducing the willingness of the elites to seek compromise.

One example of how intensifying competition for political office resulted in intraelite fragmentation is the case of Martin Van Buren, Jackson's successor in the White House from 1837 to 1841. Although Van Buren had played a key role in the Jacksonian Democracy, he was denied the Democratic nomination in 1844 and in 1848 ran as the candidate of the Free Soil Party. As Adam Rothman (2005:85) wrote in the chapter on the "Slave Power" in *Ruling America*, "Martin Van Buren, an original architect of the Democracy, turned against slavery after losing a long and bitter battle with proslavery forces in his party during the mid-1840s."

These structural-demographic processes gathered momentum during the 1850s and reached a peak when Northern elite aspirants, frustrated in their quest for power, used the new Republican Party as the vehicle for overthrowing the established elites in the election of 1860.

Elite overproduction affected the North more than the South because the great majority of immigrants during the 1840s and 1850s arrived in the Northeastern cities. So far I have focused on the cracks that fractured the American elites along the sectional (North versus South) lines. However, elite overproduction in the North also caused growing division *within* Northern elites. Some of these cracks mirrored the national issues. For example, in 1848 the Whig party in Boston split into "Cotton" and "Conscience" factions (Jaher 1982: 55). Textile magnates led the Cotton Whigs and sought to maintain friendly relations with the Southern planters. The opposition "Conscience" faction became Free Soilers and later Republicans. Interestingly, the opposition leaders tended to be younger than the Cotton Whig chieftains (Jaher 1982: 55).

Similar developments affected New York elites. Most bourgeois New Yorkers, especially merchants and bankers, were in favor of compromise with the South, because trade in cotton was their main business (Beckert 2001: 87). But a significant minority of upper-class New Yorkers, those who made their fortunes in manufacturing, railroads, and trade with the West, were more sympathetic to the Republican Party.

Slavery was not the only issue that divided Northern elites. There also was a significant tension between immigrant groups, many of whom were Catholic, and native-born Americans, who were overwhelmingly Protestant (Potter 1976: 241). After the fact, we know that in 1861 the United States split along sectional lines, but during the 1850s nativism (opposition to immigrants and immigration) was no less important than antislavery as an issue in national politics. In 1854 the Native American Party ("Know-Nothings") achieved a stunning victory in several states, carrying 63 percent of the vote in Massachusetts, 40 percent in Pennsylvania, and 25 percent in New York (Potter 1976:250). The Know-Nothings attracted substantial if short-lived support among the upper classes in New York (Beckert 2001:82). However, ultimately support for anti-immigration policies could not get traction among the Northern economic elites, especially the industrialists, because their economic wellbeing depended too much on a continuing and plentiful supply of cheap labor. As a result, later in the 1850s the upper classes switched their support to the Republican Party.

Support for the nativist cause was much stronger among the laboring classes, whose economic interests and cultural values were threatened by immigration. However, popular movements, even in democracies, are ineffectual in the absence of leadership provided by elites or elite aspirants, and the political developments during the 1850s conformed to this rule. Even though the wellbeing of urban commoners was declining and curtailing immigration could reverse this trend (as happened much later, after the Immigration Acts of the 1920s; this will be discussed in a later chapter), nativism disintegrated as a political movement. Instead, the very real dissatisfaction fueling the potential for mass mobilization was redirected by elite political entrepreneurs against the established elites, who were portrayed as the real culprits of the economic problems facing the commoners. This was accomplished by demonizing Southern elites as the Slaveocracy that was inimical to all free men (and women). As an example of such propaganda, here is Moses M. Davis of Wisconsin: "The tyrannical Slave power has got possession of the people, and will crush our liberties before many more years pass by" (quoted in Huston 2003: 83). In the end, the nativist support went to the Republican Party, and was crucial to its success in 1860 (Potter 1976:259).

Synthesis: Collapse of the Elite Consensus and the Onset of the Disintegrative Phase

The proliferation of political parties during the 1850s is another measure of the degree of political and ideological fragmentation of the American elites. As David Potter (1976:249) notes, in 1854 voters were presented with a stunning array of parties and factions: Democrats, Whigs, Free Soilers, Republicans, People's Party men, Anti-Nebraskaites, Fusionists, Know-Nothings, Know-Somethings, Main Lawites, Temperance men, Rum Democrats, Silver Gray Whigs, Hindoos, Hard Shell Democrats, Soft Shells, Half Shells, Adopted Citizens, and others. This fragmentation was a remarkable change from the situation 40 years before. During the Era of Good Feelings, after the demise of the Federalist Party, there was only one significant political party in the United States. Even when Democratic Republicans split into Democrats and Whigs, parties represented not ideologies but interests and support for specific leaders (Potter 1976: 226). The 1860 presidential election, by contrast, was a four-way race, in which Abraham Lincoln got only 39.8 percent of the popular vote, with candidates from other parties receiving 29.5, 18.1, and 12.6 percent.

Another indicator of growing intraelite conflict was the increasing incidence of violence and threatened violence in Congress, which reached a peak during the 1850s. The brutal caning that Representative Preston Brooks of South Carolina gave to Senator Charles Sumner of Massachusetts on the Senate floor in 1856 is the best-known such episode, but it was not the only one. In 1842, after Representative Thomas Arnold of Tennessee "reprimanded a pro-slavery member of his own party, two Southern Democrats stalked toward him, at least one of whom was armed with a bowie knife — a 6- to 12-inch blade often worn strapped to the back. Calling Arnold a 'damned coward,' his angry colleagues threatened to cut his throat 'from ear to ear'" (Freeman 2011). According to Senator Hammond, "The only persons who do not have a revolver and a knife are those who have two revolvers" (quoted in Potter 1976:389). During a debate in 1850, Senator Henry Foote of Mississippi pulled a pistol on Senator Thomas Hart Benton of Missouri (Freeman 2011). In another bitter debate, a New York congressman inadvertently dropped a pistol (it fell out of his pocket), and this almost precipitated a general shootout on the floor of Congress (Potter 1976: 389).

9

The Road to Civil War: A Dynamical Model of Antebellum America

Modeling Goals

In this chapter I shall construct a mathematical model that attempts to capture feedback loops and resulting dynamics of the structural-demographic variables. This model has two goals. First, in Chapter 8 I have presented a verbal argument explaining why there was a trend reversal around 1820, which led to the onset of the disintegrative phase 40 years later. The logical coherence of this verbal argument, however, needs to be tested with a formal model, because verbal arguments about dynamical systems, characterized by nonlinear feedbacks, can be easily mistaken (Turchin 2003b). Second, people who have not had extensive experience with nonlinear dynamical systems often do not appreciate how easy it is for them to transform linear, or monotonic, inputs into complex outputs, characterized by trend reversals, bifurcations, and oscillations. In the previous chapter I argued that no intervention by exogenous forces is needed to understand why a number of variables experienced trend reversals during the Jackson Era. No momentous event happened in 1830; instead, trend reversals were a result of nonlinear feedbacks driven by monotonic increases in such variables as labor supply. The model below illustrates this important point.

A few words on my modeling strategy. I aim to produce as simple a model as possible (but no simpler than that, as Albert Einstein reportedly said). The model is not predictive, but explanatory. This means that the dynamics generated by it will not be tested with independent data. Instead, I want to see whether the verbal argument of Chapter 8 is internally logical, as well as consistent with empirical patterns. Thus, the main question is: can a reasonably simple model with plausible parameter values duplicate the dynamics of structural-demographic variables and, in particular, the observed trend reversals?

The conceptual framework for the Antebellum model is the one that was introduced in Chapter 2 (*Quantifying Social Pressures for Instability*). In the next two sections I adapt this general framework to the specific conditions of Antebellum America, first focusing on demography and wellbeing, next on elite dynamics. The Antebellum model does not include a module for the state, because during the nineteenth century the American state was small and primarily concerned with external relations. As a result, it had little power and autonomy from the governing elites to influence internal social dynamics (Chapter 5). Once I have modeled demography and the elites, I will put these two components together using the PSI approach, and consider whether the model helps us explain the rising tide of sociopolitical instability that culminated in the American Civil War.

Demography and Wages

Rural population growth and urban migration

The first component of the model is demographic growth. I assume that population is divided among two "compartments": rural and urban. This is meant to approximate the situation in the Northeastern states (specifically, I focus on the four populous states of the eastern seaboard: Massachusetts, Connecticut, New York, and New Jersey). For simplicity, I begin by ignoring migratory fluxes: arrival of immigrants from Europe and emigration to Western states (I will return to this issue below). The starting point for modeling the dynamics of rural population, N, is the exponential equation (Turchin 2003a):

$$\dot{N}_{rur} = rN_{rur}$$

where r is the per capita rate of population growth and the dot over N indicates a time derivative (alternatively written as dN/dt). Between 1780 and 1860 the per capita rate of growth of American population declined from three to two percent per year, so I will set $r = 2.5$.

Naturally, rural population cannot grow without limit. There is a certain rural *carrying capacity, K*—determined by the availability of agricultural land. For example, for the four Northeastern states (MA, CT, NY, and NJ) a reasonable estimate of K is 3.5 million (because that is the level at which the rural population equilibrated in the second half of the nineteenth century, see Figure 9.1 below). As rural population approaches its carrying capacity, there will be an increasing dearth of land, which will trigger migration flows to the cities. I will assume that the migration rate is

$$M = r_{rur} \left(\frac{N_{rur}}{K} \right)^{\theta}$$

If the exponent $\theta = 1$, then the migration rate increases linearly with N and approaches r as N approaches K. In other words, when rural population reaches its carrying capacity, all "surplus" people produced by population growth immediately migrate to the cities. The assumption of linearity, however, is not a very realistic one, because the migration rate should be close to zero as long as N is low, and then accelerate as N approaches K. The exponent θ allows us to capture this nonlinearity. I set $\theta = 5$ as a reasonable compromise between 1 (linear emigration) and 10 and higher (which approximate a step function). Putting these assumptions together, we obtain the equation governing the dynamics of N:

$$(9.1) \qquad \dot{N}_{rur} = r_{rur}N_{rur} - MN_{rur} = r_{rur}N_{rur} - r_{rur}N_{rur}\left(\frac{N_{rur}}{K} \right)^{\theta}$$

Thus, the dynamics of rural population are governed by a balance between population growth and migration. Eqn. 9.1 is similar to the standard logistic model, except it introduces additional nonlinearity with the parameter θ.

The dynamics of urban population, N_{urb}, are modeled analogously:

$$(9.2) \qquad \dot{N}_{urb} = r_{urb}N_{urb} + r_{rur}N_{rur}\left(\frac{N_{rur}}{K} \right)^{\theta}$$

where the new parameter $r_{urb} = 1.5$ percent per year is the endogenous growth rate of urban population, set to a lower value than r_{rur} to reflect the increased mortality and decreased fertility rates in the cities. The second term is migration flow from the countryside to the cities. If we wished to make the model more realistic, it would be desirable to add other terms reflecting immigration from overseas and migration to the West. However, at this stage I will keep the model simple (and as we shall see below, these two flows balanced each other out).

Setting initial conditions (for the year 1790) for populations in the two compartments as $N_{rur}(1790) = 0.3K$ and $N_{urb}(1790) = 0.1N_{rur}$ (this approximates the initial rural and urban populations in the four Northeastern states), generates the trajectories depicted in Figure 9.1a. Comparing them with the data on rural and urban population in the four states in Figure 9.1b, we observe that there is a good degree of correspondence between the model and the data. This is not surprising, since certain features of the data were used in estimating model parameters; it is just a check that the model generates reasonable dynamics for population numbers. On the other hand, the model greatly simplifies the actual dynamics. Most importantly, it does not take into account immigration from Europe and migration to the West. Additionally it simplifies endogenous population growth by assuming constant per capita rates of population increase. It appears that for the period before 1880 these simplifying assumptions largely cancel each other out, since the overall dynamics of N_{urb} and N_{rur} are close to the observed trajectories.

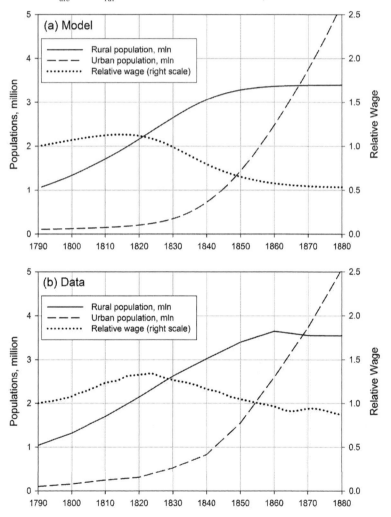

FIGURE 9.1 Population dynamics (a) generated by the model and (b) in the four Northeastern states (MA, CT, NY, and NJ). Data sources: calculations by the author and the *HSUS* (Carter et al. 2004). Model parameters assumed in calculations: $rrur = 0.025$ y–1, $rurb = 0.015$ y–1, $K = 3.5$ million, $\theta = 5$, $\beta = 0.5$, $a = 1$, $\rho = 0.03$ y–1, $\gamma = 0.01$ y–1.

Urban wages

The next step is to model the dynamics of urban wages. I will assume that there is a demand for labor, D, which grows exponentially at a rate ρ. I assume that demand for labor grew faster than the urban population, providing a powerful incentive for the bourgeoisie to encourage immigration (see Chapter 10). In other words, without that immigration from overseas, the wages of American workers would have kept pace with the GDP. As it is, D grew slowly enough to be outpaced by endogenous population growth and immigration together (which is why we observe falling relative wages and declining health indices). Thus, the value of this parameter should be between 2.5 and 3.5 percent per annum, or roughly $\rho = 3$. The equation for the demand for labor is simply

(9.3)
$$\dot{D} = \rho D$$

The model for the dynamics of urban wages is a simplified version of Eqn. (2.1):

(9.4)
$$W = ag\left(\frac{D}{S}\right)^{\beta}$$

This equation says that urban wages reflect the balance between supply and demand. When demand (D) outpaces supply (S) wages should increase, and if the reverse is true, wages should decline. Labor supply is simply modeled as a constant proportion of the urban population, $S = \lambda N_{urb}$. Additionally, increasing GDP per capita ($g = G/N$ where N is the sum of rural and urban populations) should cause wages to trend upwards. I assume that GDP per capita grows exponentially at the rate of $\gamma = 1$ percent per year, which approximates the observed rate of growth of real GDP per capita between 1790 and 1870. Note that Eqn. (9.4) excludes extraeconomic, "cultural" factors (C in Eqn. 2.1), because I assume that labor-management relations in nineteenth-century America approximated very closely a "pure" capitalist system (I have also simplified the model by setting parameter α, the exponent associated with g, to 1). Because of the problems associated with estimating the cost of living during the nineteenth century (Chapter 3), I focus here on the relative wage (scaled by GDP per capita), $w = W/g$. As a result, we have the following simple model:

(9.5)
$$w = a\left(\frac{D}{\lambda N_{urb}}\right)^{\beta}$$

Plotting the dynamics of the predicted relative wage, we observe that w exhibits nonlinear dynamics: rise until c.1820 followed by decline (the dotted line in Figure 9.1a). This is similar to what the observed relative wage did (Figure 9.1b, dotted line). At the beginning of the simulation, the growth of demand for labor in the cities outpaces the sum of endogenous growth of the urban population together with migration from rural places. Around 1820, however, the rural population approached close enough to its ceiling to generate an increasing flow of migrants to cities that, when combined with endogenous population growth there, exceeded the capacity of the growing economy to absorb them. This shift in the D/N_{urb} balance results in the trend-reversal experienced by w.

Elite Dynamics

Following the theoretical framework explained in Chapter 2 (see Eqn. 2.4), elite numbers, E, will grow as a result of endogenous population growth and due to upward mobility from the urban population, N_{urb} (I assume that the main avenue of upward mobility was urban artisans turning themselves into successful manufacturers). Accordingly, the equation for E is:

$$(9.6) \qquad \dot{E} = r_e E + \mu_0 \left(\frac{w_0}{w} - 1 \right) N_{urb}$$

The rate of elite endogenous population growth, r_e, was set to the value for rural population, on the assumption that better nutrition and the ability to escape the city in summer counteract the negative effects of urban life on elite demographic rates. The second term in Eqn. 9.6 reflects the rate at which urban commoners move into the elites. It is *inversely* related to the relative wage, w, because if wages do not keep up with the growth of GDP per capita, economic growth creates an increasingly large surplus. Parameter w_0 is the threshold level for relative wages: the more w falls below it, the more vigorous will be upward social mobility. Thus, a favorable economic conjuncture for employers creates greater upward mobility opportunities for urban entrepreneurs.

The last ingredient we need for the calculation of EMP is how average elite incomes change with time. This part of the model follows the general theoretical framework of Chapter 2 (Elite Dynamics) without modification. In particular, I use Equation 2.5 to calculate relative elite incomes:

$$(9.7) \qquad\qquad \varepsilon = \frac{1 - w\lambda}{e}$$

and multiply this quantity by GDP per capita to obtain real incomes.

The equations 9.1–9.7 describe the complete model. The elite dynamics predicted by the model are shown in Figure 9.2. At the beginning of the simulation it is assumed that the elites constitute one percent of the urban population. Initially there is little change in this parameter. In fact, the elites lose ground slightly during the 1830s as a result of rapid growth of the urban population due to migration from the countryside. After 1840, however, the economic conjuncture moves decisively in favor of the elites, causing massive upward mobility into the elite ranks. As a result, the proportion of elites grows rapidly to two percent of the population by 1860 and to three percent by 1870 (the solid curve in Figure 9.2). In absolute numbers this growth is even more remarkable: between 1840 and 1870 the elite numbers roughly triple every decade.

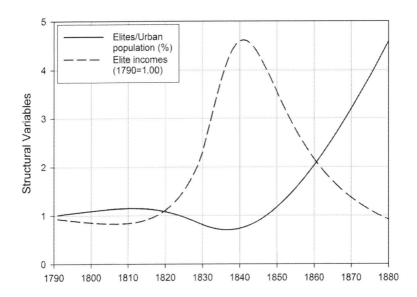

FIGURE 9.2 Elite dynamics in the Antebellum model: elite numbers relative to the urban population and average elite incomes. Parameter values: same as given in the caption of Figure 9.1, plus $\mu_0 = 0.002$ y_{-1}, $w_0 = 1$.

The average elite income (broken curve in Figure 9.2) stays roughly constant until 1820, and then begins to increase, due to the highly favorable economic conjuncture for the elites. However, after elite numbers climb, starting in 1840, the average income begins to be diluted. This happens because the amount of surplus increases less rapidly than elite numbers. It is important to note that declining average income does not mean that incomes of all elite segments are decreasing. On the contrary, as intraelite competition heats up, a few will garner an increasing share of rewards, while large segments of the elites fall further and further behind. Thus, during this period we expect to see *top* incomes continue their triumphant march upwards (which is what happened in the US after 1840).

Quantifying Social Pressures for Instability

Modeling results in the previous two sections suggest that social pressures on both the general population and the elites were building up during the Antebellum period. The next step is to quantify the magnitude of the social forces using the PSI framework of Chapter 2.

As was noted at the beginning of the chapter, the state played a minor role in the crisis of nineteenth-century America, so I focus on the first two.[8]

Social pressures arising from popular distress are indexed with Mass Mobilization Potential (MMP), which has three subcomponents: real wages, urbanization rate, and the effect of age structure:

$$\text{MMP} = w^{-1} \frac{N_{\text{urb}}}{N} A_{20-29}$$

where the first term, w^{-1}, is the inverse relative wage, the second term is the proportion of population within the cities, and the last term, A_{20-29}, is the proportion of the cohort aged between 20 and 29 years in the total population. Recollect that this parameter measures the role of "youth bulges"—the effect of the size of the youth cohorts on instability. Age structure was not explicitly modeled in the Antebellum model. Furthermore, because it made the simplifying assumption that birth rates did not vary with time, the implied age structure is constant, and there can be no youth bulges. Rather than complicate the model further, I will simply use the empirical information to estimate this parameter (Figure 9.3).

---

8   Technically this means that I set the state component to a constant value. Because we are interested in relative fluctuations in Ψ, multiplying it by a constant has no effect.

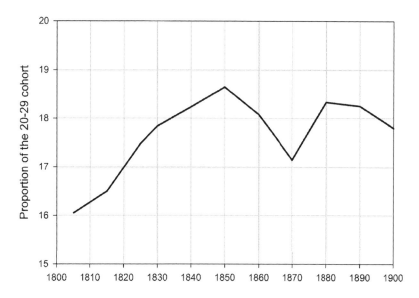

FIGURE 9.3 Proportion of the cohort aged 20–29 years among the total population of American white males. Source: calculations by the author based on data in (Carter et al. 2004: Table Aa287–364).

The formula for the second component of Ψ, which deals with the elite overproduction and competition, or Elite Mobilization Potential, is

$$\text{EMP} = \varepsilon^{-1} \frac{E}{sN}$$

The first term on the right hand side, ε^{-1}, is the inverse of the relative elite income, and the second term measures the effect of intraelite competition for government offices. It assumes that the number of positions will grow in proportion to the total population (N). The proportionality constant s is the number of government employees per total population. Empirically we know that s changed throughout the Antebellum period—the relative size of the federal government increased from roughly 0.5 to over 1 federal employee per 1,000 population (Carter et al. 2004: Table Ea894-903). I use this empirical information to track how s changed through time.

The dynamics of predicted MMP and EMP are plotted in Figure 9.4. MMP is essentially flat (actually, a slight decline) until 1820. This is followed by a rapid and accelerating rise to 1860, and slower increase after that (Figure 9.4). The dynamics of EMP are similar, but shifted in phase. The decline lasts until the 1830s, and the increase during the 1840s and especially the 1850s is extremely rapid. After 1860 the model predicts a further rise in EMP, but this prediction should not concern us, because the Civil War fundamentally changed the American sociopolitical system, and the assumptions on which the model was built ceased to hold.

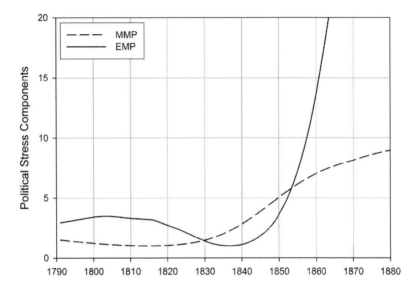

FIGURE 9.4 Dynamics of the two components of the Political Stress Index, Mass Mobilization Potential (MMP) and Elite Mobilization Potential (EMP), predicted by the Antebellum model. Both indicators were scaled to minimum = 1.

The final step is to combine these two measures within the Political Stress Index, $\Psi = MMP \times EMP$ (Figure 9.5). The calculated PSI stayed at a low level (actually, gradually declining towards a minimum in 1830. It began increasing after 1840 and exploded during the 1850s. Comparing the predicted Ψ to the empirical dynamics of sociopolitical instability measures suggests that Ψ can serve as a leading indicator of small-scale political violence which, in turn, is a leading indicator of a large-scale civil war.

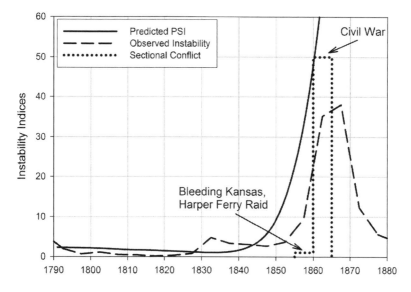

FIGURE 9.5 Predicted Political Stress Index (solid curve) compared with the observed dynamics of political instability: number of people killed in political instability events per million of population (broken curve) and a qualitative index of sectional conflict (dotted curve), which includes Bleeding Kansas and John Brown's Harper Ferry raid (1855–1860) and the American Civil War (1861–1865). Note that the two empirical indicators of instability are not shown to scale (the casualties resulting from the Civil War exceeded those of the largest riot by two orders of magnitude).

Crisis: the Civil War and Reconstruction

The Antebellum Model suggests a decline in the Political Stress Index before 1830, which was reversed at some point between 1830 and 1840 (Figure 9.5). The empirical curve of political violence also shows a decline (with the minimum in the 1820s). Indeed, after several popular insurrections of the post-Revolutionary era, Pennamite-Yankee War and Shays and Whiskey Rebellions (Table 9.1a), the United States enjoyed an unprecedented period of internal peace. The situation began changing after 1830. There was a major slave uprising (Nat Turner's Rebellion of 1831), but it was an isolated event. A more ominous trend was an increasing frequency of major urban riots (Table 9.1b), which started in the 1830s and 1840s but really exploded during the 1850s.

What the empirical curve in Figure 9.5 suggests is that the American Civil War was only one, albeit a very major one, of the political violence events that shook the United States in the middle of the nineteenth century. Sectional conflicts were less important, as a cause of urban riots, than ethnic conflicts, both between nativists and immigrants, and between different groups of immigrants (for example, between Catholic and Protestant Irish). Ethnicity, race, and labor issues all played a role, often in various combinations, in triggering urban riots during this period (Turchin 2012: Figure 6). Other kinds of instability events included vigilantism (the Regulator Movement in the Southern and Western states), the Anti-Rent War in the Hudson Valley, and even a religious war (Table 9.1c).

TABLE 9.1 Prelude to the American Civil War. Source: US Political Violence Database (Turchin 2012).

(a) Popular uprisings

Year	Killed	Where	Description
1784	7	PA	Pennamite-Yankee War
1787	20	MA	Shays Rebellion
1794	7	PA	Whiskey Rebellion
1845	1	NY	Antirent War in the Hudson Valley

(b) Major urban riots (10 or more fatalities) during the Antebellum period

Year	Killed	Where	Description
1844	14	PA	Philadelphia Nativist Riots
1849	22	NY	Astor Place Riots
1855	20	KY	Louisville Election Riot ("Bloody Monday")
1856	17	MD	Know-Nothing Riot in Baltimore
1857	10	DC	Know-Nothing Riot in Washington
1857	12	NY	The Dead Rabbits Riot
1858	11	LA	Know-Nothing Riot in New Orleans

(c) Mormon Wars

Year	Killed	Where	Description
1838	21	MO	Missouri Mormon War (Haun's Mill Massacre, Battle of Crooked River)
1844–5	2	IL	Mormon War in Illinois (assassination of Joseph and Hyrum Smith) followed by the Mormon Exodus
1856	1	MI	Assassination of James Strang, leader of Strangite Mormons, and forcible expulsion of his followers from Beaver Island, MI
1857	120	UT	Utah Mormon War (Mountain Meadows massacre)

Such a variety of issues underlying violence and the forms the violence took suggest that we need to look to deeper, structural causes of political instability. The Structural-Demographic Theory offers an internally consistent explanation for the nineteenth century's instability wave. This raises the question: can the theory also account for why this wave subsided in the early twentieth century? This issue will be addressed in the next chapter.

Aftermath of the Civil War

The victory of the North in the Civil War was a transformative event in American history. In fact, an influential school of historical thought views the Civil War and its aftermath (the Reconstruction) as the Second American Revolution (Burton 2006). In at least one important respect, however, it was an "unfinished revolution" (Foner 1988). While the Civil War freed the slaves, it failed to produce racial equality between the whites and the blacks. On the other hand, by breaking the power of the Southern slaveholding elites over the federal government and replacing them with a new ruling class dominated by Northern businessmen, the Civil War transformed power relations within the American polity. A very important part of this transformation was the economic one.

The defeat of the South in the Civil War destroyed a large part of the Southern wealth. If before 1860 the majority of wealthy Americans resided in the South, 10 years later this geographic pattern was reversed (see Figures 4 and 5 in Carson 2009). As a result of slave emancipation, wartime damage to their properties, and the repudiation of all war debts and obligations of the Confederacy (Beard 1927: 104) the average wealth of Southern whites was halved from $4,000 to $2,000 (Soltow 1975).

In the North the trend was exactly the opposite. Holding Union debt was extremely lucrative (Phillips 2002:34). Supplying the Union war effort was even more so. "A surprising number of the commercial and financial giants of the late nineteenth century—J P Morgan, John D Rockefeller, Andrew Carnegie, Jay Gould, Marshall Field, Philip Armour, Collis Huntington, and several other railroad grandees—were young northerners who avoided military service, usually by buying substitutes, and used the war to make major steps up the fortune's ladder" (Phillips 2002:36). The most remarkable statistic, however, is the increase in the number of millionaires from 41 in 1860 to 545 in 1870 (Chapter 8).

In the political arena, the secession and subsequent defeat of the Confederacy introduced a long era of dominance of the Republican Party in national politics. Between 1860 and 1932, the Democrats were able to capture the presidency in only three elections (in 1884, 1892, and 1912). The dominance of Northern business interests led to a sharp change in economic policy: the establishment of the so-called "American system" (Burton 2006: 57). New legislation, mainly passed between 1861 and 1864, protected Northern industries with high tariffs (47 percent in 1864) and established a national banking system. The Pacific Railroad Acts authorized government bonds and extensive land grants to railroad companies, reversing the previous policy that did not favor "internal improvements".

In the 1920s Charles A Beard and Mary Beard (Beard and Beard 1922, Beard 1927) argued that this economic policy reversal was one of the elements of the Second American Revolution, which shifted the balance of power from Southern planters to Northern capitalists (for the historiography of this question, see Burton 2006:58). While the new tariffs policy, internal improvements, and the national bank directly benefited Northern business interests, "other elements of the combination of power effected in 1860—namely the free farmers of the West and the radical reformers of the East—also had their rewards" (Beard 1927:114), in the form of the Homestead Grant of 1862 and the Emancipation Proclamation of 1863 (followed by the Thirteenth Amendment two years later). Emancipation of the slaves also benefited Northern capitalists, if indirectly, by impoverishing Southern elites and reducing their power to influence policy at the federal level.

The Homestead Act, on the other hand, enabled the movement of surplus labor to the land, abundant stocks of which could be found in the West. Its effect, thus, was to reduce the supply of labor and drive its price up. To counteract this undesirable consequence, Congress passed the Immigration Act of 1864, whose purpose was to ensure an adequate supply of labor, and created a Bureau of Immigration that facilitated the importation of laborers from Europe. The 1864 Republican platform explained the importance of such steps as follows: "foreign immigration, which in the past has added so much to the wealth, the development of resources, and the increase of power to this nation—the asylum of the oppressed of all nations—should be fostered and encouraged by a liberal and just policy" (Beard 1927:110).

Although the Beards' thesis enjoyed a great degree of acceptance until the 1960s, more recent scholarship has tended to be very critical of it. "Thus, as opposed to the Beards, modern scholars do not see a revolutionary or counter-revolutionary plan because there was no conspiracy on the part of the capitalist class. … In fact, no unified northern business class can be identified" (Burton 2006:58). However, nowhere do the Beards talk about a "conspiracy" by Northern businessmen (electronic search of *History of the United States*, using Google Books, yielded four instances of "conspiracy", none in the context of the Second American Revolution). Furthermore, as William Domhoff (2010a) argues, there is no need to invoke conspiracy to explain how the Northern economic elites were able to shape national economic policy to suit their collective interests.

It is also necessary to acknowledge that during the Civil War and immediately following it, Northern elites were not (yet) as consolidated and capable of pursuing a common agenda as they became several decades later. As I will discuss in the next chapter (see *Consolidation of the American Upper Class: c.1870–c.1920*), such critical upper-class institutions as the *Social Register*, the country club, the elite boarding school, and the "policy planning network" (Domhoff 2010a) coalesced gradually in the decades after the Civil War, and the process was not complete (if it ever can be called complete) until the first two decades of the twentieth century.

Nevertheless, the transformative event that created the conditions for the eventual consolidation of a true national upper class (Baltzell 1987) was the victory of the North in the Civil War (or the Second American Revolution, as the Beards would have it). The Civil War and Reconstruction eras were the period that "witnessed the political demise of the Southern planters and mercantile interests, for they were never thereafter an important force in national affairs" (Burch 1981: 46). Instead, a substantial number of high officials after 1860 were recruited from among the businessmen and corporate lawyers, and "the vast majority of these men were closely associated with railroad companies" (Burch 1981:46). Here is Philip Burch's assessment of the changes wrought by the Civil War:

> This economic transformation [a marked shift in the nation's politico-economic relations] is perhaps best reflected in the make-up of the Lincoln administration. Although not widely emphasized, Lincoln was a fairly wealthy lawyer who had been linked with certain railroads in the Midwest, especially the Illinois Central. And many of the men he appointed to major Cabinet and diplomatic office had either strong railroad or financial ties. Thus, perhaps not surprisingly, it was during the Lincoln administration that the greatest amounts of land were granted, as promotional measures, to railroads of the United States, primarily in the West. This general appointment and

policymaking trend continued into the bitterly divided Johnson administration and, in even more conspicuous manner, into the scandal-ridden Grant regime. The political influence of railroad forces also extended to the selection of Supreme Court Justices, as may be seen by the pressure generated on behalf of Noah Swayne and Stephen Field in the early 1860s, and in more direct railroad connections of William Strong and Joseph Bradley, who were appointed in 1870. These actions had some desired results, such as the controversial legal tender cases. Hence by 1876 the railroad industry had clearly emerged as the dominant politico-economic force in the nation.

This assessment fits very well with the dynamic version of Domhoff's class domination theory (see Chapter 3; *dynamic* because it emphasizes that the degree of consolidation and capacity for collective action of the capitalist class varies with time).What Burch describes is an early version of the corporate community, when it was dominated by one or two industries (railroads and banks), and lacked most of the institutions that evolved later. It was also relatively ineffective in controlling the political and economic turmoil of the post-Civil War era. As we saw in Chapter 5, political violence, while declining somewhat from the 1870 peak, remained at levels far exceeding those of the first half of the nineteenth century, and by 1920 increased toward another peak. On the economic side of things, the United States experienced a series of traumatic depressions: the Long Depression of 1873–79, the Depression of 1893–97 (sometimes known as the First Great Depression), and the Great Depression of 1929–32. The topic of continuing instability will be taken up in the next chapter.

10

From the Gilded Age to the New Deal

Persistent Instability

The Post-Civil War Period

The instability wave of the mid-nineteenth century crested in the late 1860s, but although the level of political violence declined somewhat during the 1870s and 1880s, it did not recede to the level of the early nineteenth century. The United States continued to experience elevated levels of political violence during the rest of the century, and there was another instability spike around 1920 (Figure 5.1).

As during the previous spike of 1870, rather than being driven by a single issue, instability took many forms, suggesting that the 1920 peak was also the most visible sign of structural social problems. In particular, the later decades of the nineteenth century saw a massive wave of race-motivated and vigilante lynchings and growing violence against minorities, such as the Chinese. This was also the period when two American presidents were assassinated (James Garfield in 1881 and William McKinley in 1901) as well as a number of lesser officials. A very common motive for political assassinations during this period was competition for office (Table 10.1), suggesting that high levels of intraelite competition persisted after the Civil War.

TABLE 10.1 Political assassinations resulting from disputed elections or by frustrated office-seekers. Source: USPV database (Turchin 2012).

Year	Location	Description
1870	TX	Gaylord Clark, District Judge, was shot by Frank Williams who sought the judgeship for himself
1879	MS	H M Dixon was shot by James Barksdale, Democratic Candidate for Chancery Clerk
1881	MD	President James Garfield was shot by Charles Guiteau, a frustrated office-seeker
1893	IL	Carter H Harrison, mayor of Chicago, was shot, killed by Patrick E Predergast, a disappointed office-seeker
1900	KY	William Goebel, Governor of Kentucky, was killed by Caleb Powers. Disputed election.

A very significant development during this era was increasingly violent conflicts between workers and employers. The Great Railroad Strike of 1877 began in West Virginia and spread to Maryland, Pennsylvania, Illinois, and Missouri. At least 100 people died as the strikes were suppressed by the state and federal authorities. At the time, labor violence on this scale was unprecedented in the United States.

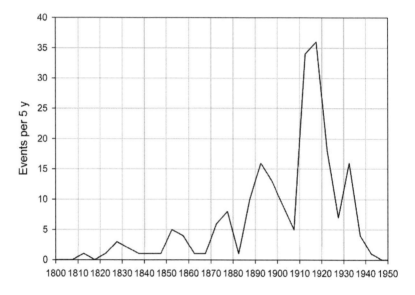

FIGURE 10.1 The occurrence of labor-related political violence (strikes resulting in at least one fatality) in the United States, 1800–1950. Source: USPV database (Turchin 2012).

At first it looked as though the Great Railroad Strike was an exception, and the American elites "put it out of mind with surprising ease" (Wiebe 1967:10). In the decades after 1877, however, violent labor disputes became increasingly common in the US (Table 10.2). The frequency of such instability events jumped in the 1890s, the decade of crisis and severe economic depression. "No depression had ever been as deep and tragic as the one that lasted from 1893 to 1897. Millions suffered unemployment, especially during the winters of 1893–4 and 1894–5, and thousands of 'tramps' wandered the countryside in search of food" (McCormick 1997).

TABLE 10.2 Violent labor strikes resulting in major loss of life (six or more fatalities), 1870–1930. Source: USPV database (Turchin 2012).

Year	Fatalities	Description
1877	100	Great Railroad Strike of 1877 (MD, PA, IL, and MO)
1886	7	Bay View (Milwaukee) massacre
1891	10	Massacre at Morewood (PA) Mine
1892	16	Homestead strike (near Pittsburgh)
1894	13	Pullman strike riots (Chicago)
1897	19	Lattimer (PA) massacre
1898	11	Battle of Virden (IL)
1909	8	Battle of McKees Rocks (PA)
1910	16	Westmoreland County (PA) coal strike
1910	7	Garment workers' strike in Chicago
1912	50	West Virginia Mine War of 1912-13
1914	26	Ludlow massacre (CO)
1916	7	Everett (WA) massacre
1917	150	East St Louis riot (IL)*
1919	6	Centralia (WA) massacre
1920	10	Battle of Matewan (WV Mine War of 1920–1)
1921	100	Battle of Blair Mountain (WV Mine War of 1920–1)
1922	23	Herrin (IL) massacre
1924	16	Hanapepe (HI) massacre
1927	8	Columbine Mine (CO) massacre

*The East St Louis riot of 1917 was due to both race and labor-related tensions

The Instability Peak of c.1920

But the scale of labor conflicts of the 1890s was easily exceeded by the peak of violence achieved during the "violent teens" and early 1920s (Figure 10.1). The worst incident in the US labor history was the West Virginia Mine War of 1920–21 (Savage 1990), which culminated in the Battle of Blair Mountain (Shogan 2004). Although it started as a labor dispute, it eventually turned into the largest armed insurrection in US history, other than the Civil War. Between 10,000 and 15,000 miners armed with rifles fought thousands of strike-breakers and sheriff's deputies, called the Logan Defenders. The insurrection was ended by the United States Army.

While such violent incidents were exceptional, they took place against a background of a general "class war" that has been intensifying during the violent teens. "In 1919 nearly four million workers (21 percent of the workforce)

took disruptive action in the face of employer reluctance to recognize or bargain with unions" (Domhoff and Webber 2011:74).

Interracial tensions were another large contributor to the 1920 violence spike. In fact, race issues were intertwined with labor issues, and in many political violence events it is impossible to separate the two. An example is the East St Louis Riot of 1917, in which at least 150 people were killed (Barnes 2008). Race-motivated riots also peaked around 1920. The two most serious such outbreaks were the Red Summer of 1919 (McWhirter 2011) and the Tulsa (OK) Race Riot (Hirsch 2002). The Red Summer involved riots in more than 20 cities across the United States and resulted in something like 1,000 fatalities. The Tulsa riot in 1921, which caused about 300 deaths, took on an aspect of civil war, in which thousands of whites and blacks, armed with firearms, fought in the streets, and most of the Greenwood District, a prosperous black neighborhood, was destroyed.

Finally, the 1910s saw the peak of terrorism activity by labor radicals and anarchists (Table 10.3). The bombing campaign by Italian anarchists ("Galleanists") culminated in the 1920 explosion on Wall Street, which caused 38 fatalities. This was followed by an even worse incident in 1927 in which 45 people were killed, among them the perpetrator, Andrew Kehoe, who was enraged by a new property tax for school construction that had, he believed, contributed to his bankruptcy.

TABLE 10.3 Political Terrorism, 1910–1930. Source: USPV database (Turchin 2012).

Year	Fatalities	Description
1910	21	Los Angeles Times bombing by Iron Worker members
1916	10	Preparedness Day bombing (San Francisco) by anarchists (?)
1917	10	Milwaukee Police Station bombing by Italian anarchists
1919	2	Eight large bombs detonated in several US cities by Italian anarchists
1920	38	Wall Street Bombing carried out by Italian anarchists
1927	45	Bath (MI) School Disaster carried out by Andrew Kehoe

Growing Insecurity of the Elites

The preceding section shows that the years around 1920 saw a culmination of several trends in sociopolitical instability, driven by such diverse issues as labor conflicts, interracial tensions, and political extremism. Many members of the political and business elites became alarmed at what amounted to multiple outbreaks of internal warfare—the Battle of Blair Mountain, the Red Summer, and the Tulsa Riot. Additionally, they were themselves direct targets—the bombing campaign of the Italian anarchists was specifically aimed at them.

A less violent, but in some ways even more threatening development was electoral challenges to their political control from the surging populist and socialist movements. Finally, American political and economic leaders were greatly concerned over the rise of communism and fascism in Europe. They perceived the gravest threat specifically in the victory of the Bolshevik Revolution in Russia and the establishment of the USSR, a country with a militant universalizing ideology that directly challenged the foundations of the American political order. It did not help that many of the counter-elites in America—labor organizers, anarchists, socialists, and communists—were recent immigrants from southern and eastern Europe (such as Italians and Jews).

All these factors heightened the fears that a Bolshevik revolution was imminent in America and led to the Red Scare of 1919–21 (also known as the First Red Scare) (Levin 1971). In 1919 and 1920, Attorney General A Mitchell Palmer and J Edgar Hoover (the future FBI director) conducted a series of raids against various radical organizations. The first target was the Union of Russian Workers, which was put out of existence as a result of arrests and deportations. Also targeted were other organizations of suspected radicals. The leader of the Italian anarchists, Luigi Galleani, and eight of his adherents were deported (this happened in June 1919, before the Palmer raids).

The First Red Scare subsided after Palmer predicted a massive uprising on May 1, 1920, which never materialized. Today there is a tendency to treat this incident as mass hysteria that had no basis in reality. However, we should consider two points. First, Palmer was not a lone crank, but a high government official, whose views were shared by substantial segments of the political and ideological elites. During 1919, in the period preceding the Palmer raids, major newspapers, such as *The New York Times* and *The Washington Post*, participated in the media campaign to convince Americans that the "Red Peril" was real. As an example, on June 8, 1919, under the headline "Russian Reds are Busy Here" (referring to the Union of Russian Workers), *The New York Times* wrote, "An organization directly connected with Russia is at work in the United States with an underground propaganda for overthrow of the Government by force."

Second, with the benefit of hindsight we know that America avoided revolution during the years around 1920. However, this does not mean that America was not in a revolutionary situation. The impressive record of intense political violence, which took so many different forms and peaked in 1919–21, suggests that it was. The scale of violence during this period exceeded the scale of violent events preceding the Civil War (see Table 8.1, although not, of course, the Civil War itself, nor the worst riots during the Civil War). A hundred or more fatalities associated with the East St Louis Riot, the Battle of Blair Mountain, and the Tulsa Riot, and a thousand deaths during the Red Summer of 1919 speak for themselves.

The Progressive Era Trend Reversal

After the 1920s the levels of political violence rapidly decreased, and during the 1940s and 50s America experienced another generation of internal peace, similar to the Era of Good Feelings of the early nineteenth century. Why this happened is the main question that this chapter seeks to resolve. It is clear that the key factor underlying this trend reversal was the series of reforms that started to be implemented during the Progressive Era (c.1900–1920s) and culminated in the New Deal (1930s). However, historians disagree about the role played by the economic elites in this process (for a historiography of this debate, see Brinkley 1997).

In one view, that of Arthur Schlesinger Jr. (1957-60), "liberal reform had been responsible for an increase in democracy and social justice in American life". In *The Triumph of Conservatism* Gabriel Kolko (1963) takes a different view. "There were any number of options involving government and economics abstractly available to national political leaders during the period 1900–1916, and in virtually every case they chose those solutions to problems advocated by the representatives of concerned business and financial interests" (Kolko 1963:2). To scholars, such as James Weinstein and (later) Jeffrey Lustig, the real story of modern America was also that of the decline of genuine democracy: "the steady increase in the power of private, corporate institutions, the growing influence of these institutions over the workings of government" (Brinkley 1997: 136). Of particular interest is the question of which social group played the key role in the Progressive movement; who were the agents that implemented the political reforms that underlied the Progressive Era trend reversal. In an influential book, *The Search for Order*, Robert Wiebe (1967) argued that it was a "new middle class". In the words of Richard McCormick, "the spirit and methods of Progressivism unquestionably emanated from the native-born, urban middle and upper-middle classes" from doctors, lawyers, ministers, businessmen, editors, school-teachers, librarians, college professors, engineers, social workers—and from their spouses" (McCormick 1997:121).

In the following pages, I attempt to chart a middle course between these extremes. Some of the disagreements are more apparent than real, stemming from different ideological stances (liberal versus leftist), focusing on somewhat different periods, and emphasizing different aspects of what might be the same phenomenon (are "lawyers" representatives of the "new middle class" or an intrinsic component of the corporate community?). However, because the primary theoretical lens through which I analyze the dynamics of American elites is that of William Domhoff (see Chapter 4: *Approaches to Studying the US Elites*), I find the views and data of Gabriel Kolko, and other New Left historians, to be particularly useful to the story below.

The basic argument is that a coalition of elites in America implemented a series of formal reforms, supplemented by a number of informal measures that were responsible for the reversal of the disintegrative trend and the beginning of the next secular cycle. Some of the reforms adopted during this period, such as the National Labor Relations Act, were highly distasteful to many members of the business and political communities, yet their resistance was overcome.

Consolidation of the American Upper Class: c.1870–c.1920

The critical dynamic was the building of consensus among the American elites about the need for, and nature of, desired change. Between the end of the Civil War, which resulted in the overthrow of the Antebellum ruling elites, and 1900, the Northern business and political elites merged into a true national upper class (Baltzell 1987, 1991). "The business and political elites knew each other, went to the same schools, belonged to the same clubs, married into the same families, shared the same values—in reality, formed that phenomenon which has lately been dubbed The Establishment" (Kolko 1963:284). As Jerome Karabel writes (2005:24–25), "the upper class developed a set of institutions that helped weld it into a national entity that bridged the cultural and social divide between the old patricians and the nouveaux riches of the Gilded Age. Among the upper-class institutions that either were invented or came to prominence in the 1880s and 1890s were the *Social Register* (its first edition was published in New York City in 1888), the country club, the exclusive summer resort, and the elite men's social clubs that arose in cities such as New York, Boston, and Philadelphia."

The key decades for the consolidation of the American upper class were the 1890s and 1900s. This was when the majority of regional *Social Registers* began publication (Table 10.4a). It was also the period when *Social Register* membership lists grew explosively. For example, the growth of the *Social Register* in Philadelphia slowed down after 1910, and especially after 1920 (Table 10.4b).

TABLE 10.4 Consolidation of the American upper class as reflected in *Social Registers*.

(a) The starting years of publication of regional *Social Registers* (Baltzell 1987:19)

year	Cities
1888	New York
1890	Boston, Philadelphia
1892	Baltimore
1893	Chicago
1900	Washington
1903	St. Louis, Buffalo
1904	Pittsburgh
1905	Providence,* Richmond-Charleston, Savannah, Atlanta*
1906	San Francisco
1907	Minneapolis-St. Paul*
1910	Cleveland, Cincinnati-Dayton
1914	Seattle-Portland,* Pasadena-Los Angeles*
1918	Detroit*

Social Registers for these cities were discontinued during the 1920s due to lack of interest

(b) The growth of the Philadelphia *Social Register*, 1890–1940 (Baltzell 1987: Table 8)

year	Number of families
1890	135
1900	1939
1910	3267
1920	4275
1930	4849
1940	5150

The rise of another upper-class institution, the elite boarding school, was less concentrated in time, with the first one, Phillips Academy, established in 1778. Nevertheless, seven of the twelve most prestigious boarding schools were founded between 1883 and 1906 (Levine 1980). Enrollment in these 12 schools grew rapidly from 936 in 1886 to 4,494 in 1926 (Levine 1980: Table 2).

Another important development was the speedy coalescence in the years around 1920 of the "policy-planning network" (Domhoff 2010a), a network of non-profit organizations, which members of the upper class and corporate leaders use to shape policy debates in the United States Table 10.5). These interlocked foundations, think-tanks, and policy-discussion organizations have close financial and trustee ties to the corporate community (Domhoff 2010a: 44). In fact, the bulk of the money came from just three members of the economic elites: Andrew Carnegie, John D Rockefeller, and a wealthy St Louis merchant, Robert Brookings.

TABLE 10.5 The Rise of the Policy-Planning Network (Domhoff and Webber 2011: 43–44)

Year	Organization
1911	Carnegie Corporation
1912	US Chamber of Commerce
1913	Rockefeller Foundation
1916	National Industrial Conference Board
1916	Institute of Government Research*
1919	National Bureau of Economic Research
1922	Institute of Economic Research*
1923	Brookings Graduate School of Economics*
1923	Social Science Research Council

*These three organizations were merged into the Brookings Institution in 1927

Consolidation of the American elite, which fused old-money families with the *nouveaux riches*, however, had definite limits. In fact, internal consolidation and the appearance of sharp boundaries between the established and aspirant elites were two sides of the same process. The members of the upper class were native-born, based primarily in Northern states, white in race, and Protestant in religion. The dynamic underlying the rise of the Establishment (to use the term anachronistically), thus, was an example of the "closing of the patriciate" (Chapter 6). At the same time that the members of the established elites took steps to reduce competition within their own ranks, they excluded (and in some cases used outright suppression) on groups that were left outside: foreigners, African- and Asian-Americans, and Jews and Catholics. As an example, in New York by the 1890s Jewish members were driven out of the Union Club, the Saratoga hotels were closed to Jews, and Jewish organizations were banned from the *Social Register* (Beckert 2001).

The Great Merger Movement, 1895–1905

The first sphere within which the elites attempted to reduce competition was economics. Gabriel Kolko (1963: 13–14) provides a number of quotes from a variety of American businesses on the need to reduce competition: "Ignorant, unrestricted competition, carried to its logical conclusion, means death to some of the combatants and injury to all"; "Unrestricted competition had proved a deceptive mirage, and its victims were struggling on every hand to find some means of escape from the perils of their environment. In this trying situation, it was perfectly natural that the idea of rational co-operation in lieu of cut-throat competition should suggest itself." Attempts to reduce "unwanted competition" were led by such business figures as John D Rockefeller and J P Morgan, whose dislike of disorder and whose pursuit of predictability are well known to historians (Diner 1998:30).

Efforts to reduce competition first resulted in the Great Merger Movement of 1895–1905. Recent research, however, has shown that in most cases these turn-of-the-century combinations were less efficient than the new rivals that appeared almost immediately, and they quickly lost their positions of market dominance (Lamoreaux 1985). The merger movement of 1895–1905, therefore, did not achieve its goal of eliminating "unwanted competition". "Private efforts to establish stability and control within various manufacturing industries had largely failed" (Kolko 1963:54). As a result, "it became apparent to many important businessmen that only the national government could rationalize the economy" (Kolko 1963:4). Federal government's interventions in the economic sphere took two forms: informal agreements between various businessmen, such as those brokered by Theodore Roosevelt, and formal legislation and the establishment of administrative commissions that supervised its application to the economy (Kolko 1963:6). In his book, Kolko marshals evidence showing that such legislation as, for example, the Federal Trade Commission Bill, was adopted with the support of the leaders of the business community; in fact, in many cases they initiated and shaped it.

Although failing in its economic goals, the turn-of-the-century merger movement had another, political aspect. Commenting on the consolidation of iron and steel manufactories in 1901, the editors of the *Bankers' Magazine* wrote about this political dimension with unusual candor:

> When business men were single units, each working out his own suc-
> cess regardless of others in desperate competition, the men who con-
> trolled the political organization were supreme. They dictated laws
> and employed the proceeds of taxation in building up the power of
> their organization. But as the business of the country has learned
> the secret of combination, it is gradually subverting the power of the
> politician and rendering him subservient to its purposes. More and
> more the legislatures and the executive powers of the Government
> are compelled to listen to the demands of organized business inter-
> ests. That they are not entirely controlled by these interests is due to
> the fact that business organization has not reached full perfection.
> The recent consolidation of the iron and steel industries is an indi-
> cation of the concentration of power that is possible. Every form of
> business is capable of similar consolidation, and if other industries
> imitate the example of that concerned with iron and steel, it is easy to
> see that eventually the government of a country where the productive
> forces are all mustered and drilled under the control of a few leaders,
> must become the tool of these forces (Anonymous 1901).

Restriction of Immigration: 1921–24

Another important area of reform during the Progressive Era was the regulation of immigration. An important study of American immigration laws
by Kitty Calavita (1984) begins by considering the following puzzle. The massive immigration influxes into the US after 1820 sparked protests among the
native-born workers and were the cause of the worst riots in American cities
during the Antebellum period (see Chapter 5). Yet, despite these violent protests and popular demand for measures restricting immigration, Congress
did not pass such laws. Instead, the legislators passed a series of measures
designed to *increase* the flow of immigrants.

It was only a century after the anti-immigration protests began, during
the early 1920s, that Congress passed several laws that effectively shut down
overseas migration into the US. Why were the nativist protests and agita-
tion unsuccessful during the nineteenth century, and why was the measure
finally adopted in the early twentieth century? Calavita uses the "dialecti-
cal-structural model" of the state to explain this apparent paradox. As with
Gabriel Kolko, the starting point for this model is Marx and Engels' classic

formulation in *The Communist Manifesto*: "The executive of the modern state is but a committee for managing the common affairs of the whole bourgeoisie." However, Calavita criticizes such analysts as Mills (1956), Domhoff, and Kolko, who explain why one interest group, the corporate community, tends to get its way consistently by focusing on the personal relations between the economic and political elites (Calavita 1984:6).

As an alternative to these "instrumentalists", Calavita proposes a structural model of the capitalist state, which emphasizes the role of the state in managing the *common affairs* of the *whole* bourgeoisie. She argues that to manage collective interests of the bourgeoisie, the state must enjoy a relative degree of autonomy. "This autonomy is 'relative' in that it is relatively free from manipulation by individual capitalists but not at all autonomous from the requirements of the political economy as a whole" (Calavita 1984:8). The capitalist state's goal is the stability and perpetuation of the whole system, which may require the sacrifice of the private interests of some segments of the economic elites. If the selfish (partisan) interests of the ruling class overwhelm the need for cooperation, the whole system is in danger of being replaced, either as a result of internal revolution, or external conquest. In this way, Calavita's model fits very well within the theoretical framework of cultural multilevel selection.

The basic argument in Calavita's book, which resolves the paradox of legislative inaction in the nineteenth century and the adoption of effective laws that restricted immigration in the early twentieth century, is as follows. The state acted not in response to the wishes of the majority of its citizens, and not in response to the wishes of individual members of the corporate community. Rather, it acted when continuing immigration threatened the existence of the state and of the business community as a whole. The immigration laws were passed and enforced when the political leaders and certain economic elites (but not all) realized that *"those very conditions that provide for and result from the maximization of profit threaten the stability upon which the political and economic system depends"* (Calavita 1984:12, italics in the original).

American economic elites were very well aware that a continuing influx of immigrants allowed them to depress worker wages and increase the returns on capital. Andrew Carnegie in 1886 compared immigration to "a golden stream which flows into the country each year" (quoted in Calavita 1984:49). During the nineteenth century the corporate community often used the state to ensure that this "golden stream" would continue to flow. For example, in 1864 (during the Lincoln administration) Congress passed the Act to Encourage Immigration. One of its provisions was the establishment of the Federal Bureau of Immigration, whose explicit intent was "the development of a surplus labor force" (Calavita 1984: 36–37). This legislation was highly effective. While in 1861, annual immigration into the US fell to about 90,000—thanks to the outbreak of the Civil War—by 1865 it had tripled to 280,000, and even exceeded the level immediately preceding the Civil War. As Calavita (1984:38) notes, strike after strike was defeated by bringing in immigrants as strike-breakers (Negroes were also used for this purpose). Between 1861 and 1865 the real wages of unskilled workers were reduced by more than a quarter.

After the Civil War, the employers organized a variety of private efforts to import immigrant workers with the explicit goal of breaking strikes. By the 1880s these efforts had led to the private labor exchange, the established system for redistributing immigrant labor (Calavita 1984:46). On many occasions the goal was not only to defeat a particular strike, but to abolish unions, by replacing a unionized labor force with immigrants (Calavita 1984:48). As Calavita demonstrates in her book with numerous examples, the private labor exchange was a highly effective system for holding labor costs down during the Gilded Age.

However, in the twentieth century, and especially in the years leading to and right around 1920, the negative aspects of unrestricted immigration began to be obvious to the political and economic leaders. As was discussed earlier in the chapter, in 1919–21 the US was experiencing a revolutionary situation, which was perceived as such and contributed to the feelings of acute insecurity among the elites. Massive immigration during the preceding decades contributed to this crisis both indirectly and directly. First, it created an oversupply of labor and high systemic unemployment. Although such an oversupply of labor was profitable to individual businesses, it also led to increasingly violent labor strikes that on several occasions grew into what were essentially popular insurrections. It also contributed to the race riots, which were motivated in large part by the threat to the whites from the competition by the blacks in the labor markets.

Immigration also directly contributed to the insecurity of the elites. As I noted above, the immigrants from Southern and Eastern Europe had become the source of counter-elites (most notably, Italian anarchists and Jewish socialists). Additionally, the danger that immigrants imported for strike-breaking would refuse to serve as "scabs" (strike-breakers), or even cross the lines and join the strike, was ever present. After 1900 immigrant workers increasingly began to organize and initiate strikes. "With the support of the Industrial Workers of the World (IWW) and a variety of small, independent unions by 1906, many spontaneous uprisings led by immigrant workers stunned both their American employers and, increasingly, their native-born co-workers" (Calavita 1984:78).

Here's an extended quote from the 1920 debates in Congress that provides an example of the anxiety felt by the political elites about the threat from immigrant radicalism:

> Beyond the seas there are being taught new and strange doctrines. Socialism, Bolshevism, and anarchy are playing unusual parts in the history and welfare of those nations, and are threatening the very foundations of their governments. Bolshevism and anarchy may draw their slimy trail across the map of Europe and write their destructive doctrines into the history of nations over there, but never with my vote or influence will they make their unholy imprint upon America or American institutions. It is absolutely imperative that this Congress close the door at this time to all immigrants except those whose entrance is provided for by the provisions of this bill... [We must be] willing to throw aside any idea of gain or commercialism for the good of America. (quoted in Calavita 1984:143)

Although policy-makers would have preferred to exclude immigrants from Southern and Eastern Europe, and to encourage immigration from Northwestern Europe (this was the intent of the 1921 legislation), gradually the feeling grew that the most effective way to eliminate the threat from immigrant radicals would be to shut down all immigration. The House Committee on Immigration and Naturalization acknowledged that "it is impossible to keep out revolutionists and Bolsheviki without keeping out substantially everybody" (Calavita 1984:144).

The "Closing of the Patriciate": Changing Admission Policies at Harvard, Princeton, and Yale

The shift in elite attitudes towards immigration is illustrated in the views of two prominent Boston Brahmins who served as presidents of Harvard University: Charles W Eliot (from 1869 to 1909) and A Lawrence Lowell (between 1909 and 1933). Eliot held liberal views on most social and political issues and opposed restricting immigration (Karabel 2005: 40).

On the other hand, Lowell, who succeeded Eliot in 1909, believed that "the masses of immigrants pouring into the United States in the late nineteenth century posed a dire threat to American democracy and to the Anglo-Saxon character of the nation's culture" (Karabel 2005:47). During the early 1920s he used his considerable ideological clout as president of America's most prestigious university in support of the legislation to limit immigration, arguing that "no democracy could be successful unless it was tolerably homogeneous" (Karabel 2005:48). This position was broadly shared by other members of the Protestant establishment, including the presidents of Stanford, Bowdoin, and Western Reserve (Karabel 2005:48).

Consistent with Eliot's liberal views on immigration was his promotion of diversity at Harvard. Towards the end of his tenure in 1909, the university acquired a remarkably heterogeneous student body, nine percent of which was Catholic and seven percent Jewish (Karabel 2005:45). Even more remarkably, in 1908 Harvard College included 29 blacks, as well as many foreigners and recent immigrants (Karabel 2005:569).

Unlike Eliot, Lowell was increasingly worried by the growing proportion of Jews in Harvard College. Following Aristotle's maxim that "the fate of empires depends on the education of youth", Lowell believed that the main function of universities was to produce a ruling elite that was socially cohesive, even if that meant some sacrifice of intellectual brilliance (Karabel 2005). When the proportion of Jews at Harvard reached 22 percent in 1922 (further increasing to 28 percent in 1925), Lowell proposed to impose a Jewish quota on Harvard's admissions. Although this proposal became a matter of considerable public controversy, by 1926 he had succeeded in imposing a new admissions regime, under which the proportion of Jews was reduced to 15 percent or less "simply by rejecting without detailed explanation" (Karabel 2005:109). As a result of this policy the proportion of Jews in the freshman class fell from 28 percent in 1925 to 12 percent in 1933 (Karabel 2005:172). Although there is no clear evidence that there was similar policy to limit African-American enrollment, the proportion of blacks in the student body had declined sharply by the late 1930s (Karabel 2005:173–4).

The other universities in the "Big Three", Yale and Princeton, dealt with the "Jewish problem" even more effectively, and without a public controversy. Jewish enrollment there was cut dramatically between 1921 and 1924 (Karabel 2005:105). This shift at the Big Three was accomplished by switching the focus of admission criteria from scholastic brilliance to "character", which was assessed, in large part, on the basis of recommendation letters and personal interviews with candidates "by the Director of Admissions and a trusted alumnus" (Karabel 2005:131).

In transforming its admissions criteria as a response to the "Jewish problem", Harvard exemplified a recurrent pattern in the history of elite college admissions: the particular definition of "merit" at a given moment reflects the ideals of the groups that hold power of cultural definition. In the case of the shift from intellect to character that took place in the 1920s at the Big Three, the redefinition of merit was a part of larger mobilization by old-stock Protestants to preserve their dominance by restricting both immigration and the educational and occupational opportunities available to recent immigrants and their children (Karabel 2005: 132).

Reductions in Jewish enrollments were a part of a broader effort by the most prestigious American universities during the 1920s to produce a more homogeneous ruling class. Other measures resulted in a decline in the proportion of students coming from public schools and an increased proportion of the sons of alumni. By 1930 just eight of the most exclusive private schools produced nearly a third of the Yale's freshman class (Karabel 2005:116).

Another aspect of this effort was a reduction in the total number of students admitted to the Big Three. Although this trend was established in the 1920s (with the sizes of freshman classes reaching peaks in the early 1920s), one of the most eloquent proponents of this policy was James Bryant Conant, who succeeded Lowell as Harvard President in 1933. Writing in 1938, Conant clearly formulated one of the central tenets of the Structural-Demographic Theory, the elite overproduction principle:

> I doubt if society can make a graver mistake than to provide advanced higher education of a specialized nature to men and women who are unable subsequently to use that training. ... The German experience in the decade after the war [*World War I*] should warn us against the perils lying in wait for a nation which trains a greater number of professional men than society can employ (quoted in Karabel 2005:153).

This observation led Conant to conclude that "there are too many, rather than too few students attending the universities of the country ... the country at large would benefit by an elimination of at least a quarter, or perhaps one-half of those now enrolled in advanced university work..." (Karabel 2005:152).

Motivated by similar concerns, although more narrowly based on its corporate interests, the American Medical Association successfully reduced competition by halving the number of medical schools (Figure 10.2; dental schools followed a similar trajectory). This resulted in the decline in the number of physicians per 100,000 population from 173 in 1900 to 137 in 1920; "as a result, the fees doctors could charge increased" (Diner 1998: 181).

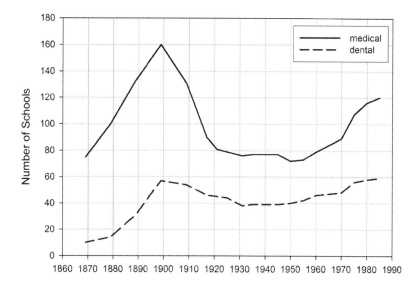

FIGURE 10.2 The number of medical and dental schools in the US, 1869–1985 (source: HSUS).

The broad effect of the new admission policies implemented at Harvard, Princeton, and Yale during the 1920s was to reduce competition within the ruling elite. The Big Three were one of the most important institutions of the American upper class. Big Three alumni dominated top government positions and were well represented among leading corporate leaders (Karabel 2005:18). During the 1920s and 1930s Big Three students became increasingly homogeneous: white, Protestant, wealthy, and with upper-class backgrounds.

The Great Depression and the New Deal

Was the Great Depression a Structural-Demographic Turning Point?

The decade of 1930s, which encompasses the Great Depression and the New Deal, is often portrayed as a fundamental turning point in American history, the "Crucial Era" (Nash 1992). There is a widely held belief among economists and other social scientists that the 1930s were the "defining moment" in the development of the American politico-economic system (Bordo et al. 1998). When we look at major structural-demographic variables, however, the decade of the 1930s does not appear to be a turning point. Structural-demographic trends that were established during the Progressive Era continued through the 1930s, although some of them accelerated (Figure 7.1 and Table 7.1).

Most notably, all the wellbeing variables went through trend reversals before the Great Depression—between 1900 and 1920 (Figure 10.3). From roughly 1910 and to 1960 they all increased essentially monotonically, with only one or two minor fluctuations around the upward trend. The dynamics of real wages also do not exhibit a breaking point in the 1930s, although there was a minor acceleration after 1932 (Figure 10.4), due primarily to falling prices.

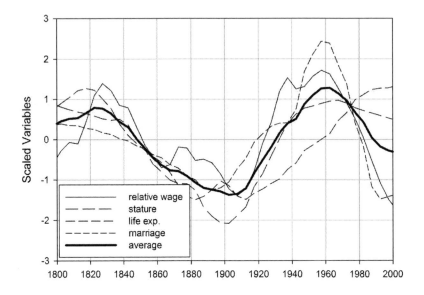

FIGURE 10.3 Wellbeing trends, 1800–2000.

The most serious negative effect of the Great Depression on wellbeing had to do with employment. The proportion of non-farm workers without jobs exceeded 30 percent in 1932 and 1933, and stayed above 10 percent until 1940 (Carter et al. 2004: Table Ba470-477). Such a deep and prolonged slump in employment is probably unique in American labor history (however we lack good employment data for the nineteenth century, and thus cannot be absolutely sure that unemployment rates during the Long Depression and the Depression of the 1890s were less).

Despite real hardship resulting from massive unemployment, wellbeing indicators suggest that the human cost of the Great Depression of the 1930s did not match that of the "First Great Depression" of the 1890s (see also Grant 1983: 3-11 for a general discussion of the severity of the 1890s Depression).

Furthermore, while the 1930s are remembered as a period of violent labor un-rest, the intensity of class struggle was actually lower than during the 1890s Depression. According to the US Political Violence Database (Turchin et al. 2012), there were 32 lethal labor disputes during the 1890s that collectively caused 140 deaths, compared with 20 such disputes in the 1930s with the total of 55 deaths. Furthermore, the last lethal strike in US labor history was in 1937 (when the police fired into the picket lines of striking steelworkers in Massillion, Ohio, killing two workers and injuring several others). In other words, the 1930s was actually the last uptick of violent class struggle in the US, superimposed on an overall declining trend.

FIGURE 10.4 Real wages of production workers, 1900–2000 (100 = 1900) (Officer 2010).

The 1930s Depression is probably remembered (or, rather, misremem-bered) as the worst economic slump in US history, simply because it was the last of the great depressions of the post-Civil War era. Generally speaking, collective memory transmitted through popular media is not as accurate as quantitative data. Such indirectly obtained beliefs are even less accurate than the recollections of the people who lived through the events themselves. In a very interesting book, *The Myth of the Great Depression*, David Potts (2006) argued that the traditional way of telling the story of the Great Depression focuses too much on the hardships and on social disruption (which undoubt-edly happened). Based on 2,000 interviews with Australians who directly experienced the Great Depression, Potts shows that, in addition to the well-known hardship caused by the economic collapse, life in the 1930s also included much resilience and happiness. Many Australians "made do" or "got by", and a significant number of people claimed that "people were happier then".

Potts' (2006) study deals with the Great Depression in Australia, but similar oral history studies in the United States (Terkel 1986) also show that the 1930s were not a uniformly bleak decade. Furthermore, Potts also points to statistical evidence indicating that the negative effects of the Great Depression on popular wellbeing are over-stated. "Despite reports in the press about increased malnutrition and homelessness, there was evidence overall that health improved and death rates declined. Suicide rates, after a sharp rise in 1930, kept falling as the Depression deepened—though the press still carried many stories of people killing themselves because of Depression impacts" (Potts 2006:1–2).

Statistical evidence from the United States suggests a very similar pattern. Expectation of life at birth continued to increase through the 1930s (Figure 10.5). While there are some fluctuations, they are much less in scale than the sharp drop caused by the 1918 flu pandemic.

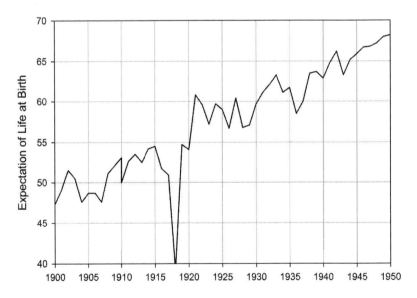

FIGURE 10.5 Expectation of life at birth, 1900–1950 (Carter et al. 2004: Table Ab644-655).

Suicide rates spiked in 1932, and then declined during the 1930s (Figure 10.6). Interestingly, the spike of 1932 was of about the same magnitude as the one during the recession that followed the Panic of 1907, but lasted only half as long. Unfortunately, the suicide data go back only to 1900, and thus we cannot use them to assess the effect of the previous great depression of the 1890s on wellbeing. This effect, however, was probably quite large, as can be seen in the data on life expectancies from the US Census. Thus, life expectancy at birth of the cohort of Americans born in 1880 was four years less than 10 years earlier, and almost six years less than 10 years later. The average heights of native-born Americans similarly reached the minimum for the cohorts born in 1880 and 1890, but grew vigorously through the 1920s and 1930s.

FIGURE 10.6 Crude suicide rates (Carter et al. 2004: Table Ec182-189)

Evidence suggests that the Great Depression of the 1930s had a much milder effect on popular wellbeing, compared with previous depressions, because the political and economic elites responded very differently to the economic hardship. This response addressed both wages and employment.

Before the Great Depression employers routinely cut wages during recessions. "Bloody strikes were fought over wage rate cuts in the 1890s, but rates were nevertheless cut just as they were in 1907–1908 and 1920–1921" (Smiley 2002:62). As a result of the recession of 1920–21, average wages of production workers declined from 54 first to 48 and then 44 cents per hour (Table 10.6; because of deflation the real wage fell less steeply). The violent labor disputes during the 1920 political violence spike, however, contributed to a change in the attitudes of business leaders and government officials.

> Herbert Hoover had been astonished and upset by the wage-rate cuts in the 1920–1921 depression. As secretary of commerce he had organized a conference on unemployment to consider how to stop this behavior. Unfortunately for Hoover, the depression ended before the conference could begin, but throughout the 1920s Hoover preached a "high wage" policy and railed against the "liquidation" of labor through wage cuts. ... By the mid-1920s such noted industrialists as Walter Teagle of Standard Oil of New Jersey, Owen D. Young of General Electric, Myron Taylor of United States Steel, Alfred P. Sloan, Jr., of General Motors, Julius Rosenwald of Sears, Roebuck, Edward Filene of Filene's Department Stores, Howard Heinz of Heinz Foods, and Pierre du Pont of the Du Pont Company were endorsing the high wage policy (Smiley 2002:62).

One particularly interesting case is that of John D Rockefeller, Jr. One of the companies owned by the Rockefellers, Colorado Fuel and Iron, was involved in a prolonged and bloody labor dispute, sometimes known as the "Great Coalfield War" (Andrews 2010). The strike culminated in the Ludlow Massacre in which more than 20 people were killed, including 11 children. In the aftermath of the event, Rockefeller was called to testify before the Commission on Industrial Relations, and he was excoriated in the press for his role in this disaster. After the Ludlow Massacre "Rockefeller began to rethink his earlier position that his money was a sign from God and that paternalism was sufficient" (Carroll et al. 2012:123). This experience was a turning point in his life (Chernow 1998:571-586) and reshaped his attitudes on the industrial-labor relations.

Rockefeller hired MacKenzie King, a Canadian labor relations expert and Liberal politician who later became Prime Minister of Canada (Domhoff and Webber 2011:52). King persuaded Rockefeller to adopt employee representation plans, which enabled workers to elect representatives who could then discuss their grievances with the company managers. "According to most analysts, employee representation plans, called 'company unions' by their critics, were designed as a way to avoid industry-wide labor unions, although Rockefeller and virtually everyone who ever worked for him always insisted otherwise" (Domhoff and Webber 2011:52).

TABLE 10.6 Wages and unemployment rates during the interwar period, 1918–1941. Nominal wage is Production Workers Hourly Compensation (dollars/hour). Real Wage is expressed in 1918 dollars. Real wage (unskilled workers) 100 = 1918. Data sources: wages (Officer and Williamson 2009), unemployment (Carter et al. 2004: Table Ba470-477).

Year	Nominal wage (production)	Real wage (production)	Real wage (unskilled)	Unemployment rate
1918	0.36	0.36	100	1.24
1919	0.43	0.37	101	2.34
1920	0.54	0.41	100	5.16
1921	0.48	0.40	93	11.33
1922	0.44	0.39	91	8.56
1923	0.48	0.42	99	4.32
1924	0.51	0.45	102	5.29
1925	0.50	0.43	99	4.68
1926	0.51	0.43	99	2.90
1927	0.52	0.45	103	3.90
1928	0.52	0.46	105	4.74
1929	0.52	0.46	108	2.89
1930	0.53	0.48	109	8.94
1931	0.51	0.50	115	15.65
1932	0.45	0.50	111	22.89
1933	0.44	0.51	118	20.90
1934	0.53	0.60	136	16.20
1935	0.54	0.59	137	14.39
1936	0.55	0.60	138	9.97
1937	0.63	0.66	151	9.18
1938	0.64	0.68	158	12.47
1939	0.64	0.69	163	11.27
1940	0.67	0.72	166	9.51
1941	0.74	0.76	176	5.99

This criticism was aired by United Mine Workers' leader John Lawson during the visit by Rockefeller to Colorado in 1915:

I believe Mr. Rockefeller is sincere … I believe he is honestly trying to improve conditions among the men in the mines. His efforts probably will result in some betterments which I hope may prove to be permanent.

> However, Mr. Rockefeller has missed the fundamental trouble in the
> coal camps. Democracy has never existed among the men who toil
> under the ground—the coal companies have stamped it out. Now,
> Mr. Rockefeller is not restoring democracy; he is trying to substitute
> paternalism for it.

While Rockefeller never turned into a supporter of the unions, he later became a leading figure among the group whom Domhoff and Webber call the "corporate moderates". Some of the ideas he expressed during this period sound quite radical. For example, in 1919 he said: "Representation is a principle which is fundamentally just and vital to the successful conduct of industry ... Surely it is not consistent for us as Americans to demand democracy in government and practice autocracy in industry ... With the developments in industry what they are today there is sure to come a progressive evolution from autocratic single control, whether by capital, labor, or the state, to democratic cooperative control by all three" (quoted in Carroll et al. 2012: 125).

The moderate segment of the economic elites came in for increasing criticism from the ultraconservatives of the National Association of Manufacturers, who were vehemently opposed to any concessions to the workers and unions. As Domhoff and Webber (2011) document in their book, the corporate moderates played an important role in shaping the New Deal reforms (although ultimately they turned against the Roosevelt administration and joined the ultraconservatives in their opposition to the National Labor Relations Act).

During the early months of the Great Depression, however, moderate business leaders stood by the consensus on the high-wage policy, which had developed during the 1920s. In December 1929 President Hoover addressed 400 key members of the business community as follows: "The very fact that you gentlemen come together for these broad purposes represents an advance in the whole conception of the relationship of business to public welfare... This is a far cry from the arbitrary and dog-eat-dog attitude of some thirty years ago" (quoted in Dawley 2005:177). Leading executives responded in 1929–30 by pledging to maintain wages at the expense of profits (Dawley 2005:177). As a result of this policy, the average nominal wage of production workers stayed essentially constant in the range of 51–53 cents per hour until 1932, when it declined to 45–44 cents, and then bounced back to 53 cents in 1934 (Table 10.6). In real terms, the wages of both production and unskilled workers actually increased, due to severe deflation in those years (Table 10.6).

The second important factor, in addition to rising real wages during the 1930s Depression, was the government programs that were designed to alleviate unemployment. It is important to remember that the unemployment rate in Table 10.6 is calculated by including all those workers who were employed in work relief programs, such as the Public Works Administration, the Works Progress Administration, the Civilian Conservation Corps, and others (Smiley 2002:126). While these programs only came in with the start of the New Deal in 1933, their effect was massive. The Works Progress Administration (WPA) alone provided eight million jobs between 1935 and 1943, with a peak employment of 3.3 million in 1938 (for comparison, the total number of unemployed in 1938, which includes those working for the WPA, was 6.8 million). Conservative commentators sometimes argue that the massive work relief programs of the New Deal, and the maintenance of money wage rates between 1929–31, prolonged the Depression and made unemployment worse (Smiley 2002: 62–63, 126).

An alternative view is presented by Ben Bernanke (2000:253):

> The New Deal era, 1933–41, was a period of general economic growth, set back only by the 1937–38 recession. This economic growth occurred simultaneously with a real wage "push" engineered in part by the government and the unions. As we normally think of higher real wages as depressing aggregate supply, how can these two developments be consistent? If the "transition to efficiency wage" hypothesis is true, part of the answer may be that the higher wages to some extent "paid for themselves" through increased productivity of labor. Probably more important, though, is the observation that with imperfectly competitive product markets, output depends on aggregate demand as well as real wage. Maybe Herbert Hoover and Henry Ford were right: Higher real wages may have paid for themselves in the broader sense that their positive effect on aggregate demand compensated for their tendency to raise costs.

Whichever of these viewpoints is correct, one thing is clear. Econometric analysis shows that government intervention in the economy during the New Deal had a strong and positive effect on popular wellbeing.

> In essence, federal relief spending provided a safety net for the unemployed and the poor that contributed to a continuation of the long-term decline in mortality rates for infants under age one, the

population most vulnerable to the effects of economic downturns. Increased relief spending had little effect on the overall non-infant death rate but contributed to reductions in suicides, deaths due to infectious and parasitic diseases, deaths from diarrheal diseases, and possibly homicides. The relief costs associated with saving a life were similar to modern estimates of the value of life in labor markets and the cost of saving lives through Medicaid (Fishback et al. 2007:13).

Decline of the Elites

There was one population group whose wellbeing took a decided turn for the worse during the Great Depression—the rich. The great depressions of the nineteenth century had no long-term effect on the triumphant march of the top fortunes. But between 1929 and the 1970s top fortunes declined not only in relative terms (in comparison with median wealth), but also in absolute terms (when inflation is taken into account). It is difficult to determine precisely when the inequality trend reversed itself. The Phillips curve (Figure 4.1) and the relative wage (Figure 3.4) point to 1910, but data on incomes of sufficient quality becomes available only after 1916, with the introduction of the income tax (Piketty and Saez 2003). From 1922 on we also have detailed data on the distribution of wealth (Wolff 1996, 2010). Both data curves (Figure 10.7) show that top income earners and wealth holders took a big hit during the Great Depression. Furthermore, the overall trend until the late 1970s was downwards, although with substantial fluctuations. Thus, although it is likely that the downward trend started around 1910, high quality data confirm that it certainly continued after 1930.

The numbers of top wealth holders also declined. If in 1900 there were 19.3 millionaires per one million of general population, in 1925 this number shrank to 13.9, and between 1925 and 1950 it plunged to 5.8 (Table 3.4). Most of this drop probably took place during the Great Depression. For example, membership of the National Association of Manufacturers collapsed from more than 5,000 in the early 1920s to 1,500 in 1933 (Phillips-Fein 2009:13).

Attrition in some economic sectors was brutal. The number of the largest banks, which were members of the Federal Reserve System, fell from 8,707 in 1929 to 5,606 in 1933. For smaller banks the failure rate was even higher: from 16,263 to 8,601 over the same period (Smiley 2002:29). This was a personal catastrophe for thousands of bank CEOs and other top officials, but it also meant that the class of top wealth-holders was shrinking in size.

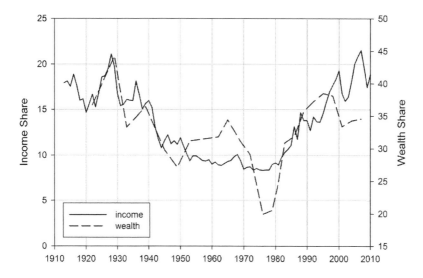

FIGURE 10.7 The share of income and wealth earned or held by the top one percent richest Americans. Income data (Piketty and Saez 2003), updated from Immanuel Saez website. Wealth data (Wolff 1996, 2010)

Assessment: the 1930s from the Structural-Demographic Point of View
Overall, data suggest that trend reversals of all major structural-demographic variables preceded the Great Depression. However, the 1930s were also a period when several important trends accelerated (for example, declines in inequality and political violence). A similar statement can be made about the important social programs that were introduced in the 1930s. As Bordo et al (1998:2) note, "many of the innovations embraced in the 1930s—most of which were part of the Roosevelt administration's New Deal—had been under consideration for some time. ... It could thus be argued that change, already proceeding, was simply accelerated by the economic collapse."

A particularly important period, when many of New Deal regulatory initiatives were first introduced, was during Woodrow Wilson's administration and, particularly, World War I. One such initiative was the government takeover of the railroads, which "fostered the belief that government could succeed when private enterprise did not" (Bordo et al. 1998:4). Another was the introduction of the income tax in 1913, which was greatly increased 1917. Other examples of government intervention in the economy were wage and price controls during World War I. This period also saw the extension of democratic institutions in the US: the seventeenth and nineteenth amendments, passed in 1913 and 1920, respectively, provided for direct elections to the Senate and guaranteed women's right to vote.

Nevertheless, although many of the New Deal initiatives were introduced in the preceding decades, the atmosphere of crisis induced by the Great Depression was very important in cementing these changes in social policy in place. Additionally, the deep and persistent economic crisis helped to discredit laissez-faire ideologies and provided added legitimacy for an expanded role of the federal government in economy. As a result, the federal government's spending as a fraction of GNP was permanently doubled during the 1930s (Bordo et al. 1998:10).

The ideological and cultural shift that occurred during the 1930s was a particularly important, albeit hard-to-quantify, development.

Proposals for minimum wage, social security, unemployment compensation, public ownership, public works, securities regulation, and deposit insurance were already on the table. Having studied reforms instituted in Europe, Canada, Australia, and at the state level in the United States, economists generally found favorable, supporting empirical evidence.

The experts were convinced of the need for more government intervention, but it took the depression to damage the public's strong ideological bias against it. Once established, the public's predisposition towards intervention endured for several decades. Beginning with the stagflation of the 1970s, skepticism about government intervention began to reappear. A shift in public opinion, like that in the 1930s, was preceded by a shift in opinion among economists. The 1930s was a defining moment in the conception of government's role (Bordo et al. 1998:11).

This observation suggests that long-term cycles in economic development, the Kondratiev Waves with periods of 40–50 years, may interact with factors shaping cultural and ideological shifts. Although not all economists accept that Kondratiev Waves are real, prolonged periods of economic malaise do tend to recur with roughly the same timing that was identified by Kondratiev himself in the 1930s. Thus, the Great Depression was followed by the stagflation and the Bear Market of the 1970s, and we may be living through yet another Kondratiev downturn, following the Great Recession of 2009. A prolonged period of economic malaise tends to delegitimize the prevailing ideology and pave the way for an ideological shift.

Synthesis: Structural-Demographic Causes of the Progressive Era Trend Reversal

Although the American political system has been under the influence of wealthy elites ever since the American Revolution, in some historical periods it has worked primarily for the elite benefit, but in others it has implemented policies that benefited society as a whole. It is relatively easy to understand the periods in which the wealthy and powerful shape the political agenda to suit their own interests, as happened in the Gilded Age, when economic inequality grew by leaps and bounds. But how can we account for the policies of the Great Compression era, during which inequality of income and wealth tended to decrease? And what caused the reversal that ended the Gilded Age and ushered in the Great Compression?

Investigations of historical case-studies suggest that the key role in such trend reversals is played by long periods of persistent political instability. Eventually the elites become alarmed at incessant violence and disorder. They realize that they need to pull together, suppress their internal rivalries and switch to a more cooperative way of governing. Such a shift in the social mood is observed repeatedly in history (Turchin and Nefedov 2009)—towards the end of Roman civil wars (first century BC), following the English Wars of the Roses (1455–85), and after the Fronde (1648–53).

As I discussed at the beginning of this chapter, the years around 1920 induced a feeling of unprecedented insecurity among the American elites. The United States was essentially in a revolutionary situation.

By 1920 the American economic and political elites had consolidated into a true upper class, which had acquired a number of institutions that promoted cohesive political action (the elite boarding schools, the Ivy League universities, exclusive country clubs, and, most notably, the policy planning network). Gradually, a realization grew among many American leaders that in order to reduce instability, steps had to be taken to decrease "unwanted competition" in both the economic and political arenas and to ensure a more equitable division of the fruits of economic growth (for the corrosive effect of within-group competition on cooperation see Chapter 2: *Explaining Trend Reversals*).

Early steps to deal with cut-throat economic competition took the form of the Great Merger Movement, but were not as effective as business leaders hoped. Immigration laws of 1921 and 1924, on the other hand, succeeded in effectively shutting down immigration into America. Much of the motivation behind these laws was to exclude "dangerous aliens" such as Italian anarchists and Eastern European socialists, and indeed the political threat from these counter-elites subsided in the post-1920s period. But a broader effect was to reduce labor oversupply. Although such political and business leaders as Herbert Hoover and Henry Ford had favored increased worker wages before 1920, shutting down immigration reduced labor supply and provided a powerful boost to real wages for many decades to come.

During the nineteenth century, American employers ("capitalists") had essentially no concern for the wellbeing of the working classes. The politico-economic system characterizing the United States before the Progressive Era can be characterized as "pure" capitalism (for this reason, the wages submodel in Chapter 9 only included purely economic forces). Things began to change after 1900. "The Progressive Era provides the first examples of the "business case" for socially responsible corporate behavior. ... By the late 1910s, a number of the nation's leading firms were beginning to take a long-term view of their relationship to their employees" (Carroll et al. 2012:116–121). This period saw an introduction of employee stock plans by several corporations.

A very important aspect of this "search for order" was steps taken to reduce intraelite competition and limit upward social mobility. These steps took the form of limiting the numbers graduating from the prestigious universities, such as Harvard, Princeton, and Yale, and implementing discriminatory admission policies favoring white Protestant wealth-holders coming from upper class families.

During the New Deal all these trends were helped along by the economic and social turbulence brought on by the Great Depression. In particular, new legislation legalized collective bargaining through unions, introduced a minimum wage and established Social Security. American elites essentially entered into a "fragile, unwritten compact" (Fraser 1978) with the working classes. This implicit contract included the promise that the fruits of economic growth would be distributed equitably among both workers and owners. In return, the fundamentals of the political-economic system would not be challenged. Avoiding revolution was one of the most important reasons for this compact (although not the only one). As Douglas Fraser wrote in his famous resignation letter from the Labor Management Group, at the point when the compact was about to be abandoned, "the acceptance of the labor movement, such as it has been, came because business feared the alternatives" (Fraser 1978).

In addition to the internal threat due to the spike in political violence around 1920, another, external threat loomed large in the minds of American elites—Bolshevik Russia. The Soviet Union's model of welfare statism and state intervention in the economy could also be a source social innovations. As Kiran Patel writes in *The New Deal*, "Experts around the country associated the whole concept of 'social experiment' with the Soviet Union, resulting from the experience of several hundred Americans who traveled East in the years prior to the New Deal". President Roosevelt himself admitted to Harold Ickes, his Interior Secretary, that "what we were doing in this country were some of the things that were being done in Russia" (Patel 2016: 117).

In this account it is important not to over-emphasize the degree of unity of the American power elites. There was no hidden capitalist conspiracy, and there was no monolithic ruling class. In their analysis of the origin and implementation of New Deal reforms, Domhoff and Webber (2011) stress that there were at least six recognizable power networks that participated in shaping New Deal legislation. It was a complex pattern of conflict and cooperation between these power actors that determined the success or failure of various reforms (and different legislation could be supported by different alliances).

The Progressive Era trend reversal introduced the Great Compression, a long period of decreasing (although with fluctuations) economic inequality. However, while such "quantitative" inequality declined, there was an underside to this arrangement. The cooperating group comprised mainly native-born white Protestants. African-Americans, Jews, Catholics and foreigners were excluded or heavily discriminated against. Nevertheless, while making such "categorical inequalities" worse, the compact made a dramatic reduction in overall economic inequality possible in the first place. As Digby Baltzell, the sociologist of American elites, noted, "the patrician reformers who led the Progressive movement eventually took the steam out of the populist revolt" (Baltzell 1964: 179).

PART FOUR

The Current Secular Cycle: from the Great Depression to the Present, c.1930–2010

11

Long-Term Trends, 1930–2010: a Synthesis

While Part III was concerned with understanding and modeling the dynamical feedbacks between structural-demographic variables operating during the first American secular cycle (1780–1930), the main goal of Part IV is to do the same for the second, incomplete secular cycle (1930–present). Again, of particular interest is the period when structural-demographic variables went through their "trend-reversals". A survey of long-term structural-demographic dynamics in Part II suggested that the key period, when most reversals occurred, was around 1970 (the significant decades were 1960–1980). As we approach the present, more and better-quality data become available to proxy various structural-demographic processes, enabling us to fine-tune our estimate of the timing of that turning point. Accordingly, the first goal of this chapter is to present a summary of empirical trends during the period 1930–2010. The second goal is to provide a temporal framework for the rest of Part IV, a periodization of recent American history from the point of view of Structural-Demographic Theory.

Summary of the Dynamics

Table 11.1 summarizes the story told by various proxies. Beginning with factors affecting labor supply and demand, we observe that the proportion of the American population born outside the country fell to less than five percent (see Figure 3.2b) in 1970, and has been growing vigorously since then. Currently it has reached and even exceeded the level achieved during the previous cycle. Another process affecting the demand for labor is the balance of foreign trade. Prior to 1970–75 the United States was a net exporter, which generated additional demand for labor to produce the exported goods. Since 1975, however, the rising tide of imports has steadily reduced the demand for American labor.

TABLE 11.1 Timing of trend reversals of structural-demographic variables in the current secular cycle, with references to the relevant graphics elsewhere in the book.

Structural variable	Proxy	Reversal	Figure
Labor oversupply	Proportion Foreign Born	1970	3.2b
Labor oversupply	Foreign Trade Balance	1975	12.7
Labor oversupply	Demand/Supply ratio, estimated	1970	12.1
Wellbeing, economic	Real wage	1978	3.3
Wellbeing, economic	Relative Wage	1960	3.4
Wellbeing, health	Average stature	1970	11.1
Wellbeing, health	Life expectancy	none	3.5
Wellbeing, social	Marriage Age (–)*	1960	3.6
Wellbeing, social	Proportion Married	1960 (1970)	11.2
Wellbeing, social	Children in 2-parent household	1960	11.2
Inequality, economic	Extreme Value Index	1980	4.1
Inequality, economic	Top 1% income share	1975	11.3
Inequality, economic	Top 1% wealth share	1975	11.3
Elite overproduction	Lawyers/population ratio	1970	4.4b
Elite overproduction	Medical internships	1975	12.9
Intraelite competition	Yale tuition	1950 (1980)	4.7
Intraelite competition	College and law school tuition	1980	4.6
Intraelite fragmentation	Polarization	1950 (1980)	4.8
Intraelite cooperation	Filibusters (–)*	1960 (1970)	11.4
Intraelite cooperation	Judicial Confirmations	1965 (1980)	11.5
Social cooperation	Tax rate on top incomes	1965 (1980)	5.6
Social cooperation	"Cooperation" in Google Ngram	1975	12.3
Cooperation and Equity	Real minimum wage	1970 (1980)	12.4
Cooperation and Equity	Labor union coverage	1955 (1970)	12.2
Cooperation and Equity	Labor union suppression (–)*	1980	12.2
Patriotism	Visits to national monuments	1970	5.5
State legitimacy	Trust in government	1965	5.3
State capacity	Public debt/GDP (–)*	1981	5.1
Sociopolitical instability	USPV events per 5y	1960 (1980)	6.1a

*The minus sign indicates that this proxy correlates negatively with the structural variable.

Immigration and trade deficits are only two of the contributing factors that affect the balance of labor demand and supply. This complex of factors will be analyzed in the next chapter (*Estimating Labor Demand and Supply*), where I show that prior to 1970 demand for labor grew faster than supply, but then the situation was reversed.

Measures of wellbeing also went through trend reversals between 1960 and 1980 (with one exception, life expectancy). On the economic side, the relative wage reached a peak in 1960, but real wages continued to grow for another decade. It was only during the 1970s that real wages of unskilled workers reached their peak, going into a decline after 1978. Real wages regained some ground during the 1990s, but again declined after 2003 (these dynamics will be studied and modeled in greater detail in Chapter 12).

With respect to health variables, expectation of life has continued to grow essentially monotonically since 1945 (see Figure 3.5 inset). This is what should be expected, given the great advances in medicine and public health during the twentieth century.

What is a real shocker is the dynamics of average heights of Americans. We would expect that in the modern world and in a highly developed nation, crude Malthusian forces would no longer operate, and that phases of the secular cycle would stop affecting biological aspects of wellbeing. That expectation is borne out by the continuing growth of life expectancy, but the situation is very different for stature.

Figure 11.1a plots average heights for native-born Americans, separately for men and women and for whites and blacks. Prior to 1970, despite some divergence among different segments of the population, the overall pattern was vigorous advance, resulting in gains of about 5cm across the board. After 1970, however, this vigorous growth regime was transformed into one of stagnation and even decline. The timing of the break point is somewhat difficult to determine, because adult height can be affected by environmental conditions at any point during the first two decades of life. I follow the practice established in Chapter 3 and plot data not by the year of birth, but by the year when individuals reached age 10, the midpoint of the growth period.

Using this convention we see that the overall average (averaging over both gender and race, while weighting by the number of observations in each category) peaks during the early 1970s (Figure 11.1b). Comparing the dynamics of this index to real wages we observe that ups and downs in the average height tend to precede the ups and downs in the real wage by another 5–10 years (in addition to the shift of 10 years, resulting from plotting the heights data by the data of age = 10y). In other words, when the average population height is plotted not by the date of birth, but by the date of reaching the age of 15–20 years, there is a large degree of parallelism between the fluctuations of the real wage and average stature. A possible explanation is that the level of wages experienced by the *parent* generation has a most direct effect on the biological wellbeing of their *children* when they are going through their adolescent growth spurt. If this explanation is correct, then we expect that average stature will again decline as a result of decreasing real wages after 2003 and especially following the Great Recession.

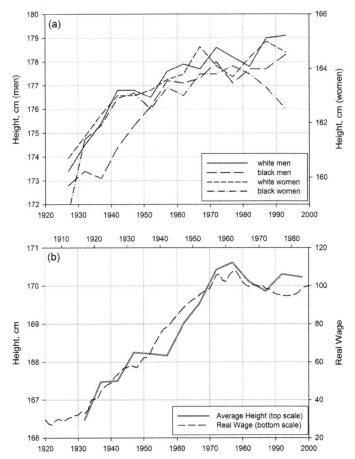

FIGURE 11.1 Changes in average height, 1925–1995. (a) Average heights of white and black men (left scale), and white and black women (right scale). Data source: (Komlos 2010). Data are plotted by year of reaching age 10. (b) A weighted mean (averaging over gender and race) plotted together with real wages for unskilled labor. Average height is plotted by the year of birth (top scale) which is shifted by 15 years with respect to the calendar year (bottom scale).

Proxies for social wellbeing tell a similar story to that of economic and biological indicators. Age at first marriage (Figure 3.6), proportion of the cohort aged 25–34 who are married, and proportion of children living in two-parent families (Figure 11.2) all go through trend reversals around 1960.

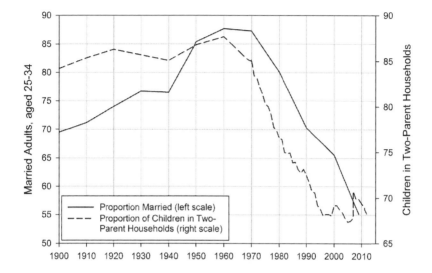

FIGURE 11.2 Two proxies for social wellbeing: proportion of adults aged 25-34 who are married or have been married at least once (source: US Census Bureau) and proportion of children living in households where both parents are present (source: Carter et al. 2004: Table Ae128-190 and US Census Bureau).

Next, we turn to elite-related variables. Measures of economic inequality went through trend reversals around 1975–1980. During the twentieth century, in addition to the cruder Extreme Value Index (whose virtue is that it is also available for the nineteenth century, Figure 4.1) we have much more detailed data on both the distribution of incomes and wealth. These data allow us to refine the estimate of when economic inequality went through the trend reversal. It was 1975, with a particularly vigorous period of growth following 1980 (Figure 11.3).

A direct proxy for elite overproduction, as I argued in Chapter 4, is provided by the number of lawyers in relation to general population. Before 1970 the numbers of lawyers increased at about the same rate as the general population, so that there were roughly 1.5 lawyers per 1,000 population. After 1970, numbers of lawyers began growing much faster and today approach the level of four lawyers/1,000 population (Figure 4.4b). An even more direct indicator

of elite overproduction will be discussed in the next chapter, the balance between the number of available medical internship positions and the number
of applicants for them. As we shall see, the balance shifted in c.1975 (Figure
12.9).

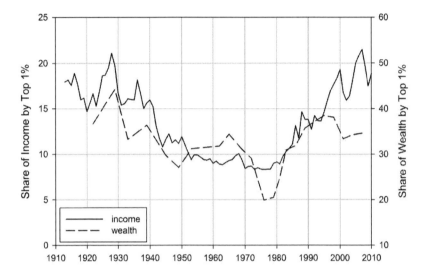

FIGURE 11.3 Proportion of income and wealth concentrated by the top one
percent. Sources: income inequality (Piketty and Saez 2003, Saez 2013);
wealth inequality (Wolff 1996, 2010).

Trends in elite competition proxies paralleled the dynamics of elite overproduction, although the break point came somewhat later, in 1980. Detailed
data on inflation-adjusted cost of college education suggest that during the
1960s and 1970s real tuition at both public and private universities increased
more or less at the rate of inflation (Figure 4.6). Starting in 1980, however,
tuition at both the undergraduate level and for post-graduate education (law
schools) started growing much faster than inflation. The overall increase in
the 25 years following 1980 was roughly threefold (Figure 4.6). Note, however,
that tuition at Yale University, for which much longer time-series data are
available, actually fell to its lowest in 1950, but its growth also accelerated in
1980. Because we lack more general data on the costs of college education for
the period before 1960, it is possible that that the actual trough was in 1950.

An index of intraelite fragmentation, political polarization in Congress,
shows similar dynamics. The twentieth century low point was in c.1950, but
it was followed by a very gradual increase. The actual breakpoint was 1980,

when the index of polarization started growing very rapidly. Other measures of intraelite polarization and conflict show very similar dynamics (Figures 11.4 and 11.5). Especially after 1980, politics at the federal level have become increasingly contentious and uncooperative.

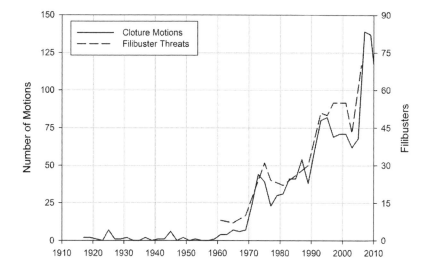

FIGURE 11.4 A proxy for intraelite conflict: the use of filibuster in the Senate. Two measures are shown: the number of cloture motions filed per legislative period (two years) and the proportion of measures filibustered or threatened with a filibuster. Sources: US Senate and (Sinclair 2006, 2009).

Finally, there are a number of measures that can go under the general rubric of "commonwealth": social cooperation, patriotism, and state legitimacy. Some of these measures were discussed in Chapter 5 and others will be treated in the next chapter (*Looking for a Proxy for "Culture"*). The summary in Table 11.1 shows that all these proxies went through trend reversals between 1960 and 1980 (except participation in labor unions, which peaked in 1955).

The overview of variables in this section and Table 11.1 shows that a large number of economic, social, and political indicators went through "regime changes" between 1960 and 1980. Most such regime changes were trend reversals, when a long-term (on the decadal time-scale) trend in one direction was succeeded by a trend moving in the opposite direction. In other cases, a trend was succeeded by stagnation, or vice versa, a variable that had been fairly constant for several decades suddenly plunged (or climbed). Out of roughly 30 structural-demographic variables and proxies in Table 11.1, only one (life expectancy) did not experience a regime change. Furthermore, the direction of trend reversals was not random; rather they all conformed to the predictions of the Structural-Demographic Theory. This striking pattern suggests that something very fundamental changed in the American social system around 1970. In Chapter 12 I will present a structural-demographic model that attempts to make sense of this secular trend reversal. Before doing that, however, I shall briefly review the timing of various events during the post-war period of American history.

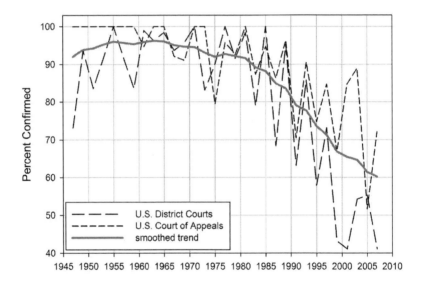

FIGURE 11.5 A proxy for intraelite conflict: percentage of judicial nominations confirmed. Source: (Binder and Maltzman 2009).

A Time Framework for the Current Secular Cycle

The "Second Era of Good Feelings"

The two decades following World War II were a remarkable period in American history. All measures of popular wellbeing grew vigorously (with wages even faster than the overall economic growth), while all variables associated with negative aspects of secular cycles—inequity, political fragmentation and infighting, lack of cooperation and social distrust—bottomed out. Lethally violent labor strikes went away, there were very few riots, and even the frequency of racial lynchings declined. Homicide rates dropped to a very low level (by US standards).

The only other period in American history when the structural-demographic indicators were at such positive levels was the first three decades of the nineteenth century. For this reason, it would be appropriate to refer to the period 1945–60 as the Second Era of Good Feelings. Like the 1820s, the 1950s were a period of remarkable feelings of concord on the part of political elites.

As the journalist Bill Bishop wrote in a recent book,

> The American ideal was to get along. The national goal was moderation and consensus. … In Congress, members visited, talked across party boundaries. They hung out at the gym, socialized at receptions, and formed friendships that had nothing to do with party and ideology. (After all, members had been elected more on their personal connections at home—what V. O. Key called "friends and neighbors" politics—than by the force of party or policy.) … Concerned about electoral torpor and meaningless political debate, the American Political Science Association in 1946 appointed a committee to examine the role of parties in the American system. Four years later, the committee published a lengthy (and alarmed) report calling for the return of ideologically distinct and powerful political parties. Parties ought to stand for distinct sets of politics, the political scientists urged. Voters should be presented with clear choices. …
>
> A call for greater partisanship appeared to be a grand lesson in the downside of wish fulfillment during the presidential campaign of 2004. (Bishop 2008:82–83)

Indeed.

It is true that the spirit of consensus and cooperation had well-defined limits. In the political arena, it certainly did not include the Communist Party. The 1950s were also a period when discrimination against blacks, Jews, and Catholics was the norm. Many commentators also addressed the downside of consensus—social conformity and political passivity. Characters such as *The Man in the Grey Flannel Suit* in Sloan Wilson's 1955 novel became symbols of rejecting conformity in the business world. In the international arena, the United States pursued a very muscular policy, fought a bloody war in Korea and was gradually drawn into Southeast Asian conflicts.

The point of this is to acknowledge that the 1950s were not a Golden Age for all. But they were the Golden Age for common Americans. During the two post-war decades the majority of the American population experienced a historically-unprecedented growth in their quality of life (and it was not limited just to the economic side of things).

The Reagan Era Trend Reversal

Like all Golden Ages, the post-war one did not last very long. A few warning signs appeared as early as the 1950s, when, for example, the unionized proportion of the labor force stopped growing. More structural variables began experiencing trend reversals in the 1960s, but the overwhelming majority hit turning points between 1970 and 1980 (Table 11.1). When Ronald Reagan was elected President in 1980, the structural-demographic trend reversal was an accomplished fact.

I think it appropriate to refer to this turning point as the *Reagan Era Trend Reversal*, because the presidencies of Ronald Reagan and George Bush (who had been Reagan's Vice President) were the period when the new economic and social regime became obvious to all observers, characterized by the suppression of the labor unions, falling real minimum wage, galloping income and wealth inequality, and political polarization. In any case, Reagan was not the cause of this great turning point, but rather a consequence—and symbol—of it (the change came about not because of the actions of any particular individual, but as a result of deeper structural shifts involving myriads of people). Reagan's political rise (Governor of California from 1967 to 75, his first and second presidential campaigns in 1976 and 1980) actually coincides very closely with the period when different variables went through their regime changes. There is, thus, a direct parallel with the Jackson Era Trend Reversal, which largely took place before Andrew Jackson became President.

The Second Gilded Age

There is generally an agreement that Ronald Reagan was one of the most consequential American Presidents, and that his presidency introduced a new era in American history. The past three decades have been characterized by declining wellbeing indicators and growing economic and political polarization of American society. There are many clear parallels with the Gilded Age (c.1870–1900) and a number of political commentators have dubbed the period we are living in as the "Second Gilded Age".

The Rest of Part IV

The next chapter (12: *From the New Deal to the Reagan Revolution: A Dynamical Model*) will follow in the footsteps of Chapter 9 by developing a quantitative model (using the conceptual framework of Chapter 2). A major focus will be the dynamics of general population and wellbeing since 1930 and why real wages stopped growing in the 1970s.

In Chapter 13 (*Social Pressures towards Instability: From the Reagan Revolution to the Troubles of Our Times*), I focus on elite overproduction, intensified intraelite competition and conflict during the 1990s. I combine the trends in wellbeing and elite overproduction with state variables (public debt and trust in the state institutions) and bring the three major structural-demographic components (population–elites–state) together in a single measure of the Political Stress Indicator, Ψ.

The final chapter (14: *Conclusion: Two Ages of Discord*) provides an overview of the book's results and discusses how the fundamental predictions of the Structural-Demographic Theory (listed in Table 1.2) fared when confronted with the data.

12

From the New Deal to the Reagan Revolution: A Dynamical Model

Goals of the Chapter

The overview of major structural-demographic variables in Chapter 11 demonstrates that the integrative trend, which was established during the Progressive Era, reversed itself during the 1970s (for reasons explained in the previous chapter, I refer to this turning point as the Reagan Era Trend Reversal). This pattern of an integrative trend changing to a disintegrative trend is very similar to what happened in the 1820s (the Jackson Era Trend Reversal, see Chapter 8), and the goal of this chapter is to determine whether the mechanisms responsible for the Reagan Era trend reversal were, at a fundamental level, the same as those operating in the early nineteenth century. I will address this question with the general structural-demographic model that traces internal feedbacks within the population-elite system (Chapter 2; a version of this model was deployed to understand the Jackson Era Trend Reversal in Chapter 9). Naturally, the specific implementation of the general model needs to reflect the very different characteristics of American society in the second half of the twentieth century.

Modeling Labor Oversupply and General Wellbeing

In this section I focus on the economic aspect of popular wellbeing—primarily, real wages, although later I also discuss the additional forces that affected the dynamics of household incomes. The chief empirical observation that we need to understand is why the robust and virtually monotonic pattern of real wage growth ended in the 1970s and was replaced by a regime of stagnation and decline.

The general modeling approach that I will use has already been introduced in Chapter 2:

$$(12.1) \qquad W_{t+\tau} = a \left(\frac{G_t}{N_t} \right)^{\alpha} \left(\frac{D_t}{S_t} \right)^{\beta} C_t^{\gamma}$$

Where W is the real wage, G/N is the real GDP per capita, D/S is the balance of labor demand and supply, and C stands for the effect of non-market forces ("culture"). The subscripts index time (years) and τ measures the "stickiness" of wages (time lag before wages respond to a shift in the labor supply/demand balance).

An investigation of the empirical adequacy of the model (its ability to explain the long-term dynamics of W) requires data on the predictor variables (G/N, D/S, and C). Where direct data are not available, I need to find reasonable proxies. The first quantity, real GDP per capita, is readily available from a number of sources. The wages and GDP data are taken from MeasuringWorth (Officer 2007, Officer and Williamson 2009).

Estimating Labor Demand and Supply
Estimates of labor demand and supply require more work. To a first approximation, we can estimate demand for labor by dividing the total amount of goods and services produced, G, by labor productivity, P (Blanchard 1997:512). Since P is usually measured as productivity per hour, the G/P ratio tells us how many hours were needed to produce the GDP for that year. Assuming a 40-hour work week, there are roughly 2,000 hours per year per (fully employed) worker, so

$$D_t = \frac{G_t}{2000 P_t}$$

(actually, a constant factor, such as 2,000 hours, does not affect the results of the analysis because all such factors are folded into the scale parameter a in Eqn. 12.1).

I used the Bureau of Labor Statistics (BLS) data for labor productivity from 1947 to the present. For the period before 1947, I consulted Ferguson and Wascher (2004: Table 1). These authors give an overall estimate of labor productivity growth between 1927 and 1948 as 1.8 percent per year. Accordingly, I used 1927 as the first year of the data series for analysis.

Because real wages are expected to change slowly and in response to long trends in predictor variables (rather than short-term fluctuations of the business cycle), I smoothed all predictor variables using an exponential kernel smoother (Li and Racine 2006) with bandwidth $h = 4$ years. A smoothed GDP, in particular, is known as "potential" or "trend" level of output (Samuelson and Nordhaus 1998:376). Real wage data, W, on the other hand, were not smoothed, because smoothing the response variable introduces biases into statistical estimation. (I also re-ran the analyses using unsmoothed predictor variables; the results were qualitatively similar, but the regression model explained a lower proportion of variance).

A reasonable first approximation of labor supply is the total labor force in the United States. I took the data from HSUS (Carter et al. 2004) and the BLS for years after 1990. There is one problem: while BLS data include unemployed workers searching for work, they do not include those unemployed who gave up on finding a job and dropped out of the work force. The recent trend of declining labor participation rate suggests that the Great Recession of 2007–9 caused increasingly large numbers of potential workers to withdraw from the labor force.[9] For this reason, my estimate of S probably underestimates the true labor supply, a problem that has become especially severe in the last few years.

Plotting the estimated trends in labor demand and supply on the same graph shows that at the beginning of the period the demand curve grew faster than the supply curve (Figure 12.1). During the late 1960s, however, the supply curve accelerated and quickly outpaced the growth in demand. Two processes explain this acceleration. One was the reversal of immigration policy in 1965 that facilitated the arrival of workers from overseas. By the early 2000s, one in six American workers were foreign-born. However, the initial rise during the late sixties and the seventies was primarily driven by the second factor, internal demographic growth. The generation that reached marriageable age during the Great Depression and World War II had fewer babies than the post-war generation (the parents of baby-boomers). When baby boomers began entering the job market in massive numbers after 1965, they quickly drove the supply curve up above the demand (see Easterlin 1980, Macunovich 2002).

Another turning point was reached around 2000, when the demand curve stopped growing altogether. This remarkable occurrence was due to a combination of sluggish economic growth and rapid gains in labor productivity, which put a lid on the number of workers needed to satisfy the demand for labor. Notice that the plateau occurred before the Great Recession, and it provides one possible explanation for the "jobless recovery" following the Recession of 2001.

---

9   "Three reasons the U.S. labor force keeps shrinking" by Brad Plumer (*Washington Post*, September 6, 2013)

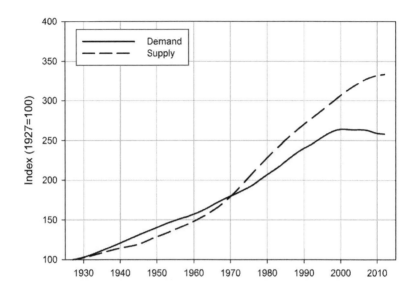

FIGURE 12.1 Trends in labor demand and supply (the United States, 1927–2012). Both time series have been scaled so that 1927 = 100. Source: calculations by the author based on data from MeasuringWorth, HSUS, and BLS.

Overall, the trends in demand and supply curves appear to yield interesting insights into the forces shaping the dynamics of American real wages. However, before we can quantitatively estimate the relative effects of the *D/S* ratio on wages, we need to quantify the dynamics of extra-economic factors.

Looking for a Proxy for "Culture"

Non-market forces affecting real wages include a whole host of potential mechanisms. These mechanisms can either promote growth of wages, or hold them down. For example, in Chapter 10 I discussed how during the Great Depression there was a broad consensus among the political and business elites that worker wages should not be lowered. As a result, real wages actually grew quite vigorously between 1929 and 1941, helped along by a deflation of prices.

During World War II, on the other hand, millions of Americans were put into uniform and sent to fight overseas. The supply of labor dropped (even despite many women entering the labor force for the first time). At the same time, the war demanded a huge increase in output. During this period, worker wages grew, but much less than if they had been driven up by purely economic forces of demand and supply. The reason was that the government (through the National War Board created by President Roosevelt in 1942) actively intervened in suppressing labor disputes and restraining wage growth (Schumann 2001).

Over the long term, the whole period from the New Deal through the Great Society was characterized by government policies that promoted labor unions and outlawed various business practices designed to suppress unionization. As a result, the proportion of unionized workers increased from seven or eight percent in the early 1930s, before the passage of the National Labor Relations Act (NLRA) in 1935, to over 25 percent between 1945 and 1960 (Figure 12.2). In the 1970s and 1980s, union coverage of workers rapidly declined, and currently it is at the level of 12 percent. The decline of union membership in the private sector was even more pronounced: from 35 percent in the 1950s to 7.6 percent in 2008 (Schmitt and Zipperer 2009).

Various explanations have been proposed for this decline, but recent research, summarized and extended by Schmitt and Zipperer (2009) indicates that the most important factor was efforts by the firms to derail unionization campaigns. One of the methods used to defeat union drives was firing pro-union workers, which is illegal under the NLRA. The frequency of union election campaigns in which employers used illegal firings as a disruptive and intimidating tactic grew during the 1970s and reached a peak in the early 1980s, when roughly one in three unionization campaigns was marred by illegal firings (Figure 12.2). Between the 1950s and 1980s the probability that a pro-union worker would be fired during a union drive increased more than tenfold (Schmitt and Zipperer 2009: Figure 2).

There is no consensus among economists on whether a decline in unionization has contributed to wage stagnation. While labor unions definitely increase the wages of unionized workers, by an estimated 10–15 percent on average, most economists believe that labor unions distribute income from non-union to union workers, and that the effect on the overall real wages is negligible (Samuelson and Nordhaus 1998: 238). Whether this assessment is correct, or not, the undeniable fact is that the social mood among the American elites with respect to labor unions underwent a sea change during the 1970s.

To put this shift in perspective, consider the social mood that became established in America following the New Deal Era. As the historian Kim Phillips-Fein wrote in *Invisible Hands* (2009:33), despite their initial resistance to the New Deal policies regulating labor-corporate relations, by the 1950s many managers and stockholders, executives and owners, did in fact make peace with the liberal order that had emerged. They began to bargain regularly with the labor unions at their companies. They advocated the use of fiscal policy and government action to help the nation to cope with economic downturns. They accepted the idea that the state might have some role to play in guiding economic life.

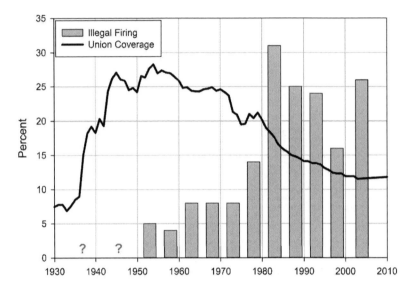

FIGURE 12.2 Labor union dynamics. The curve indicates the proportion of workers covered by unions, 1930–2010. The bar chart traces the proportion of union election campaigns in which pro-union workers were illegally fired, 1951–2007. Data sources: union coverage (Mayer 2004), supplemented by BLS data; illegal firing (Schmitt and Zipperer 2009).

Here are additional quotes illustrating this new attitude.

- In 1943 the President of the US Chamber of Commerce told the Chamber, "Only the willfully blind can fail to see that the old-style capitalism of a primitive, free-shooting period is gone forever" (cited in Phillips-Fein 2009:31).

- In 1954 President Eisenhower said, "Should any political party attempt to abolish social security, unemployment insurance, and eliminate labor laws and farm programs, you would not hear of that party again in our political history. There is a tiny splinter group, of course, that believes you can do these things. Among them are H. L. Hunt … , a few other Texas oil millionaires, and an occasional politician or business man from other areas. Their number is negligible and they are stupid" (Hacker and Pierson 2010: 189).

- In 1964 corporate support went overwhelmingly to the Johnson candidacy. Business leaders abandoned the Goldwater campaign despite Goldwater's focus on low taxes and his anti-union rhetoric (Phillips-Fein 2009: 139-142).

However, the social mood among the American elites began to change during the 1970s. As a result, that decade saw a spurt of growth in pro-business lobbying (Hacker and Pierson 2010:118). By the late 1970s a new generation of political and business leaders had come to power. This change of guard was particularly noticeable in the Republican Party. The Young Republicans, who included Newt Gingrich (elected to Congress in 1978), Vin Weber (1980), Dick Armey and Tom DeLay (1984), were critical of the old-guard congressional GOP leadership that, in their opinion, was too comfortable with the art of compromise (Hacker and Pierson 2010:190). To them the revolutionary situation of 1919–21 and the Great Depression (see Chapter 10) were just history.

These political leaders took the smooth functioning of the American political-economic system for granted, but they and their supporters within the business community were deeply dissatisfied with the declining top incomes and wealth. During the Bear Market of 1973–82 capital returns took a particularly strong beating and the high inflation of that decade ate into inherited wealth. A fortune of $2 billion in 1982 was a third smaller, when expressed in inflation-adjusted dollars, than $1 billion in 1962, and only a sixth of $1 billion in 1912.

There is an interesting parallel here between the Great Depression and the 1970s Bear Market. Both periods of economic hardship (although it goes without saying that the Great Depression was a much more severe crisis) were broadly interpreted as empirical evidence against the prevailing economic doctrine – the naked, *laissez faire* capitalism in the first instance, more cooperative relations between business and labor in the second. Yet it is much more likely that the primary mechanism, responsible for long-term economic decline/stagnation in each case, was the negative phase of the Kondratiev cycle, perhaps supplemented by exogenous shocks (eg, the 1973 oil embargo). Yet in each case a prolonged period of economic troubles helped to delegitimize the prevailing ideological regime (Chapter 9).

Although the election of President Ronald Reagan in 1980 and the beginning of "Reaganomics" was its most visible symbolic manifestation, the actual cultural shift had taken place several years earlier. While the presidency of the Republican Richard Nixon continued the Great Society policies of

Lyndon Johnson's era, policy under the Democrat Jimmy Carter bore more resemblance to that of the subsequent Reagan era.

The United Auto Workers president Douglas Fraser described this cultural shift in his famous resignation letter to the Labor-Management Group (Fraser 1978) as follows.

> I believe leaders of the business community, with few exceptions, have chosen to wage a one-sided class war today in this country—a war against working people, the unemployed, the poor, the minorities, the very young and the very old, and even many in the middle class of our society. The leaders of industry, commerce and finance in the United States have broken and discarded the fragile, unwritten compact previously existing during a past period of growth and progress.

> For a considerable time, the leaders of business and labor have sat at the Labor-Management Group's table—recognizing differences, but seeking consensus where it existed. That worked because the business community in the US succeeded in advocating a general loyalty to an allegedly benign capitalism that emphasized private property, independence and self-regulation along with an allegiance to free, democratic politics...

> The acceptance of the labor movement, such as it has been, came because business feared the alternatives. ... But today, I am convinced there has been a shift on the part of the business community toward confrontation, rather than cooperation. Now, business groups are tightening their control over American society. As that grip tightens, it is the "have-nots" who are squeezed.

> The latest breakdown in our relationship is also perhaps the most serious. The fight waged by the business community against that Labor Law Reform bill stands as the most vicious, unfair attack upon the labor movement in more than 30 years. ... Labor law reform itself would not have organized a single worker. Rather, it would have begun to limit the ability of certain rogue employers to keep workers from choosing democratically to be represented by unions through employer delay and outright violation of existing labor law...

The new flexing of business muscle can be seen in many other areas. The rise of multinational corporations that know neither patriotism nor morality but only self-interest, has made accountability almost non-existent. At virtually every level, I discern a demand by business for docile government and unrestrained corporate individualism. Where industry once yearned for subservient unions, it now wants no unions at all…

Business blames inflation on workers, the poor, the consumer and uses it as a club against them. Price hikes and profit increases are ignored while corporate representatives tell us we can't afford to stop killing and maiming workers in unsafe factories. They tell us we must postpone moderate increases in the minimum wage for those whose labor earns so little they can barely survive.

Our tax laws are a scandal, yet corporate America wants even wider inequities. … The wealthy seek not to close loopholes, but to widen them by advocating the capital gains tax rollback that will bring them a huge bonanza.

I have quoted this remarkable and, in many ways, prophetic letter at length, because it is an excellent summary of the structural-demographic variables that are relevant to the cultural shift, which took place during the 1970s. What is particularly remarkable about the letter is that it was written in 1978—the year when real wages stopped growing. However, it was not at all clear at the time that it was not just a "blip", but actually the beginning of a new long-term trend. Furthermore, economic inequality did not really start growing until 1980 (Figure 10.7). Similarly, the anti-labor union push from the corporations only gathered momentum in the 1980s (Figure 12.2), during the Reagan presidency (with the defeat of the 1981 air controllers' strike as the symbolic turning point). And while the first big reduction in the federal tax rate on top incomes took place in the 1960s, it only brought the top rate to the pre-World War II level (around 70 percent, see Figure 5.6). Much more drastic decreases occurred during the 1980s (eventually to ~30 percent). In other words, the cultural and ideological shift that Fraser describes preceded the shift in economic and state-related structural-demographic variables. This observation is consistent with the idea that cultural factors were one of the causes of the 1970s trend reversal.

One particularly important aspect of Fraser's letter is his emphasis on what he perceives as a shift by the business community from "morality" and "cooperation" to "self-interest", "unrestrained corporate individualism", and "confrontation". It is interesting that "culture-metric" data support Fraser's subjective perception. For example, the frequency of the word "cooperation" in the corpus of American books grew rapidly during the Progressive Era and somewhat less so during the New Deal (Figure 12.3). After reaching a peak in 1940, there was a minor decline during the 1950s, followed by an increase towards the second peak of 1975. After 1975, however, the frequency of this word went into a sustained decline.

Google Ngram is an imperfect instrument with which to trace cultural shifts. One problem is that the same word (eg, "capitalism") can be used with either positive or negative valence, and Ngram does not allow one to separate these different meanings. "Cooperation", however, is rarely used in the negative sense. Because of its predominantly positive valence, its overall frequency should provide us with a proxy for how much a society values cooperative values. Checking different variants (cooperation, Cooperation, cooperative, etc) yields the same overall rise-fall dynamics during the twentieth century (and up to 2008, where the current Google book database stops).

Furthermore, a more specific phrase, "labor-business cooperation" again traces out the same secular cycle, although with significant differences during some decades (eg, the 1920s). Finally, "corporate greed" with its predominantly negative valence is another check on the validity of this result, and it is reassuring that during the twentieth century its frequency moved in the opposite direction from the two positive terms (to show this parallelism more clearly, Figure 12.3 plots "corporate greed" on an inverse scale).

Another significant point that Fraser raises (which was later echoed by many political commentators) is the erosion of the real minimum wage due to inflation and the failure of the American political system to increase the nominal minimum wage to counteract inflationary pressures. Prior to 1970, the overall (smoothed) trend in the real minimum wage was up, and between 1950 and 1970 the real wage doubled (Figure 12.4). After 1970, however, the wage declined before equilibrating at a lower level during the 1990s and 2000s.

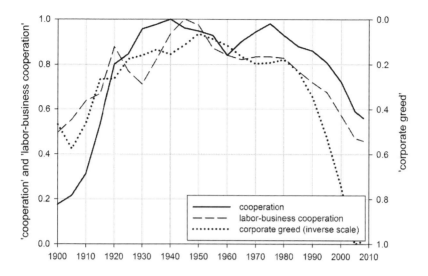

FIGURE 12.3 The frequency of the word "cooperation" and the phrases "labor-business cooperation" and "corporate greed" in the American English corpus of literature (1900–2008), according to the Google Books Ngram Viewer (http://books.google.com/ngrams/, read on May 11, 2013). All frequencies have been scaled to maximum = 1. Note the inverse scale for "corporate greed" (right axis).

The dynamics of the minimum wage, thus, trace a cycle that shares many similarities with variables reflecting employer-employee relations. This is not surprising, because the value of the minimum wage reflects the shifting cultural and political attitudes toward what is the appropriate level of pay for unskilled labor. From the New Deal to the Great Society, these non-market forces pushed the wage up faster than inflation. During the 1970s, however, an opposing trend gained the upper hand, allowing the minimum wage to decay as a result of inflation.

These considerations suggest that the smoothed trend of the real minimum wage may serve as a reasonable proxy for the hard-to-quantify effect of the non-market forces. An additional advantage of this particular variable is that it is expressed in the same units as the quantity that we aim to model and understand (inflation-adjusted dollars per unit of work time).

It is worth emphasizing that what is important here is not the direct effect of the minimum wage on overall wages. The direct effect of changing the minimum wage on worker wages is likely to be slight, because it affects a small proportion of the American labor force. Furthermore, many states set their minimum wages above the federal level. Thus, the primary value of this variable in the analysis is as a proxy for the complex of non-market forces.

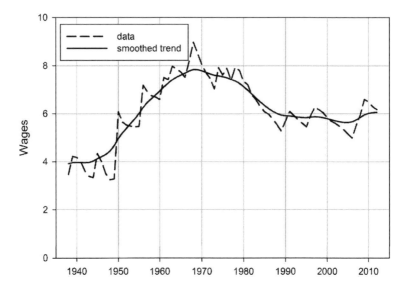

FIGURE 12.4 Dynamics of the real minimum wage, 1938–2012 (data source: US Department of Labor).

Regression Analyses

We now have all the quantitative ingredients—GDP per capita, labor demand/supply ratio, and a proxy for non-market forces. In this section I put it all together in a statistical analysis that quantifies the effects, if any, of these three factors on real-wage trends. My modeling strategy is to add one explanatory variable at a time to the regression model (see Eqn. 2.2 in Chapter 2):

$$(12.2) \qquad \log W_{t+\tau} = A + \alpha \log\left(\frac{G_t}{N_t}\right) + \beta \log\left(\frac{D_t}{S_t}\right) + \gamma \log C_t + \varepsilon_t$$

and at each step evaluate the improvement (if any) of the fit between data and model quantitatively (with the coefficient of determination, R^2) and qualitatively (by observing whether the regression reproduces upward and downward trends in the data). Once this process is completed, I estimate the values of parameters by fitting a regression model with autocorrelated errors. The overall goal of the analysis is to determine whether the three-factorial model can explain why real wages stopped growing during the late 1970s.

The regression that includes only the effect of growth in GDP per capita predicts a steady and monotonic increase in real wages (Figure 12.5a). There is no hint of a break in the GDP curve during the late 1970s, because GDP per capita grew fairly steadily, although sometimes at a faster, and at other times at a slower rate. However, the growth rate of real wages outpaced that of GDP per capita before 1970s, while the growth rate of GDP per capita outpaced that of real wages after that date.

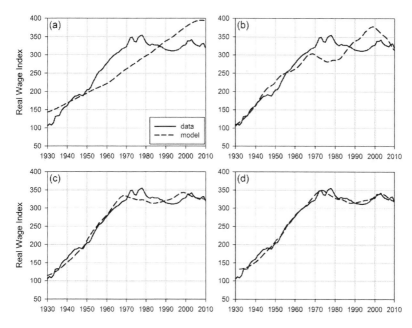

FIGURE 12.5 Results of fitting various forms of the regression model (12.2) to the data. (a) Including only the effect of GDP per capita (no time lag). (b) Including both GDP and labor demand/supply ratio (no time lag). (c) Including all three factors (no time lag). (d) The full model, time lag = 5 years.

The regression model that takes into account both GDP (per capita) and labor supply/demand ratio generated the fitted curve that is shown in Figure 12.5b. The two-factorial model explains data substantially better than the model with just GDP (the coefficient of determination, R^2 = 0.93, compared with R^2 = 0.73 for the one-factorial model). The predicted curve hints that demand/supply ratio may be responsible for some of the trend reversals in the data, but overall, the model is not particularly satisfactory.

Adding minimum wage as the proxy for non-market forces results in a dramatic improvement in the match between the model-generated trajectory and data (R^2 = 0.98). The three-factorial model now predicts both regimes of vigorous growth and stagnation (Figure 12.5c). However, notice that the break point in the fitted curve, when it shifts from the growth to the stagnation regime, occurs several years before the break point in the data. As I discussed earlier, this is the expected pattern. As economic conditions change (for example, supply begins to overtake demand for labor), wages do not adjust to the new situation immediately. Labor contracts need to run their course and be renegotiated, and neither employers nor employees know yet whether this year's conditions are part of a long-term trend, or just a temporary spike. This means that real wages this year actually reflect the social and economic conjuncture that obtained several years ago.

Setting the lag time to five years yields a trajectory that accurately predicts the switch point from growth to stagnation regime (Figure 12.5d). This is, of course, not surprising, because the delay parameter was selected to account for this feature of the data. What is surprising is that the model now accurately predicts fluctuations of real wages during the stagnation phase: down during the 1980s, up until the early 2000s, and then down again. Such fine-scale correspondence between the model trajectory and data is entirely unexpected, and serves to strengthen further our confidence in the ability of the model to capture the forces driving the dynamics of real wages.

Formal statistical analysis with a regression model that accounts for autocorrelated errors (Table 12.1) confirms that all three components are needed to replicate the data pattern. The conclusion is that real wages grow faster or slower than "per capita income" as a result of an interplay between market forces (captured by the labor demand/supply ratio) and cultural influences (proxied by the real minimum wage).

TABLE 12.1 Results of regression analysis of real wage data using the R function arima (and checking the results with the function auto.arima in R package "forecast"). Model selection with the Akaike Information Criterion (AIC) suggested that the best model includes all three predictors, as well as ARIMA(1, 0, 1) terms.

Factors	Estimate	Standard error
GDP per capita	0.60	0.07
Labor demand/supply	1.65	0.31
Real minimum wage	0.45	0.08
AR1	0.74	0.09
MA1	0.65	0.10

Synthesis: Relative Contributions to the Real Wage Trend Reversal

Model (12.1) is deceptively simple. It has only three parameters (α, β, γ) measuring the contributions of each of the three factors to the dynamics of real wages (the scale parameter a is of no interest and can be set to 1 without any loss of information). However, this parsimonious form in fact incorporates many more mechanisms that have been proposed to explain trends in real wages.

For example, immigration (both legal and illegal) enters the equation by making the labor supply increase faster. Trade deficit, on the other hand, subtracts from the GDP, and thus decreases the demand for labor. The proxy that I used for the operation of non-market forces, the minimum wage, trended up and down together with a number of other cultural and political indicators. Because the regression model captures 98 percent of variation in the real wage data, the implication is that this particular proxy is all we need to represent the action of various non-market forces.

The model, thus, can be used as a common framework within which different explanations can be compared with each other quantitatively. An imbalance between labor supply and demand clearly played a very important role in driving real wages down after 1978. As Harvard economist George J Borjas recently wrote, "The best empirical research that tries to examine what has actually happened in the US labor market aligns well with economy theory: An increase in the number of workers leads to lower wages" (Borjas 2013).

Between 1977 and 2012 demand for labor increased only by 31 percent, while labor supply grew by 56 percent (Figure 12.1). A big chunk of the increase in the labor supply was simply the overall population growth. Between 1977 and 2012 the native-born population of the United States increased by roughly 33 percent (or roughly the same magnitude as the growth of demand).

There are several reasons why labor supply grew faster than overall population growth, of which two appear to be most important. One big factor is immigration. In 2011 the total American work force was 153 million, of which 24.4 million workers were foreign-born (this number includes both legal and illegal immigrants). The proportion of foreign-born in the labor force is currently around 16 percent (compared with five percent 40 years ago).

The second factor was the increasing number of women working. In the 1970s only 40 percent of women were in the labor force; today this proportion is close to 60 percent. If the labor participation rate of native women (so that we don't double-count foreign-born women in the labor force) stayed at its

1970s level, today there would be 20 million fewer workers—an effect of nearly the same magnitude as that of immigration.

Before the turning point of the 1970s the American work force was predominantly male and native-born. In the last few decades, the oversupply of labor, resulting from the operation of these two factors, drove down the wages of typical, or median, male workers (Figure 12.6)

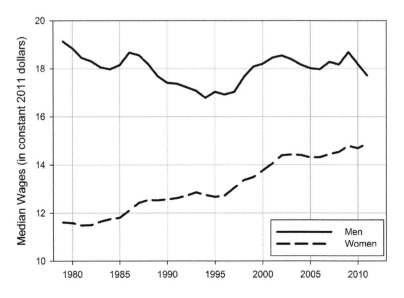

FIGURE 12.6 Dynamics of real median wages for men and women. Source of data: Economic Policy Institute (http://stateofworkingamerica.org/).

If median wages of men declined, why did the median household incomes continue to rise after 1979, even if more slowly than the growth in GDP per capita? The answer is an increasing proportion of married women working and women earning more, as a result of their wages gradually converging with those of men (Figure 12.6). As men's real wages declined, an increasing number of families switched to two-earner households, which allowed them to increase their combined income.

The supply of labor is affected by additional factors, such as changing age composition of the population, but these factors are of lesser magnitude. Thus, in 1978 individuals aged between 20 and 64 years were 55 percent of the total population, and by 2012 this proportion increased to nearly 60 percent. Had it stayed at a constant level, there would be 7–9 million fewer workers in the labor force (depending on various assumptions about their workforce participation rates).

We are also interested in forces that operate on the labor demand side. The most important of these (or, at least, among those that operate in the short-term) is the balance of trade. During the 1970s the balance of trade changed from positive to negative (the first postwar year of trade deficit was 1971, the last year of trade surplus was 1975).

We can express this factor in the same units, full-time worker equivalents, by dividing the "missing" part of GDP due to trade deficit by the average annual productivity of American workers (Figure 12.7). Trade deficit has fluctuated substantially in recent years—from 3.5 percent of GDP in 2001 to a peak of 5.6 in 2005 and 2006, and then down to 3.4 percent in 2010, corresponding to 4–8 million worker equivalents (Figure 12.7). Averaging these numbers over the decade suggests that trade deficit resulted in a loss of roughly 6.5 million jobs in any of those 10 years. The effect of trade imbalance, thus, is of a substantially lesser magnitude than such labor supply factors as immigration and growing participation of women in the work force, and similar to the effect of the changing age composition of the US population.

FIGURE 12.7 Foreign Trade Balance, 1927–2011, expressed in terms of full-time worker equivalents.

13

Social Pressures towards Instability:
From the Reagan Revolution
to the Troubles of Our Times

Whereas the previous chapter examined the structural-demographic causes of the decline in popular wellbeing, Chapter 13 focuses on the consequences of labor oversupply and declining relative wages for elite dynamics. This chapter also moves us forward in time, from the focus on the Reagan-era reversal to the development of elite overproduction in the 1990s.

Modeling Elite Overproduction and Intraelite Competition

The relative wage (wage in relation to GDPpc) is a fundamental driver in the Structural-Demographic Theory (see Chapter 2). In addition to having a direct effect on the wellbeing of the general population, the level of the relative wage has important implications for the dynamics of the elites. I now apply the general structural-demographic model of Chapter 2 to investigate the dynamics of relative elite numbers, e (the numbers of elites in proportion to the total population), during the contemporary secular cycle. This variable is governed by the following equation:

(13.1)
$$\dot{e} = \mu_0 \frac{w_0 - w}{w}$$

where the dot over e indicates that it is e's rate of change, w is the relative wage (a dynamical quantity) and μ_0 and w_0 are fixed parameters. The main implication of this equation is that elite numbers relative to the general population should increase when relative wages are low and decline when relative wages are high (reflecting the balance of upward versus downward social mobility).

Our investigation in Chapter 12 showed that as a result of a complex interplay between market forces (labor supply vs demand) and non-market influences (socio-cultural norms and institutions), the relative wage increased between 1930 and 1960, lost some ground between 1960 and 1977, and took a plunge during the last two decades of the twentieth century (see the dotted curve in Figure 13.1).

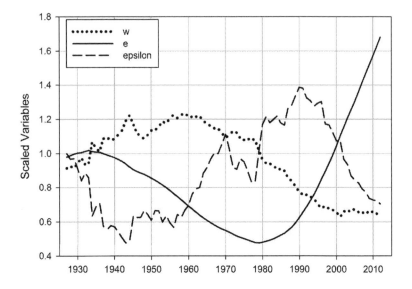

FIGURE 13.1 Dynamics of the elite module (submodel) of the general structural-demographic model, 1927–2012: relative wage (dotted line), relative elite numbers (solid line), and relative elite income (dashed line). All relative variables were scaled to mean = 1 for the pre-war period (1927–40).

Using the data on w as the driver in equation (13.1) predicts two distinct dynamical regimes for e. First, there is a long period of gentle decline starting after the Great Depression and continuing to the eve of the Reagan Revolution. After 1980, however, the relative elite numbers begin to increase at an accelerating rate (the solid curve in Figure 13.1). The dynamics shown in Figure 13.1 were generated using parameter values $\mu_0 = 0.1$ and $w_0 = 1$, but the behavior is generic for any reasonable parameter values. Variation in w_0 advances or delays the turning point by a few years, while μ_0 determines solely the amplitude (the difference between trough and peak). Essentially, the shape of the e-curve is determined by the shape of the w-curve.

The second aspect of elite dynamics is relative elite income, ε (the average elite incomes scaled by GDP per capita). Recollect (Chapter 2) that this quantity in the model is determined by two factors. First, falling relative wages increase the proportion of GDP that is shared among the elites. However, and second, the more elites there are, the smaller the share of each (on average).

Interplay between these two factors results in complex dynamics for this variable (the dashed curve in Figure 13.1).

The Great Depression was associated with a rapid plunge of elite incomes. During the first post-war decade ε stabilized at a relatively low level. After 1955, however, ε began to recover, driven primarily by declining elite numbers in relation to the general population. This period of recovery was interrupted by the Bear Market of 1973–82. After 1978 elite income growth resumed, this time driven primarily by the precipitous fall in w, the wellbeing of the general population. However, at the same time elite numbers began to grow, and when this process became explosive, expanding e started to dilute average elite incomes, which began their decline after 1990.

It is important to remember that ε does not index income (scaled by GDPpc) of some "typical" elite household. Because the distribution of top incomes follows a power law, there is no "typical" elite income. In some extreme cases, when there are too many aspirants to elite positions, the frequency distribution of incomes may become even more unequal than the one described by a power law with a "thick" tail. One such example, the development of a bimodal distribution of salaries to recent law school graduates, will be discussed later in this chapter.

It is better, instead to think of ε as an overall index of elite wellbeing. Low ε can result either from too small a pie that the elites divide among themselves, or too many eaters at the table. Recollect also that the inverse of this quantity, ε^{-1}, enters the elite submodel of the Political Stress Indicator, elite mobilization potential (EMP). As explained in Chapter 2 (*Quantifying Social Pressures for Instability*), EMP has two components: ε^{-1} (which measures the intensity of competition in the economic domain) and e/s (which reflects competition in the political domain—for a limited supply of public offices). Thus, high ε corresponds to low ε^{-1} and a low level of competition for economic resources among the elites. Conversely; low ε/high ε^{-1} indicates a high level of intraelite competition in the economic domain.

Development of Elite Overproduction in the 1990s: Empirical Results

The elite submodel, thus, predicts a very substantial increase in relative elite numbers—roughly, threefold since 1980. After 1990 elite overproduction, according to the model, should lead to an intensification of intraelite competition. How do these predictions square with data?

Overproduction of Top Wealth-Holders

One way to check this result is to examine the dynamics of the numbers of top wealth-holders in proportion of the overall population. Data collected by the New York University economist Edward N Wolff suggest that the percentage of millionaires and multimillionaires expanded between 1983 and 2010 several-fold (Table 13.1). In particular, the expansion rate of households with net worth exceeding 1 million and 10 million (doubling and quadrupling, respectively) brackets the theoretical prediction (threefold increase, see the solid curve in Figure 13.1).

TABLE 13.1 Proportion of millionaires and multimillionaires in relation to the total population, 1983–2007 (Wolff 2012: Table 3). Net worth is calculated in constant 1995 dollars.

Year	Percentage of households with net worth exceeding:		
	1 mln	5 mln	10 mln
1983	2.9	0.29	0.08
1986	3.3	0.32	0.07
1992	3.3	0.29	0.04
1995	3.0	0.48	0.19
1998	4.7	0.74	0.23
2001	5.5	1.00	0.32
2004	5.8	1.00	0.31
2007	6.3	1.26	0.40
2010	6.5	0.90	0.30

There is also evidence that growing numbers of wealth-holders have resulted in greater competition for political office. The clearest evidence of competition is the exploding "price" of election. Thus, the cost of getting elected to the House of Representatives has more than doubled (in inflation-adjusted dollars) between the 1980s and 2012 (Figure 13.2). The total amount spent per House election grew even faster, approaching a billion dollars in 2010.

Even more direct evidence of elite overproduction comes from the data compiled by the Center for Responsive Politics on the number and composition of candidates that compete for House and Senate seats. Between 2000 and 2010, the number of contenders for the House grew by 54 percent, and for the Senate by 61 percent. Note that the number who actually run understates demand for political office. As the price rises (Figure 13.2), it deters an increasing proportion of potential candidates.

Beginning in 2002, the Center for Responsive Politics started keeping track of how many "millionaires" run for Congress (adding together the Senate and the House). The Center's research staff defines millionaire candidates as those who spend at least half a million dollars of their own money on the campaign. According to this definition, between 2004 and 2010 the number of such millionaire candidates nearly doubled. In summary, the empirical trends are entirely consistent with the structural-demographic prediction. Both the candidate numbers and the growing cost of running for office appear to reflect intensifying intraelite competition.

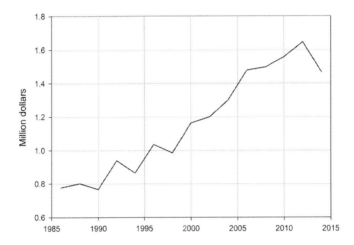

FIGURE 13.2 The average cost of winning an election to the House, 1986–2014 (in millions of inflation-adjusted 2014 dollars). Data source: The Campaign Finance Institute (http://www.cfinst.org/pdf/vital/VitalStats_t1.pdf).

TABLE 13.3 Numbers of candidates (including the primaries) that ran for House and Senate seats: 2000–2012. (Source: Center for Responsive Politics, OpenSecretes.org)

Year	House	Senate	Both chambers	Millionaires
2000	1233	191	1424	*no data*
2002	1299	146	1445	32
2004	1212	189	1401	30
2006	1317	166	1483	42
2008	1377	168	1545	51
2010	1897	308	2205	58
2012	1711	251	1962	48

Overproduction of Elite Aspirants: the MDs

Let us now look at other kinds of elites: highly-paid professionals. As I noted in Chapter 10, during the Progressive Era the medical profession collectively managed to impose a quota on the numbers of Americans receiving MDs. Between 1900 and 1920 the number of medical schools in the US was halved (Figure 10.2). During the late 1950s, and especially after 1970 the trend reversed. This new development resulted in greater numbers of Americans obtaining medical education. Additionally, and perhaps more importantly, more American students went to study at medical schools abroad. Finally, increasing numbers of foreigners holding MDs began emigrating to the US.

By the 1990s these processes had resulted in the overproduction of medical school graduates. We can quantify how this condition developed using the data gathered by the National Resident Matching Program, which has recorded the numbers of applicants for medical residency and internship positions in the US and the supply of positions since 1952.

Before 1970 the number of applicants increased very gradually, and there were many more internships than could be filled (Figure 13.3). During the 1970s, however, the number of applicants surged due to the factors described above. As a result, after 1980 the situation reversed: there were more applicants than positions, and the gap between the two curves grew. Whereas the supply of post-graduate positions for new MDs increased just slightly faster than the general population in the US, which doubled between 1952 and 2012, the number of aspirants to become physicians (which is a direct route to the upper middle class, if not to the wealthiest one percent) increased even faster. Between 1970 and 2012 the number of applicants grew three times as fast as the overall population. The gap between the demand and supply of MD positions became particularly large during the 1990s.

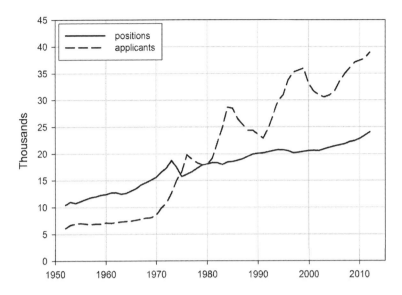

FIGURE 13.3 Total number of first-year post-graduate medical-school positions and the number of applicants, 1952–2012. Data: (NRMP 1985, 2012)

Elite Overproduction and Intraelite Inequality: Emergence of a Bimodal Distribution in JD Salaries

One of the key processes in the Structural-Demographic Theory is the effect of elite overproduction on increasing economic inequality. What is particularly important is that inequality increases not only population-wide (that is, between the elites and the commoners), but also among the elites themselves. The mechanism postulated by the theory that leads to growing intraelite inequality works as follows. When conditions of labor oversupply create a favorable economic conjuncture for the elites, upward social mobility into the elite strata begins to swell elite numbers. After a time lag, the elite numbers increase beyond the ability of society to support all of them. As a result, intraelite competition for the limited number of positions in business and government becomes very intense. The problem is exacerbated by rapidly increasing expectations of the income levels needed to maintain elite status (in part, resulting from conspicuous consumption, which is, in turn, fueled by intraelite competition).

As intraelite competition intensifies, it results in a "winner-take-all" mentality (Frank and Cook 1996). The elite aspirants who end up among the winners tend to be rewarded disproportionately, but at the same time there is a growing proportion of losers. As a result, intraelite inequality explodes:

while a minority enjoys runaway incomes and fortunes, a growing majority are frustrated in their attempts to attain elite status (that is, to secure the income level necessary for maintaining elite status).

Growing intraelite inequality typically results in the distribution of incomes becoming increasingly more right-skewed, with a long "fat tail" reflecting the incomes of the winners. In more extreme cases, however, it is also possible that the distribution of incomes actually becomes bi-modal. That is, it develops two humps, one for the winners and another for the losers, with very few individuals in between.

An example of this dynamic in action is provided by the evolution of the distribution of starting salaries of law school graduates during the 1990s. As we saw earlier in this chapter, starting in the 1970s the numbers of lawyers began to grow much more quickly than the general population, so that over the last 40 years the number of lawyers per 1,000 population has increased from 1.6 to 3.9 (Figure 4.5b). Twenty years into this period, in 1991, the distribution of starting salaries was still unremarkable. There was a mode at $30,000 and a "fat tail" extending to $90,000 (Figure 13.4a). In other words, it was a fairly typical income distribution (which usually have longer right tails, reflecting the incomes of the well-off).

In 1996 the right tail becomes even thicker, and a minor peak appears at $85,000 (Figure 13.4b). But the most dramatic change develops over the next four years. By 2000 there is a second peak at $125,000 which is nearly as high as the peak at $40,000 (Figure 13.4c). In the following years the right peak shifts even farther away from the left peak, to $160,000, and grows in magnitude, reaching an astonishing 25 percent of the total by 2008–9. In the aftermath of the Great Recession and collapsing demand for law school graduates, however, the right peak started declining, although its location, at $160,000 did not shift left (due to, probably, the stickiness of starting lawyer salaries).

During the same period the left peak has hardly advanced and by 2011 was still located at $50,000. Given that the debt burden of an average law school graduate is twice that (over $100,000), it means that many (or even most) of the individuals in the "loser" category will never be able to repay their loans. In other words, the group of elite aspirants who have gone to law school since 2001 have been sorted into two completely separate categories: those who succeeded in entering the top ranks of the elites and those who have failed utterly, with very few people in between.

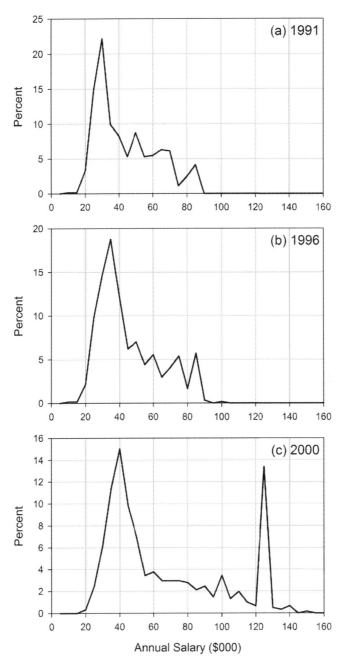

FIGURE 13.4 Frequency distributions of starting full-time salaries for law school graduates. (a) The Class of 1991. (b) The Class of 1996. (c) The Class of 2000. Source: (NALP 2008).

Estimating the Political Stress Indicator (PSI)

We are now in position to estimate the Political Stress Indicator. Combining definitions of PSI components (see *Quantifying Social Pressures for Instability*) yields

$$(13.2) \qquad \Psi = \text{MMP} \times \text{EMP} \times \text{SFD} = w^{-1} \frac{N_{urb}}{N} A_{20-29} \frac{\varepsilon^{-1} e}{s} \frac{Y}{N} (1 - T)$$

Most of the quantities in this equation can be estimated directly. Thus, the main component of MMP, the relative wage w, is the worker wage scaled by GDP per capita (data source: Officer and Williamson 2013). As for the other components of MMP: the urbanization rate, N_{urb}/N, is given in the *Historical Statistics of the United States* (Carter et al. 2004) and the youth bulge index, A_{20-29}, was obtained from the US Census Bureau. On the other hand, the EMP components (relative elite numbers, e, and relative elite incomes, ε) need to be estimated indirectly (see Figure 13.1).

To complete the estimation of PSI we need state-related variables, national debt scaled by GDP (Y/N), and a measure of distrust in government institutions. These quantities are plotted in Figure 13.5.

Prior to 1980, the US national debt behaved in a very predictable way. Each major war (the Revolutionary War, the War of 1812, the Civil War, and World War I) generated a spike in public debt, which was quickly repaid during the post-war years. The same pattern held for World War II. Beginning in 1980, however, the national debt began growing much faster than GDP. This was the first time this had happened during a period of peace.

Unfortunately, data on trust in government institutions (T) is available only from 1958, when the Pew Research Center conducted its first study of this key social indicator. It is likely, however, that the post-war decade enjoyed a low level of distrust in government, similar to the one observed in the late 1950s and 1960s (Figure 13.5). State legitimacy was badly damaged during the 1970s, as a result of the Watergate affair, which led to the resignation of President Richard Nixon. Since the 1970s the levels of social distrust have fluctuated in a cyclic manner. However, each succeeding peak has been higher than the preceding one.

Growing distrust in state institutions is particularly worrying because it can combine with exploding public debt in unpredictable ways. So far, the United States has enjoyed a very low cost of servicing its public debt. However, given a very shallow level of generalized trust in state institutions, there is a real danger that investors in the US debt may suddenly lose confidence in the specific institution: in the willingness and ability of the US government to pay on its obligations. Political polarization and intraelite conflict (themselves a result of elite overproduction and internal competition), which contributed to such policy failures as the 2013 government shutdown, are putting additional stresses on the social system. Sudden collapse of the state's finances has been one of the common triggers releasing pent-up social pressures toward political instability, including in such well-known cases as the English Civil War and the French Revolution (Goldstone 1991).

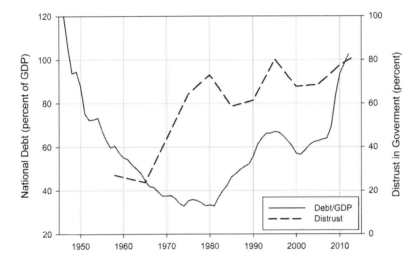

FIGURE 13.5 National debt scaled by GDP and proportion of people who distrust government institutions. Debt/GDP data are taken from the US Department of the Treasury. Distrust in government data are taken from the Pew Research Center (proportion responding "some of the time" or "never" to the question, "How much of the time do you trust the government in Washington?").

With all the ingredients of Eqn. 13.2 accounted for, I can put them together and estimate the dynamics of the overall measure of social pressures for instability, the Political Stress Indicator. Because data for D, a proxy for public distrust in state institutions, is not available for the period before 1958, I focus on the period from 1958 to the present (Figure 13.6).

The Forecast: the "Turbulent 2020s"

The Political Stress Indicator was developed by Goldstone (1991) with the concrete goal of quantifying structural-demographic pressures leading to the English Revolution. His results showed that the PSI can serve as a leading indicator of an outbreak of major political violence in this historical case study—the English Civil War. Goldstone also showed that the method works for the French Revolution of 1789 and the nineteenth-century revolutions in France and Germany. Here I have used the same approach to study social pressures toward instability in the period preceding the American Civil War and in contemporary America. Although I use modified functional forms, the logical core of the approach is the same.

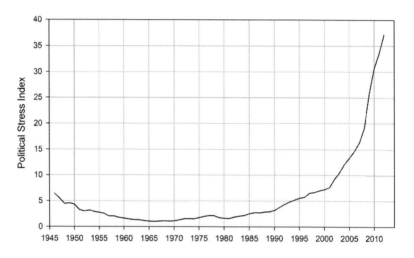

FIGURE 13.6 Estimated Political Stress Indicator, 1946–2012.

The core of Structural-Demographic Theory is concerned, as its name implies, with how the effects of demographic processes on political instability are channeled through social structures. In the case of seventeenth-century England, the chief engine of change was simply a prolonged period of vigorous population growth. Its effects were labor oversupply, elite overproduction, and the increasing fragility of state finances, eventually resulting in the English Revolution and Civil War.

As the Antebellum model shows, the engine of change in the nineteenth-century US was in one way more complex, in another simpler. As in England, there was vigorous rural population growth, resulting in massive migration to the cities. But there were additional processes: immigration from Europe and migration to the West (these processes were roughly of the same order of magnitude and tended to cancel one another out). On the other hand, given the very limited autonomy of the state from the elites, we did not need to track the state's fiscal distress (SFD).

In contemporary America, forces driving structural-demographic dynamics are much more complex. They include internal population growth, immigration, globalization, increased labor participation by women, and changing cultural attitudes (which I proxied by real minimum wage). The end result, however, was the same in all three cases—agrarian England, the industrializing United States, and post-industrial America. A growing gap between labor supply and labor demand led to falling relative wages. This was then followed by elite overproduction, intraelite competition and conflict, and increasing sociopolitical instability.

In the two historical cases, pent-up structural-demographic pressures eventually found a release in bloody civil wars. Similar to the case of England in the seventeenth century, investigated by Goldstone, the Antebellum model, developed here for nineteenth-century America, shows that PSI was an accurate leading indicator of these catastrophic outbreaks of political instability. However, the Antebellum model is not limited to constructing the PSI; it also delves into the interlinked mechanisms explaining why the PSI components, specifically MMP and EMP, grew in the decades preceding the American Civil War. Thus, the Antebellum model provides an explanation of why relative wages began declining after 1820 and why an elite overproduction problem developed after 1840 (Figure 9.4).

The contemporary model also investigates the causal factors responsible for trend reversals in the relative wage and relative elite numbers. Note that the dynamics of these variables during the twentieth century follow the same qualitative pattern as in the nineteenth century. In particular, the relative wage began declining roughly 20 years before relative elite numbers started increasing (Figure 13.1).

In the contemporary case we have, so far, avoided a full-blown civil war. Nevertheless we should pay close heed to the lessons from the historical cases, in which the PSI was a reliable lead indicator of catastrophic outbreaks of political violence. The estimated PSI began increasing after 1980, and has grown very rapidly after 2000 (Figure 13.6). Furthermore, during the decade of 2011–20, the structural conditions continue favoring an increase in social pressures toward instability (Turchin 2010).

We saw that demand for labor has been stagnating since 2000, and this trend is likely to continue to 2020. The reason is that we are currently in the negative phase of the Kondratiev cycle, and are unlikely to emerge from it until after 2020 (Akaev and Sadovnichiy 2009). At the same time, the supply of labor continues to increase due to population growth. According to the projections of the US Census Bureau, the numbers of youths aged 20–29 will peak in 2017–18, before they begin declining. In other words, the youth bulge is set to continue growing until the end of the decade and the growing gap between the supply and demand for labor will continue to depress real wages. Falling wages, in turn, will feed into the elite submodel; so both MMP and EMP are expected to rise.

As I wrote in 2010 (Turchin 2010), we are rapidly approaching a historical cusp at which American society will be particularly vulnerable to violent upheaval. However, a disaster similar in magnitude to the American Civil War is not foreordained. On the contrary, we may be the first society that is capable of perceiving, if dimly, the deep structural forces pushing us to the brink. This means that we are uniquely equipped to take policy measures that will prevent our falling over it.

14

Conclusion: Two Ages of Discord

A central goal of this book (Chapter 1) has been to test the predictions of the Structural-Demographic Theory (SDT) using the history of the United States as an empirical case-study. Because SDT was developed, and first tested, on pre-industrial states, applying it to an industrializing (and post-industrial) society represents a major extension of the theory's scope. This required a certain degree of reformulation, especially of SDT's neo-Malthusian component (see Chapter 1: *From Agrarian to Industrial Societies*). Nevertheless, the comparisons between theoretical predictions and data in this book represent a true test of the theory, because data were not used when deriving predictions. In the statistical jargon, such a comparison represents an "out-of-sample" test.

Let's begin the overview of empirical results with the observed dynamics of political instability. As I discussed in Chapter 1, all large-scale, state-level historical societies experience multicentennial waves of political instability—secular cycles. In many cases, there is an additional cycle of roughly 50 years in period superimposed on the longer secular cycles. My analysis (Chapter 6) found that a very similar pattern holds for the United States. There were two periods in American history that were remarkably free of political violence: the Era of Good Feelings (the 1820s) and the post-war prosperity of the 1950s, which I termed the Era of Good Feelings II. Between these two dates, the United States experienced a massive wave of sociopolitical instability (Figure 6.1). After the quiet 1950s, however, incidents of political violence again became more frequent and now we may be in the middle of another wave of sociopolitical instability.

The 50-year periodicity was also prominent in the data on American political violence. Instability spikes were observed around 1970, 1920, and 1870 (Figure 6.1a). Extending this sequence back, we would expect a spike at 1820, which is missing in the data. It is interesting that the American Revolutionary War (1775–83) fits the 50-year pattern quite well, especially if we note that the political upheavals, which eventually blew up into a full-scale revolt, started with resistance against the Stamp Act, passed by the British Parliament in 1765. Thus, we have the following progression (now going forward in time):

1770–80, (missing 1820 spike), c.1870, c.1920, c.1970, and—extending the sequence to the near future—c.2020?

The missing 1820 spike is not particularly bothersome because my analysis of structural-demographic pressures for instability showed that the 1820s were remarkable in having high and growing popular well-being, and absence of any signs of elite overproduction (Chapter 9). Thus, the 1820 spike was probably suppressed due to very favorable structural-demographic conditions obtaining at the time. The mathematical model that incorporated both secular and 50-year cycles shows that favorable structural-demographic conditions indeed suppress the 50-year cycle (Chapter 2: *Fathers-and-Sons Cycles and Secular Waves: A Model with Multiple Feedbacks*).

Secular movements of internal instability were generally paralleled by the waxing and waning of other structural-demographic variables (Figure 7.1). For easy reference, Figure 14.1 reproduces the overall secular trend, obtained by averaging all time-series in Figure 7.1. When the curve is above 0 (horizontal broken line), the social system is in the disintegrative phase (and vice versa, the integrative phases are when the curve is below 0). Note that the first (complete) disintegrative phase ends in c.1930. Following the convention that we used in *Secular Cycles* (Turchin and Nefedov 2009), I date the end of American Secular Cycle I to 1930. Part III of this book traced the structural-demographic during this complete secular cycle, Paying particular attention to the Jackson Era and Progressive Era trend reversals (the periods when the secular curve reversed its direction). Part IV, correspondingly, looked at the developments since 1930—the second, incomplete secular cycle in American history.

The duration of the first American cycle (1780–1930) at 150 years was somewhat shorter than periods typical for pre-industrial European societies (around two centuries, and sometimes longer). Models of demographic-structural dynamics, developed in *Historical Dynamics* (Turchin 2003b), suggest why. One general finding there was that the periods of secular cycles are mostly determined by population growth parameters. In the American case, growth of the native population has been supplemented by massive immigration waves. In the middle of the nineteenth century immigration essentially doubled population growth rates. The direct effect of such inflows was that the conditions of labor oversupply were achieved more rapidly than in typical agrarian societies, which relied on predominantly internal sources for population growth.

In summary, the empirical analysis of the overall structural-demographic trend (Part II) showed that the various indicators waxed and waned roughly in agreement with the predictions of the SDT. Next, let's consider more formally the three fundamental SDT predictions that explain the dynamics of instability (Table 1.2).

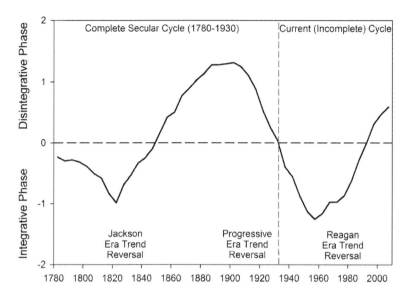

FIGURE 14.1 Anatomy of American secular cycles. The solid curve traces out the average secular trend (it is the same as the thick gray curve in Figure 7.1).

Labor oversupply principle. Labor supply/demand ratio is affected by a complex interplay of factors. Because the combination of factors affecting this quantity changed over American history, I used two versions of the general model (developed in Chapter 2), one for the nineteenth century (the Antebellum Model, Chapter 9) and another for the twentieth century (the Contemporary Model, Chapter 12). Both models were successful in summarizing the empirical trends, and confirmed the key role of labor oversupply in depressing wages. However, whereas in the Antebellum model labor supply/demand ratio was the main factor determining relative wages, in the Contemporary Model there was an additional factor capturing the influence on non-market, "cultural" forces.

The conclusion, thus, is that the labor oversupply principle is empirically supported, although in contemporary societies this is not the only factor that influences wages. Unlike the laissez-faire capitalism of the nineteenth century, today social norms and institutions can play a major role in restraining the influence of the supply/demand ratio on the price of human labor.

Elite overproduction principle. Overall, we saw that the relative wage (typical wage divided by GDPpc) went through two cycles since 1780 (see Figure 3.4). The second general principle states that declining relative wages (thus, shifting the rewards of economic growth from commoners to the elites) should result in growing numbers of elites (and elite aspirants), as well as an increase in their consumption levels. This development, in turn, leads to the conditions of elite overproduction: growing wealth inequality, increased intraelite competition, and political fragmentation. The data reviewed in Chapters 3 and 4 strongly support such a relationship (see Figure 14.2).

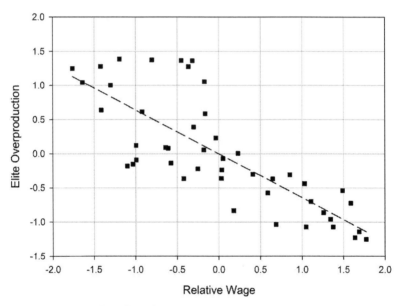

FIGURE 14.2 The effect of relative wage (typical wages scaled by GDPpc, from Figure 3.7) on elite overproduction (the average of three elite proxies in Figure 4.10a). Both variables were standardized to mean = 0 and variance = 1.

Instability principle. The final general principle connects sociopolitical instability to demographic-structural pressures. In order of importance, these pressures are (1) **elite overproduction** leading to intraelite competition and conflict, (2) **popular immiseration**, resulting from falling living standards, and (3) the **fiscal crisis of the state** (Table 1.2). Figure 14.3 shows that there is a strong positive relationship between instability and a measure that combines the first two pressures, elite overproduction and popular immiseration. I focus here on the first two factors because the fiscal crisis of the state is not always present as a factor contributing to sociopolitical instability, as discussed in *Secular Cycles* (Turchin and Nefedov 2009: Section 10.4) and in Chapter 1 of this book (*Reformulating the Theory for Modern Societies*).

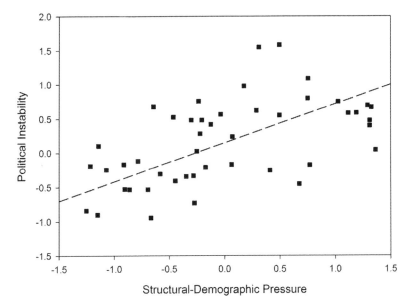

FIGURE 14.3 The effect of structural-demographic pressure (combining popular immiseration and elite overproduction proxies) on political instability in the United States (1780–2010).

Finally, let us review the results of a more quantitative approach: using the Political Stress Index (PSI) as a predictor of mounting political violence. Because state-related pressures for instability were not important in the nineteenth century, the Antebellum Model (Chapter 9) only includes two components: Mass Mobilization Potential and Elite Mobilization Potential. The Contemporary Model (Chapters 12 and 13), on the other hand, includes all three components (adding State Fiscal Distress). The outputs of these two models are depicted in Figure 14.4 together with additional relevant data.

Figure 14.4 brings together several major strands developed in this book and, thus, can serve as a graphical summary of its main conclusions. First, it plots the long-term dynamics of a population wellbeing index, which averages economic, health, and social measures of wellbeing (Figure 3.7). Second, it traces the dynamics of the PSI calculated by the Antebellum and Contemporary Models. These two sets of curves focus on slowly developing structural variables—on the *longue durée*, to borrow the terminology use by the French Annales School. The figure then maps a number of significant events and key periods of American history on these *longue durée* dynamics.

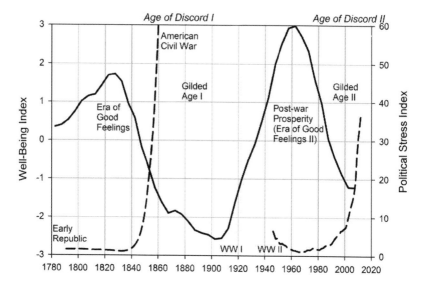

FIGURE 14.4 Ages of Discord: mapping the *longue durée* dynamics of popular wellbeing index (solid curve) and the Political Stress Index (broken curve) onto American "event history".

What we see is that the PSI was an accurate leading indicator of rising tide of political instability in the Antebellum America, which culminated in the American Civil War. As to the present, we live in times of intensifying structural-demographic pressures for instability. The PSI has not yet reached the same high level that triggered the Civil War of 1861–65. However, its explosive growth should be a matter of grave concern for all of us—our economic and political elites, as well as the general public. Will we be capable of taking collective action to avoid the worst of the impending demographic-structural crisis? I hope so. More, I hope that the theory and data explained in this book will contribute to finding solutions that will help us find a non-violent escape from the crisis.

References Cited

Akaev, A. A., and V. A. Sadovnichiy. 2009. [Акаев, А.А., Садовничий, В.А. О новой методологии долгосрочного циклического прогнозирования динамики развития мировой и российской экономики].

Allen, R. C. 2003. Farm to Factory: A Reinterpretation of the Soviet Industrial Revolution. Princeton University Press Princeton, NJ.

Ames, M. 2005. Going Postal: Rage, Murder, and Rebellion from Reagan's Workplaces to Clinton's Columbine and Beyond. Soft Skull Press, Brooklyn, NY.

Andrews, T. G. 2010. Killing for Coal: America's Deadliest Labor War. Harvard University Press, Cambrdige, MA.

Angeles, L. 2007. GDP per capita or real wages? Making sense of conflicting views on pre-industrial Europe. Explorations in Economic History 45:147-163.

Anonymous. 1901. Editorial Comment. The Bankers' Magazine 62:497-514.

Ashworth, J. 1997. The Sectionalization of Politics, 1845-1860. Pages 33-46 *in* W. L. Barney, editor. A Companion to 19th Century America. Blackwell, Oxford.

Baltzell, E. D. 1964. The Protestant Establishment: Aristocracy and Class in America. Yale University Press, New Haven.

Baltzell, E. D. 1987. Philadelphia Gentlemen: The Making of a National Upper Class. Transaction Publishers, New Brunswick (USA).

Baltzell, E. D. 1991. The Protestant Establishment Revisited. Transaction Publishers, New Brunswick.

Barnes, H. 2008. Never Been a Time: The 1917 Race Riot That Sparked the Civil Rights Movement Walker, New York.

Beard, C. A. 1927. The rise of American civilization. Macmillan, New York.

Beard, C. A., and M. R. Beard. 1922. History of the United States. Macmillan, New York.

Beckert, S. 2001. The Monied Metropolis: New York City and the Consolidation of the American Bourgeoisie, 1850-1896. Cambridge University Press, Cambridge.

Bernanke, B. S. 2000. Essays on the Great Depression. Princeton University Press, Princeton.

Binder, S., and F. Maltzman. 2009. The politics of confirming federal judges. Judicature 92:320-329.

Bishop, B. 2008. The Big Sort: Why the Clustering of Like-Minded America Is Tearing Us Apart. Houghton Mifflin, Boston.

Blanchard, O. 1997. Macroeconomics. Prentice Hall, Upper Saddle River, NJ.

Blee, K. M. 2005. Racial violence in the United States. Ethnic and Racial Studies 28:599-619.

Blumstein, A., and R. Rosenfeld. 1998. Explaining Recent Trends in U.S. Homicide Rates. Journal of Criminal Law and Criminology 88:1175-1216.

Bois, G. 1984. The Crisis of feudalism. Cambridge University Press, Cambridge.

Bois, G. 2000. La grande dépression médiévale: XIVe-XVe siècles. Presses Universitaires de France, Paris.

Bordo, M. D., C. Goldin, and E. N. White. 1998. The Defining Moment Hypothesis: The Introduction. Pages 1-20 in M. D. Bordo, C. Goldin, and E. N. White, editors. The Defining Moment: The Great Depression and the Americna Economy in the Twentieth Century. Universtiy of Chicago Press, Chicago.

Borjas, G. J. 2009. The Analytics of the Wage Effect of Immigration (March 2009). NBER Working Paper Series No. 14796.

Borjas, G. J. 2013. Immigration and the American Worker: A Review of the Academic Literature. Center for Immigration Studies. April 2013.

Bowles, S. 2006. Group competition, reproductive leveling and the evolution of human altruism. Science 314:1569-1572.

Bowles, S. 2009. Did Warfare Among Ancestral Hunter-Gatherers Affect the Evolution of Human Social Behaviors? Science 324:1293-1298.

Bowles, S., and H. Gintis. 2011. A Cooperative Species: Human Reciprocity and Its Evolution. Princeton University Press, Princeton.

Braudel, F. 1988. The Identity of France. Volume II. People and Production. Harper Collins, New York.

Brinkley, A. 1997. Prosperity, Depression, and War, 1920-1945. Pages 133-158 in E. Foner, editor. The New American History. Temple University Press, Philadelphia.

Burch, P. H. 1981. Elites in American History. Vol. II: The Civil War to the New Deal. Homes & Meier, New York.

Burton, V. 2006. Civil War and Reconstruction, 1861-1877. Pages 47-60 in W. L. Barney, editor. A Companion to 19th Century America. Blackwell, Oxford.

Calavita, K. 1984. U.S. Immigration Law and the Control of Labor: 1820-1924. Academic Press, London.

Carroll, A. B., K. J. Lipartito, J. E. Post, and P. H. Werhane. 2012. Corporate Responsibility: The American Experience. Cambridge University Press, Cambridge.

Carson, S. A. 2009. Health, Wealth, and Inequality: A Contribution to the Debate about the Relationship between Inequality and Health. Historical Methods 42:43-54.

Carter, S. B., S. S. Gartner, M. R. Haines, A. L. Olmstead, R. Sutch, and G. Wright, editors. 2004. Historical Statistics of the United States: Millennial Edition. Cambridge University Press, New York.

Casti, J. L. 2010. Mood Matters: From Rising Skirt Lengths to the Collapse of World Poers. Copernicus Books, New York.

Chernow, R. 1998. Titan: The Life of John D. Rockefeller, Sr. Warner Books, London.

Choi, J.-K., and S. Bowles. 2007. The coevolution of parochial altruism and war. Science 318:636-640.

Chojnacki, S. 1994. Social Identity in Renaissance Venice: The Second Serrata. Renaissance studies 8:341-358.

Clark, D. S. 2003. American legal education: yesterday and today. International Journal of the Legal Profession 10:93-108.

Collins, R. 1979. The credential society: an historical sociology of education and stratification. Academic Press, New York.

Cornell, T. J. 1995. The beginnings of Rome: Italy and Rome from the Bronze Age to the Punic Wars (c.1000-264 BC). Routledge, London.

Coser, L. A. 1956. The Functions of Social Conflict. Free Press, Glencoe, IL.

Dahl, R. A. 1961. Who Governs? Democracy and Power in an American City. Yale University Press, New Haven.

Dawkins, R. 1976. The Selfish Gene. Oxford University Press, New York.

Dawley, A. 2005. The Abortive Rule of the Big Money. Pages 149-180 in S. Fraser and G. Gerstle, editors. Ruling America: A History of Wealth and Power in a Democracy. Harvard University Press, Cambridge, MA.

de Sanctis, G. 1953. Storia dei Romani. Nuova Italia, Firenze.

Diamond, J., and J. A. Robinson. 2010. Natural Experiments of History. Belknap, Cambridge, MA.

Diner, S. J. 1998. A Very Different Age: Americans in the Progressive Era. Hill and Wang, New York.

Domhoff, G. W. 2010a. Who Rules America" Power, Politics, and Social Change. 6th ed. McGraw-Hill, New York.

Domhoff, G. W. 2010b. WhoRulesAmerica.net http://sociology.ucsc.edu/whorules-america/index.html.

Domhoff, G. W., and M. J. Webber. 2011. Class and Power in the New Deal: Corporate Moderates, Souhtern Democrats, and the Liberal-Labor Coalition. Stanford Univbersity Press, Stanford, CA.

Dye, T. R., and L. H. Zeigler. 1970. The Irony of Democracy: An Uncommon Introduction to American Politics. Wadsworth, Belmont, CA.

Easterlin, R. 1980. Birth and Fortune. Basic Books, New York.

Easterlin, R. A. 1976. Population change and farm settlement in the northern United States. Journal of Economic History 36:45-75.

Eckberg, D. L. 1995. Estimates of Early Twentieth-Century U.S. Homicide Rates: an Econometric Forecasting. Demography 32:1-16.

Eisner, M. 2003. Secular trends of violent crime: evidence and theoretical interpretations. Crime and Justice: an Annual Review 31.

Epperson, J. F. 2005. Causes of the Civil War. OTTN Publishing, Stockton, NJ.

Ferguson, R. W., and W. L. Wascher. 2004. Distinguished Lecture on Economics in Government: Lessons from past Productivity Booms. Journal of Economic Perspectives 18:3-28.

Fishback, P. V., M. R. Haines, and S. Kantor. 2007. Births, Deaths, and New Deal Relief During the Great Depression. Review of Economics and Statistics 89:1-14.

Fogel, R. W. 1966. The New Economic History. I. Its Findings and Methods. Economic History Review 19:642-656.

Fogel, R. W. 1986. Nutrition and the decline in mortality since 1700: some preliminary findings.*in* S. L. Engerman and R. E. Gallman, editors. Long-term factors in American economic growth. University of Chicago Press, Chicago.

Fogel, R. W. 2004. The escape from hunger and premature death, 1700-2000. Cambridge University Press, Cambridge.

Fogel, R. W., R. A. Galantine, and R. L. Manning, editors. 1992. Without Consent or Contract: The Rise and Fall of American Slavery. Vol. II. Evidence and Methods. W. W. Norton, New York.

Foner, E. 1988. Reconstruction: America's Unfinished Revolution, 1863-1877. Harper & Row, New York.

Foner, E. 1997. Slavery, the Civil War, and Reconstruction. Pages 85-106 *in* E. Foner, editor. The New American History. Revised and Expanded Edition. Temple University Press, Philadelphia.

Frank, R. H., T. Gilovich, and D. T. Regan. 1993. Does Studying Economics Inhibit Cooperation? Journal of Economic Perspectives 7:159-171.

Frank, S. A. 2003. Repression of competition and the evolution of cooperation. Evolution 57:693-705.

Fraser, D. 1978. Resignation Letter from the Labor-Management Group. July 17, 1978.

Freeman, J. B. 2011. When Congress Was Armed and Dangerous. New York Times (January 11, 2011).

Gardner, A. 2008. The Price equation. Current Biology 18:R198–R202.

Gilje, P. A. 1996. Rioting in America. Indiana University Press, Bloomington, IN.

Gleick, J. 1987. Chaos: Making a New Science. Viking, New York.

Goldin, C., and R. A. Margo. 1992. The Great Compression: the Wage Structure in the United States at Mid-Century. Quarterly Journal of Economics 57:1-34.

Goldstone, J. A. 1991. Revolution and Rebellion in the Early Modern World. University of California Press, Berkeley, CA.

Grant, H. R. 1983. Self-Help in the 1890s Depression. Iowa State University Press, Ames, Iowa.

Griffin, P. 2007. American Leviathan: Empire, Nation, and Revolutionary Frontier Hill and Wang, New York.

Grimstead, D. 1998. American Mobbing, 1828-1861: Towards Civil War. Oxford University Press, New York.

Hacker, J. S., and P. Pierson. 2010. Winner-Take-All Politics: How Washington Made the Rich Richer - and Turned its Back on the Middle Class. Simon and Schuster, New York.

Haines, M. R. 1996. Long-term marriage patterns in the United States from colonial times to the present. The History of the Family 1:15-39.

Hajnal, J. 1965. European Marriage Patterns in Perspective. Pages 101-143 in D. V. Glass and D. E. C. Eversley, editors. Population in History. Arnold, London.

Hirsch, J. S. 2002. Riot and Remembrance: The Tulsa Race War and its Legacy. Houghton Mifflin, New York.

Howe, D. W. 2008. What Hath God Wrought: The Transformation of America, 1815-1848. Oxford University Press, New York.

Huston, J. L. 2003. Calculating the Value of the Union: Slavery, Property, and the Economic Origins of the Civil War. University of North Carolina Press, Chapel Hill.

Jaher, F. C. 1982. The Urban Establishment: Upper Strata in Boston, New York, Charleston, Chicago, and Los Angeles. University of Illinois Press, Urbana, IL.

Johnston, L., and S. H. Williamson. 2013. What Was the U.S. GDP Then? http://www.measuringworth.org/usgdp/. MeasuringWorth.

Jones, A. H. 1977. American Colonial Wealth: Documents and Methods, Volume 3. Arno Press, New York.

Kane, T. 2004. Global U.S. Troop Deployment, 1950–2003. A Report of The Heritage Center for Data Analysis. CDA04-11 October 27, 2004.

Kane, T. 2011. Boots on the ground: Where American troops have served during the past 60 years. The Economist online. Nov 21st 2011.

Karabel, J. 2005. The Chosen: The Hidden History of Admission and Exclusion at Harvard, Yale, and Princeton. Houghton Mifflin, Boston.

Kay, A. C., S. C. Wheeler, J. A. Bargh, and L. Rossa. 2004. Material priming: The influence of mundane physical objects on situational construal and competitive behavioral choice. Organizational Behavior and Human Decision Processes 95:83-96.

Kelly, R. C. 2000. Warless Societies and the Origin of War. University of Michigan Press, Ann Arbor, MI.

Klein, H. S. 2004. A Population History of the United States. Cambridge University Press, Cambridge.

Kohn, G. C., editor. 2001. Encyclopedia of Plague and Pesilence: From Ancient Times to the Present. Revised Edition. Checkmark Books, New York.

Kolko, G. 1963. The Triumph of Conservatism: A Reinterpretation of American History, 1900-1916. Free Press, New York.

Komlos, J. 1985. Stature and nutrition in the Habsburg Monarchy: the standard of living and economic development in the eighteenth century. American Historical Review 90:1149-1161.

Komlos, J. 2010. The recent decline in the height of African-American women. Economics and Human Biology 8:58-66.

Komlos, J., and M. Baur. 2004. From the tallest to (one of) the fattest: the enigmatic fate of the American population in the 20th century. Economics and Human Biology 2:57-74.

Korotayev, A., A. Malkov, and D. Khaltourina. 2006. Introduction to Social Macrodynamics: Secular Cycles and Millennial Trends. URSS, Moscow.

Korotayev, A., J. Zinkina, S. Kobzeva, J. Bozhevolnov, D. Khaltourina, A. Malkov, and S. Malkov. 2011. A Trap at the Escape from the Trap? Demographic-Structural Factors of Political Instability in Modern Africa and West Asia. Cliodynamics 2:276–303.

Krauthammer, C. 2009. Medicalizing mass murder. Washington Post, November 13, 2009.

Lamoreaux, N. R. 1985. The Great Merger Movement in American Business, 1895-1904. Cambridge University Press, Cambridge.

Lee, J. S. 1931. The periodic recurrence of internecine wars in China. The China Journal (March-April Issue):111-163.

Levin, M. B. 1971. Political Hysteria in America: The Democratic Capacity for Repression. Basic Books, NY.

Levine, S. B. 1980. The Rise of American Boarding Schools and the Development of a National Upper Class. Social Problems 28:63-94.

Levy, S. G. 1969. A 150-year study of political violence in the United States. Pages 84-100 in H. D. Graham and T. R. Gurr, editors. The History of Violence in America: Historical and Comparative Approaches. Praeger, New York.

Levy, S. G. 1991. Political violence in the United States, 1819-1968 [Computer File]. Inter-University Consortium for Political and Social Research, Ann Arbor, MI.

Li, Q., and J. S. Racine. 2006. Nonparametric Econometrics: Theory and Practice. Princeton University Press, Princeton.

Lieberman, V. 2003. Strange Parallels: Southeast Asia in Global Context, c.800-1830. Volume I: Integration on the Mainland. Cambridge University Press, Cambridge.

Lynch, M. J. 2007. Big prisons, big dreams: crime and the failure of America's penal system. Rutgers Uuniversity Press, New Brunswick.

Macunovich, D. J. 2002. Birth Quake: The Baby Boom and Its Aftershocks. Universtiy of Chicago Press, Chicago.

Madden, T. F. 2008. Empires of Trust: How Rome Built - and America Is Building - a New World. Dutton, New York.

Maguire, K., editor. 2010. Sourcebook of Criminal Justice Statistics. http://www.al-bany.edu/sourcebook/index.html.

Malamud, M. 2008. Ancient Rome and Modern America Wiley-Blackwell, New York.

Mann, M. 1986. The sources of social power. I. A history of power from the beginning to A.D. 1760. Cambridge University Press, Cambridge, UK.

Margo, R. A. 1992. Wages and prices during the Antebellum period: a survey and new evidence. Pages 173-210 *in* R. E. Gallman and J. J. Wallis, editors. American Economic Growth and Standards of Living before the Civil War. University of Chicago Press, Chicago.

Margo, R. A. 1994. The price of housing in New York City. NBER Historical Paper No. 63.

Margo, R. A. 2000. The Labor Force in the Nineteenth Century. Pages 207-243 *in* S. L. E. a. R. E. Gallman, editor. The Cambridge Economic History of the United States Vol. 2: The Long Nineteenth Century. Cambridge University Press, Cambridge.

Marwell, G., and R. Ames. 1981. Economists Free Ride, Does Anyone Else? Journal of Public Economics 15:295-310.

May, R. M., and R. M. Anderson. 1991. Infectious diseases of humans: dynamics and control. Oxford University Press, Oxford.

Mayer, G. 2004. Union Membership Trends in the United States. Congressional Research Service, Washington, DC.

McCarty, N., K. T. Poole, and H. Rosenthal. 2006. Polarized America: The Dance of Ideology and Unequal Riches. MIT Press, Boston.

McCormick, R. L. 1997. Public Life in Industrial America, 1877-1917. Pages 107-132 *in* E. Foner, editor. The New American History. Temple University Press, Philadelphia.

McWhirter, C. 2011. Red Summer: The Summer of 1919 and the Awakening of Black America. Henry Holt, New York.

Mills, C. W. 1956. The Power Elite. Oxford University Press, New York.

Monkkonen, E. 2001. Murder in New York City. University of California Press.

Murphy, C. 2008. Are We Rome? The Fall of an Empire and the Fate of America Houghton Mifflin, New York.

NALP. 2008. Salaries for New Lawyers: How Did We Get Here? NALP Bulletin, January 2008. .

NALP. 2010. Market for Law Graduates Changes with Recession: Class of 2009 Faced New Challenges. NALP Press Release, July 22, 2010. National Association for Law Placement, Washington, DC. URL: http://www.nalp.org/09salpressrel.

Nash, G. D. 1992. The Crucial Era: The Great Depression and World War II, 1929-1945. Waveland Press, Prospect Heights, Ill.

Nefedov, S. 1999. The method of demographic cycles in a study of socioeconomic history of preindustrial society. PhD dissertaion, Ekaterinburg University (in Russian), Ekaterinburg, Russia.

Newman, K. S. 2004. Rampage: The Social Roots of School Shootings. Basic Books, New York.

NRMP. 1985. NRMP Data: March 1985. NRMP.org.

NRMP. 2012. Results and Data: 2012 Main Residency Match. NRMP.org.

Officer, L. H. 2007. An improved long-run consumer price index dor the United States. Historical Methods 40:135-147.

Officer, L. H. 2010. Annual Wages in the United States Unskilled Labor and Manufacturing Workers, 1774-Present," MeasuringWorth. URL: http://www.measuringworth.com/uswage/.

Officer, L. H., and S. H. Williamson. 2009. Annual Wages in the United States, 1774-2008. MeasuringWorth. URL: http://www.measuringworth.org/uswages/.

Officer, L. H., and S. H. Williamson. 2013. Annual Wages in the United States, 1774-Present. MeasuringWorth. URL: http://www.measuringworth.com/uswages/.

Okasha, S. 2007. Evolution and the Levels of Selection Oxford University Press, New York.

Patel, K. K. 2016. The New Deal: A Global History. Princeton University Press, Princeton, NJ.

Pessen, E. 1973. Riches, Class, and Power before the Civil War. D. C. Heath, Lexington, MA.

Phillips, K. 2002. Wealth and Democracy: A Political History of the American Rich. Broadway Books, New York.

Phillips-Fein, K. 2009. Invisible Hands: The Businessmen's Crusade against the New Deal. Norton, New York.

Pierson, G. W. 1983. A Yale Book of Numbers: Historical Statistics of the College and University 1701-1976. Yale University Press, New Haven.

Piketty, T., and E. Saez. 2003. Income Inequality in the United States, 1913-1998. Quarterly Journal of Economics 118:1-39.

Poole, K. T., and H. Rosenthal. 1984. The Polarization of American Politics. Journal of Politics 46:1061-1079.

Poole, K. T., and H. Rosenthal. 1997. Congress; A Political-Ecojnomic History of Roll Call Voting Oxford University Press, New York.

Portes, A., and E. Vickstrom. 2011. Diversity, Social Capital, and Cohesion. Annual Review of Sociology 37:461-479.

Potter, D. M. 1976. The Impending Crisis, 1848-1861. Harper and Row, New York.

Potts, D. 2006. The Myth of the Great Depression. Scribe, Melbourne.

Price, G. R. 1970. Selection and covariance. Nature 227:520–521.

Price, G. R. 1972. Extension of covariance selection mathematics. Annals of Human Genetics 35:485–490.

Putnam, R. D. 2000. Bowling Alone: The Collapse and Revival of American Community. Simon and Schuster, New York.

Putnam, R. D. 2007. E Pluribus Unum: diversity and community in the twenty-first century: the 2006 Johan Skytte Prize lecture. . 30:137–74

Rosenblum G. 1973. Immigrant Workers: Their Impact on. Scandinavian Political Studies 30:137-174.

Reinhart, C. M., and K. Rogoff. 2009. This Time is Different: Eight Centuries of Financial Folly. Princeton University Press, Princeton.

Richards, L. L. 2000. The Slave Power: The Free North and Southern Domination, 1780-1860. Louisiana State University, Baton Rouge.

Richerson, P., and J. Henrich. 2012. Tribal Social Instincts and the Cultural Evolution of Institutions to Solve Collective Action Problems. Cliodynamics 3:38-80.

Richerson, P. J., and R. Boyd. 2005. Not by Genes Alone: How Culture Transformed Human Evolution. University of Chicago Press, Chicago.

Roth, R. 2001. Child murder in New England. Social Science History 25:101-147.

Roth, R. 2009. The American Homicide. Harvard University Press, Cambridge, MA.

Rothman, A. 2005. The "Slave Power" in the united States, 1783-1865. Pages 64-91 in S. Fraser and G. Gerstle, editors. Ruling America: A History of Wealth and Power in a Democracy. Harvard University Press, Cambridge, MA.

Saez, E. 2013. Striking it Richer: The Evolution of Top Incomes in the United States (Updated with 2011 estimates). January 23, 2013.

Samuelson, P. A., and W. D. Nordhaus. 1998. Economics. 16th edition. McGraw-Hill, New York.

Sanderson, W. C. 1979. Quantitative Aspects of Marriage, Fertility and Family Limitation in Nineteenth Century America: Another Application of the Coale Specifications. Demography 16:339-358.

Savage, L. 1990. Thunder in the Mountains: The West Virginia Mine War, 1920-21. University of Pittsburgh Press, Pittsburgh.

Schapiro, M. O. 1982. Land availability and fertility in the United States, 1760-1870. Journal of Economic History 42:577-600.

Schlesinger, A. M. J. 1957-60. The Age of Roosevelt. 3 vols. Houghton Mifflin, Boston.

Schlesinger, A. M. J. 1986. The cycles of American history. Houghton Mifflin, Boston.

Schmitt, J., and B. Zipperer. 2009. Dropping the Ax: Illegal Firings During Union Election Campaigns, 1951-2007. Center for Economic and Policy Research.

Schumann, R. E. 2001. Compensation from World War II through the Great Society. Compensation and Working Conditions Fall 2001:23-27.

Shoemaker, N. 2004. A Strange Likeness: Becoming Red and White in Eighteenth-Century America. Oxford University Press, New York.

Shogan, R. 2004. The Battle of Blair Mountain: The Story of America's Largest Union Uprising. Westview Press, Boulder, CO.

Shouter, D. C. 2010. A Classification of American Wealth: History and genealogy of the wealthy families of America. Internet Resource. http://www.raken.com/american_wealth/encyclopedia/index.asp

Silver, P. 2008. Our Savage Neighbors: How Indian War Transformed Early America. W. W. Norton, New York.

Simmel, G. 1955. Conflict. The Web of Group-Affiliations. Free Press, Glencoe, IL.

Sinclair, B. 2006. Party wars: polarization and the politics of national policy making. University of Oklahoma Press, Norman.

Sinclair, B. 2009. Partisan Polarization, Rule Divergence and Legislative Productivity. Prepared for the Conference on Bicameralism Sponsored by the Political Institutions and Public Choice Program, Duke University; March 27 & 28, 2009.

Skocpol, T. 1979. States and social revolutions: a comparative analysis of France, Russia, and China. Cambridge University Press, Cambridge, UK.

Smil, V. 2010. Why America Is Not a New Rome. MIT Press, Cambridge.

Smiley, G. 2002. Rethinking the Great Depression. Ivan R. Dee, Chicago.

Solometo, J. 2006. The dimensions of war. Pages 24-65 in E. N. Arkush and M. W. Allen, editors. The Archaeology of Warfare: Prehistories of Raiding and Conquest. University Press of Florida, Gainesville, FL.

Soltow, L. 1975. Men and Wealth in the United States, 1850-1870. Yale University Press, New Haven, CT.

Sorokin, P. A. 1937. Social and cultural dynamics. Vol. III. Fluctuations of social relationships, war, and revolution. American Book Company, New York.

Steckel, R. H. 1995. Stature and the standard of living. Journal of Economic Literature 33:1903-1940.

Stevens, R. 1983. Law School: Legal Education in America from the 1850s to the 1980s. University of North Carolina Press, Chapel Hill.

Stiglitz, J. E. 2012. The Price of Inequality. Norton, New York.

Terkel, S. 1986. Hard times : an oral history of the great depression. Pantheon Books, New York.

Tocqueville, A. d. 1984. Democracy in America. Anchor Books, Garden City, NJ.

Toynbee, A. J. 1957. A study of history. Volume II. Oxford University Press, London.

Trevor-Roper, H. R. 1966. The Crisis of the Seventeenth Century; Religion, the Reformation, and Social Change. Harper & Row, New York.

Tuchman, B. W. 1978. A distant mirror: the calamitous fourteenth century. 1st edition. Knopf, New York.

Turchin, P. 2003a. Complex Population Dynamics: A Theoretical/Empirical Synthesis. Princeton University Press, Princeton, NJ.

Turchin, P. 2003b. Historical dynamics: why states rise and fall. Princeton University Press, Princeton, NJ.

Turchin, P. 2005. Dynamical feedbacks between population growth and sociopolitical instability in agrarian states. Structure and Dynamics 1(1):Article 3.

Turchin, P. 2006a. Scientific prediction in historical sociology: Ibn Khaldun meets Al Saud. Pages 9-38 *in* P. Turchin, L. Grinin, A. Korotayev, and V. C. de Munck, editors. History and Mathematics: Historical Dynamics and Development of Complex Societies. URSS, Moscow.

Turchin, P. 2006b. War and Peace and War: The Life Cycles of Imperial Nations. Pi Press, NY.

Turchin, P. 2008a. Arise 'cliodynamics'. Nature 454:34-35.

Turchin, P. 2008b. Modeling periodic waves of integration in the Afro-Eurasian world-system. Pages 163-191 *in* G. Modelski, T. Devezas, and W. R. Thompson, editors. Globalization as Evolutionary Process: Modeling Global Change. Routledge, London.

Turchin, P. 2010. 2020: Political Instability May Play a Role. Nature 463:608.

Turchin, P. 2011. Warfare and the Evolution of Social Complexity: a Multilevel Selection Approach. Structure and Dynamics 4(3), Article 2:1-37.

Turchin, P. 2012. Dynamics of Political Instability in the United States, 1780–2010. Journal of Peace Research 4:577-591.

Turchin, P. 2016. Ultrasociety: How 10,000 Years of War Made Humans the Greatest Cooperators on Earth. Beresta Books, CHaplin, CT.

Turchin, P., and S. Nefedov. 2009. Secular cycles. Princeton University Press, Princeton, NJ.

Turchin, P., H. Whitehouse, P. Francois, E. Slingerland, and M. Collard. 2012. A Historical Database of Sociocultural Evolution. Cliodynamics 3:271-293.

Turner, F. J. 1921. The Frontier in American History. H. Holt and Company, New York.

Veblen, T. 1973 [1899]. The Theory of the Leisure Class: An Economic Study of Institutions. Houghton Mifflin, Boston.

Wallis, J. J. 2006. Government Finance and Employment. Pages 5.3-5.9 *in* S. B. Carter, S. S. Gartner, M. R. Haines, A. L. Olmstead, R. Sutch, and G. Wright, editors. Historical Statistics of the United States, Millennial Edition on Line. Cambridge University Press, Cambridge.

Walsh, L. S. 1992. Consumer behavior, diet, and the standard of living in late colonial and early antebellum America, 1770-1840. Pages 217-261 *in* R. E. Gallman and J.

J. Wallis, editors. American Economic Growth and Standards of Living before the Civil War. University of Chicago Press, Chicago.

Waters, B., editor. 2001. A Yale Book of Numbers, 1976-2000. Office of Institutional Research, Yale University. URL: http://www.yale.edu/oir/pierson_update.htm.

Wiebe, R. H. 1967. The Search for Order, 1877-1920. Hill and Wang, New York.

Williamson, J. G. 1992. Comment. Pages 210-216 in R. E. Gallman and J. J. Wallis, editors. American Economic Growth and Standards of Living before the Civil War. University of Chicago Press, Chicago.

Wilson, D. S. 2007. Evolution for Everyone: How Darwin's Theory Can Change the Way We Think About Our Lives. Random House, New York.

Wolff, E. N. 1996. Top Heavy. The New Press, New York.

Wolff, E. N. 2010. Recent Trends in Household Wealth in the United States: Rising Debt and the Middle-Class Squeeze - an Update to 2007. The Levy Economics Institute of Bard College Working Paper No. 589.

Wolff, E. N. 2012. The Asset Price Meltdown and the Wealth of the Middle Class. NBER Working Paper No. 18559.

Zelinsky, W. 1988. Nation into State: The Shifting Symbolic Foundations of American Nationalism. University of North Carolina Press, Chapel Hill.

Index

Made in the USA
Columbia, SC
19 June 2020